M000033727

Stone Boat Odyssey

Stone Boat Odyssey

Ralph and Phyllis Nansen

Copyright © 2011 by Ralph and Phyllis Nansen.

Library of Congress Control Number: 2011908368
ISBN: Hardcover   978-1-4628-7590-0
                 Softcover   978-1-4628-7589-4
                 Ebook   978-1-4628-7591-7

All rights reserved. No part of this book may be reproduced or transmitted in
any form or by any means, electronic or mechanical, including photocopying,
recording, or by any information storage and retrieval system, without
permission in writing from the copyright owner.

Cover Photo courtesy of Joe Fern s/v *Champagne*
Drawing of *Fram* courtesy of Lynn Nansen-Dale

This book was printed in the United States of America.

To order additional copies of this book, contact:
Xlibris Corporation
1-888-795-4274
www.Xlibris.com
Orders@Xlibris.com
83237

Contents

Part III
Living the Dream

Part IV
Conclusion of the Dream

Dedicated to our children

David, Lynn, and Lisa

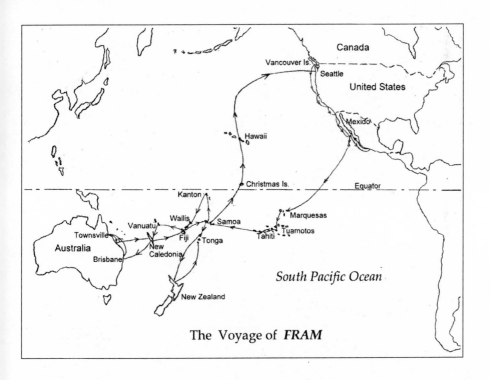

The Voyage of **FRAM**

Prologue

May 1989

We are sitting at anchor in the crystal-clear water of Kauehi lagoon in the Tuamotus, French Polynesia. The wind is calm, and the boat is still as if on a solid foundation. The sky is a mosaic of towering white clouds and brilliant sunshine. The white sandy beach glistens below the fringing palms. It takes little effort to walk to the rail, dive in, and enter the warm wonderland on which we float. The shadow of the hull shelters a school of passing fish. Nearby coral heads are home to many other colorful residents of the sea. Life is slow and easy. No need to set the alarm with no job to get up for in the morning, but the sun is a reliable alarm clock, which calls us to the start of another beautiful day in paradise.

Our requirements are simple—what to have for dinner; collecting water from the occasional shower, deciding which *motu* to explore next, wondering if it's a good time for a little nap, choosing the next book to read, should we take the dinghy or swim over to one of the other boats to say hello and maybe have a beer. Oh yes, once in a while some necessary boat maintenance. Our only time pressure being that we must move on when our visas expire. We also must decide where to spend the cyclone season.

We are here, living our dream. It is a dream that did not come easily but, rather, developed slowly through the years. Fortunately, it is a shared dream with my wife, Phyllis. It required years of determination and focused dedication to endure the long hours of work, the financial burdens, and sacrifices of other activities. As it often happens with dreams, the reality is not the same as the dream. For us, the reality surpassed our expectations. Now we are here with others, who share our dream and vision of cruising the oceans of the world. Our dream was born one evening many years ago . . .

Part I

Birth of the Dream

Sailing the good ship *Koru*

Chapter 1

The Ship *Koru*

The day had been long and the flight even longer. Through the late evening, as the big jet headed west out of Kennedy International in New York City to make the long transcontinental flight to Seattle, I could only think of getting home and letting some of the tension of the last few days drain away. This past week, Boeing began a new program to develop the Space Shuttle. We have been given a second chance after losing the original competition. It will be a long uphill climb, against big odds, to be successful this time. Two drinks on the six-hour flight did little to dull the senses and dim the view of the task before us, if we are to win this time.

In my profession, winning a contract was significant. My company won when men left the earth on our creation for their voyage to the moon. My lifelong dream of going to the moon was fulfilled when I helped design the rocket that made it happen. This accomplishment was the pinnacle of my life and career, one which would be hard to reach again. However, it whetted my appetite to again experience the excitement and fulfillment of achieving a great goal. Thus, this second chance to design the Space Shuttle held out the possibility of a new goal in space, which I could once again grab on to and hold. But I was tired, so terribly tired, and the flight was long.

That was the night I first saw the little ship *Koru*. We landed at SeaTac Airport in the waning light of a summer evening in the month of June 1970. As I walked from the plane, my wife, Phyllis, and my fifteen-year-old son, David, were waiting for me. The first thing they said as I walked through the gate was, "We have something to show you. We found a boat!"

When Boeing moved us back to Seattle from New Orleans several months before, we were forced to sell our twenty-three-foot sailboat. Now we wanted a bigger boat to take our family on sailing adventures in the Pacific Northwest.

Oh, and it also had to be one we could afford. With this fuzzy idea, we looked at just about everything afloat or nearly so. After months of searching, we reached a state of never expecting to find the right boat at a reachable price. Therefore, my attitude that evening was, "Well here's another one we ought to look at."

It was in this state of mind, along with my total exhaustion, that I greeted the suggestion of looking at another boat. There was no way out, however, as their exuberance over this great find meant I just had to see it that very night. The drive from the airport to Shilshole Marina, where this great prize was hidden, was another hour added to an already endless day. Looking back, I now realize how carefully they tried to prepare me for what I would find.

First, the buildup. It was a classic wooden thirty-five-foot sloop with a towering mast and a long slender counter ending in a small graceful transom. An Ed Monk design built at Vic Franks, the finest boat builder in Seattle. The cabin has full headroom, even for me (and I am six foot two). To top it all off, the hull was painted black, and I liked black boats. It was beginning to sound pretty good.

But then I began to suspect that all was not well. The price: best offer, as is. I could understand the best-offer bit, but when I asked about the as is part, the true story seeped forth. It seemed the boat was in a cradle onshore, and there seemed to be a little bitty hole in the bottom, which probably should be patched before it was put back in the water.

"But Dad, with your wood-working talent plus your structural design knowledge, it is undoubtedly a minor matter," David said as we were nearing the marina.

"Besides, it has the cutest little wood-burning stove," added Phyllis.

That was when the warning flags went up. With great foreboding, I swung into the parking lot at Shilshole that night past acres of masts to a small fenced haul-out area. There, bathed in the headlights of the car, stood a snub-nosed black hulk, with an unbelievably ugly blue cabin.

This is the boat? I wondered.

No one said a word when we got out of the car and walked through the gate. As we approached the bow, I realized the first impression of it being snub-nosed wasn't exactly true. The spoon bow had a graceful sweep from the long keel to the deck, and only the last few perpendicular inches created the impression of bluntness. The hulking mass of the underbody of a heavy displacement hull was awe inspiring to someone like me, whose sole experience with sailboats had been a light displacement twenty-three-foot fiberglass fin-keel Ericson. This hulk towered over our heads. Silence prevailed as we walked aft around the hull to her stern. There, on her graceful teak transom, was her name, *Koru*; but as my eyes wandered down her stern, my heart sank as I saw the little bitty hole in her bottom. Apparently, that little bitty hole had conceived and had babies in the last few hours. At any rate, there were now many little holes and other areas of depressed, wrinkled appearance under the new paint, which even I could recognize after months of looking at boats as that insidious evil of wood boats—dry rot! The new holes had, in fact, been created by curious lookers probing for the extent of the sickness, as evidenced by the innumerable knife-blade and ice-pick marks on the hull. It was obvious the rot extended over at least eight feet of her stern from the transom to the rudder.

This was the crushing end to an endless day, on top of a looming professional challenge already too heavy. There was no way I could even think of taking on the project of rebuilding *Koru*. The drive home was in icy silence, and Phyllis cried most of the night.

In the bright sunlight of a warm summer day, after a good night's sleep—and on a Saturday at that—the world and all of one's problems seem much less formidable. Add to that the guilt feelings of having hurt someone you love. So we drove back to the marina to have another look at *Koru* and her problems.

The resilience of the human spirit is a wonderful thing, particularly when coupled with the rationalization one can use to convince oneself that nothing was impossible. Thus, on that Saturday morning, as we drove back to look at the rotting hulk, in my mind's eye I saw her stripped bare to the skeleton and rising again in grandeur. I have learned through the years that a fundamental quirk of my personality was an immediate negative response to anything new and then, with time, the development of an overwhelming enthusiasm to proceed. The bigger the problem, the better I like it. As a result, I have gained the reputation of being an eternal optimist. Phyllis, however, was just the opposite. She was usually bubbly with enthusiasm about new things that strike her fancy and then has second thoughts about them later. However, with *Koru*, she was obviously convinced it was the boat for us, with no second thoughts about it.

With all these things in mind, we approached the prize again, this time prepared for the worst. Also, I planned to make as thorough an investigation as a landlubber turned sailor knew how. I came prepared with a pocket knife and an ice pick to probe and stick as many before had already done. By phone, we received the owner's permission to board and look her over. He arranged to meet us later. There was no hurry; we had all day. First, of course, I had to see the cabin and the cute little stove and the separate enclosed head and the stand-up headroom in the cabin (our Ericson 23 was strictly sit-down headroom) and the cozy forward cabin and the nice four-cylinder inboard auxiliary (our 23 was outboard power) and the wonderful bronze portholes, which opened, and the beautiful nautical wooden blocks. It went on and on, and pretty soon, I too was in love with *Koru*.

The mere fact of eight feet of dry rot in the stern seemed inconsequential. The other fact that emerged from the long morning of crawling and probing and gazing was that *Koru* was a beautifully designed and built vessel. By this time, I could no longer call her a hulk. She was a beautiful little ship. Even with the love affair, which was obviously growing, my feet were planted firmly enough on the ground to probe long and hard.

As near as I could tell, the cold hard facts were these: the horn timber, beginning eighteen inches from the transom to one foot forward of the rudder post, was rotten; the deadwood above the propeller cutout to the horn timber was rotten; nine planks from the horn timber forward, averaging about five feet each, were rotten; several ribs in the same area were rotten; the underside of the decking over the counter and stern area was rotten; and the deck beams under the counter were rotten. So other than having to rebuild the entire stern of the boat, there was nothing wrong with her.

During the time we were methodically covering the boat from stem to stern, several prospective buyers stopped by to see the bargain offered for sale in the enticing newspaper ad.

"Are you the owners?" they inquired, as we had apparently adopted the subtle mantle of possession.

"No," we said, "we're only looking."

Then uncertainty began to build as each nautical-looking professional came by. The comments were all similar and disheartening.

"I wouldn't take her if she was free," they would say.

As a result, two strong deep feelings swelled up within me. The first was, "Run, you fool, this is junk, worth little or nothing." The second was, "You just do not know the true gallantry of this wonderful ship, and she will live to prove you wrong."

We were in this mood when the owner arrived, and I liked him immediately. His heart seemed to bleed for his stricken vessel. It was with great trepidation that I gave him our offer for his soul. It was easy to see he was hurt. So it came as no surprise when he said, "I've been offered much more than that."

By this time, I was panic-stricken; I had blown the first feeling sky-high (the one about "run, you fool"), and now it was pure love and what it would take to possess my new love. So I upped the ante another thousand dollars, and my stomach began to twist. By this time, he hesitated, and I knew I had found a kindred spirit. Now was the time to give him the sales pitch. Not money this time; it was pure passion. A mistress, from one man to another. However, love was a bond not easily broken, and the heart must have time for the wound to heal before the mind can say yes.

So it was we waited! All afternoon and then the evening before the fireplace, knowing in our hearts it was *our boat*. Sunday morning of another beautiful day and through the long afternoon we waited for a call, which did not come. Finally, Phyllis, in her wisdom, said, "Call him." It was nearly that simple, except for hearing the anguish in his voice and the hesitation. I added another $100 to our offer, but it was not the money. He loved his boat. I waited two minutes, in nerve-racking silence, for his answer.

At the end of a couple of minutes, *Koru* was ours.

Chapter 2

The Rebirth

Now it was a great feeling to own a yacht, and we celebrated with a bottle of champagne and an evening dreaming dreams and imagining exotic places we could go. Our home stood high on a hill. As we sat in the darkened living room in the light of a flickering fireplace, looking through a wall of windows, at Puget Sound, we had the feeling it was the gateway to the world, which had been closed, but now, suddenly, was open. The pathway was inviting, with the flashing beacon on Point Robinson saying, "I will show you, I will show you the way. Just come to me, come to me."

We were carried away with the euphoria of the evening, dreaming of the joy of things to come. But the next morning, the stark reality of what had to be done sank into our conscious minds. Shilshole Marina did not allow for major repairs, and they wanted the boat moved out, *now*! She had already exceeded their normal limits.

"But," I told them, "she has holes in her bottom, and the forestay is gone, and I have to fix her first."

"Sorry," the manager said, "but there can't be an exception. You've got to get her out."

So with those words, we looked for some place to take her. I planned to do the work myself, because after paying the purchase price, I could not afford to have the work done. The previous owner had not been able to afford it either, and now the problem was mine. The estimate he had for repairs equaled what we paid him for the boat. For two days, Phyllis and I set out in separate directions to find a place for *Koru*. Finally after many discouraging headshakes, Phyllis came up with the perfect spot, so she said.

When I went to look at this wonderful place, my heart sank. Hylebos Boat Haven in Tacoma looked like a land-locked graveyard of old wooden hulks in various stages of ruin. Some were from natural causes, and others showed the heavy hand of man. The most sobering of all were those in apparent abandonment, with their weathered, rotted skeletons laid bare and then left to seek their own end in the company of their peers. For long moments I stood in contemplation, wondering, *Is this how* Koru *will end after I cut into her bowels?* Will I, too, stand convicted of failure by this sad evidence? Will the brave dreams in the firelight die like the smoldering coals on the hearth—in rotten pulp around me?

No! They will not! The heart had resolved, and now the mind and hands must produce. The perfect spot began to reveal why it was so perfect. First, it was cheap (fifty cents a day including electricity); second, they had a nice open space close to the office with a water faucet nearby; third, you did your own work (obviously), and they were always open. Last, but not least, they had a mobile crane big enough to haul out *Koru* and deposit her ashore.

Now my problem was how to get her there. Of the two options available, land or sea, land just wasn't practical because of cost and certainly not proper for a lady like *Koru*. By water, it was thirty miles from Shilshole. We had to make her seaworthy or at least calm-water worthy for the voyage south to Tacoma. By this time, I was back at work full time with all its pressing problems. The fix had to be easy and fast, because we were scheduled to get the boat back into the water at Shilshole on Friday morning of the Fourth of July weekend at seven, three days hence, arriving in Tacoma by five thirty in the evening to haul out at Hylebos.

After talking with my fellow workers, many of whom were boaters, the logical fix became self-evident. Put a canvas patch over the holes with tacks and paint it to seal out the water. Thus, the elegant lady, *Koru*, in her dignified black, suffered the indignity of having a large white diaper pinned around her graceful bottom.

I had one more chore before she was launched, and that was to change her registry. To those of you like me, who have never had a documented vessel, the experience was both pleasant and interesting. For example, the terminology was strange. *Koru* was not a sailboat, she was a Gas-screw. The coast guard officer explained the complex document, being helpful and patient with such an obvious fool. I also found the compete history of my boat—the designer, builder, and all previous owners (including their financial problems with *Koru*). The result of this visit to the coast guard registry office was a formal-looking envelope, which came in the mail a few days later and proclaimed to the world that I was the owner of the Gas-screw *Koru* of the port of Seattle with the permanent registry number 217438, which was carved into the shelf beam inside the head in three-inch-high numerals.

Now we were ready to go! Friday morning dawned bright and clear and early. We were up at first light to get everything ready by seven—the long drive to Shilshole; loading all the necessities for our big adventure; up the high ladder to the deck, twelve feet off the ground; and then the frantic search for a place to buy ice at six thirty in the morning. We decided to make a festive day out of our first voyage on *Koru*, because it might be her last for a while. Our three children, David, Lynn, and Lisa, were there; and Phyllis's brother, Ted, came along to lend a helping hand. All was set, and there came the big four-legged monster on wheels that would lift us up and deposit us in the water. As the young crane operator stopped just short of the boat and came down to talk to me, I felt pretty insecure. He first asked me if I was familiar with the operation of putting a boat in the water.

"No," I said.

"Well," said he, "it goes like this. First, you have to take off the forestay to clear the rig (partner to the one they had broken hauling her). Then just as she touches the water, start the engine so you'll have control when she floats free of the slings."

"But, but, but . . . I don't know how to start her." I admitted with the awful realization that I truly did not. How could I have forgotten that?

"*Ooooh*," he said with a disgusted look on his face. "I'll hold you up for a while, so you can figure it out, but there isn't much time. The tide is going out fast."

Ted and I scrambled onboard. He, to let go the remaining forestay at the bow, being careful it did not fall from the mast at the broken fitting; and I to search for the ignition key, the gas valves, and battery switch. By this time, the slings were under the hull, and we were suspended in the air. The rocking motion was gentle as we were carried across the asphalt to the launching dock—then the thrill of being lowered onto the water. But time was wasting. Now was when the engine was supposed to be running. I found the key, the gas valve was on and, I think, the battery switch, which did not say "off" or "on," just "turn." Everything was ready. The only thing was nothing happened. I could not find the starter switch! Ted was down below, fiddling with gadgets on the engine. I was in the cockpit, pulling switches, pushing levers, and was not able to hear anything happening because of the crane's roaring diesel engine reverberating in the confined area of the launching dock.

Suddenly, Ted stuck his head up and yelled, "Do what you did again. She turned over."

Well now, that was a lot easier to say than do, because I had just done about ten different things in my panic to get that hunk of iron going. Then to my utter embarrassment, I realized that in my perception of my vessel as a grand old lady, I had completely discarded the possibility of a modern and simple device such as a key switch starter.

Seconds later, above the diesel roar, came one of the finest sounds I have ever heard. All my life, since I was a little boy, I wanted an inboard-powered motorboat, and even though I had gone to sails, the deep-seated longing was still there. This I suddenly realized, as with a deep-throated roar, *Koru*'s unmuffled engine sprang into life, and the satisfaction was overwhelming.

With a new surge of confidence, I waved to the crane operator, and we were totally waterborne. The shift lever seemed self-explanatory, so I casually pushed it back, and we made sternway out of the slip. It was a good thing that a lot of waterway was available, because I learned another lesson very fast. Long keel sailboats are nearly impossible to steer in reverse. After this revelation, I gingerly approached the public dock and picked up Phyllis and the kids. Sixteen-thousand-pound sailboats do not stop very fast either.

With our new yacht tied to the dock, sitting quietly in her element, her real qualities again reached out to renew my determination to make her live. She was built for the water, and that is where I would make it possible for her to stay. A few minutes to hoist David up the mast to secure a line as a temporary forestay and we were ready to go.

I had not turned off the engine during this time, because I liked the soft burbly music it made in my ears. It is odd. I do not like the sustained noise of a boat engine, but somehow the quiet idle and first roar of power at acceleration appeals to my mechanical mind as symbolic of man's dominance over his environment. We ghosted slowly from the marina into Puget Sound, gradually acquiring a feel for the boat, happy with the smooth steady beat of the little four-cylinder, thirty-year-old Kermith engine.

The day was one of the rare great ones to remember. With ideal weather, we anchored for lunch in Port Blakeley, a beautiful little cove across Puget Sound from Seattle. The canvas patch held perfectly, the engine ran without hesitation, and we even practiced sailing under main alone. All in all, it was great! In fact, it was so great we dallied along the way and, as a result, arrived in Tacoma after the drawspan in the opening bridge was closed to boats during the hours of heavy automobile traffic. All was not lost, however. We turned back from the bridge to a nearby marina, found an open slip, and boldly landed. A call to Hylebos sufficed to keep the crane operator there until the bridge reopened. Meanwhile, we spent an enjoyable hour in a universal pastime—talking to other boaters about boats.

Thus, with mixed emotions, we slipped through the bridge raised high for our mast and came slowly to the haul-out dock. Our thoughts were filled with the satisfaction of a memorable first cruise. Then there was anticipation of the future, tempered with the knowledge of what lay hidden under the embarrassing white diaper. The ancient Travelift trudged out over us, and the slings dipped under the keel. The operator this time was a withered little old man, hunched over his levers, who symbolized the weathered boats he hauled and launched. He worked alone with great patience and quiet competence, and soon our wounded ship hung dripping from the slings. There she would hang all night, as the job of blocking her up was longer than the sun. So it would be Saturday morning when *Koru* took the ground again to rest and be healed.

The goal I set for myself to accomplish this job was one month. I had to meet this formidable schedule for two reasons: first, we planned our vacation for the last two weeks in August (on the boat of course), and second, I was going to be in New York on business the first two weeks of August. It was now the Fourth of July.

The previous owner told us about a book written by Ed Monk, the boat's designer, about boat building in 1939 and featured the construction of a boat named *Kilitan* as an example of sailboat design and construction. *Kilitan* was a thirty-four footer but otherwise identical to *Koru*. Phyllis found the book in the educational section of the library. It was dog-eared and worn from use. Inside was the story of how to build boats the way *Koru* was built. Not only did the book feature the construction of *Kilitan* in photos, but there, in great detail, were the lines, the design, and construction specifications for the thirty-five-foot sailing yacht *Koru*! With this knowledge and a deadline, how could I fail?

The next day, the last block had just been set under the boat, and the crane was waddling away when I drove a chisel into the rotten horn timber, which was the backbone of the stern overhang. I was determined to find the extent of the damage and planned to cut and chisel until all was gone. I would use both the ancient art of boat building and the modern technology of bonding with epoxies to renew the backbone and frame. I did not want to remove any piece unless it was rotten throughout.

Slowly, the first few chips were joined by others until there was a little mound, and then the big mound became a heap, and still later, I had to push it away just to get close enough to work. The progress was both heartening and discouraging. Then the great pleasure when the chisel rang solid, and the champagne color of sound clear fir, freshly cut, gleamed out of the dull gray mass of decay. A happy end to the first day of *Koru's* resurrection, but this was not the end of the rot.

Then came the night of the second day. My back ached, my hands were covered with blisters, my knuckles were skinned and bleeding, my arms so tired I could hardly lift them, and then the next blow broke through, with the chisel buried two inches deep in the shaft log, where it joined the horn timber. The spirit has trouble rising when the body is bone tired. I slowly picked up my tools, turned out the light, and stood in the darkness surrounded by the shadowy derelicts of man's folly. I was beat.

The next evening after work, I came to stare at the gaping cavity that had once been a proud ship's stern and pondered what to do now. Was there no end, or would the rot go on and on and on until there would only be an ugly mountain of chips? Absent-mindedly, I picked up the hammer and chisel and casually worried away at the rot before me. Soon, great chunks fell to the ground. Without conscious thought, my protesting muscles were again forging on, and I sweat with exertion. The mind once more picked up the task before it and discarded the lethargy of the last twenty-four hours. A necessary new plan came forth. The engine had to come out. The rudder had to be removed, and so it went.

Now it was time for others to join the battle. Phyllis and David worked during the day, and I worked at night. David cleaned out the engine compartment. Phyllis stripped the deck for refinishing. Ted came again, and the old Kermith gas engine lifted reluctantly from her bed and lay inanimate on the cabin sole. There, her rusty body was sanded and painted a glistening white. The propeller and shaft were removed, revealing the ravages of time. The inch-and-a-quarter bronze propeller shaft had turned to copper sponge at the bearing. The alloy was gone after thirty years of turning. This time, a sympathetic neighbor offered to machine a new shaft. With the care of a true craftsman, it materialized in perfect form in his hands.

The real stumper occurred when I asked David to remove the rudder. He was left to his own devices for a day with the general instruction, "Dig a hole so it can be dropped out of its post."

When I arrived that evening, the rudder remained boldly in place with a little six-inch cavity dug in the sandy soil beneath. My first reaction and exclamations are not worthy of repeating, but needless to say, I expressed the opinion that mighty little had been done for a day's work. I should have known better, because David was extraordinarily conscientious and tried hard to please. It was only after I grabbed the shovel in disgust and rammed it into the sandy soil that I stopped to listen to his explanation, for I nearly broke my foot as the shovel penetrated exactly one inch of sand and stopped!

One of the advantages of the spot where the boat rested was the nearby water faucet. It was also a major disadvantage, because one of the requirements of a water faucet was a pipe to carry the water. Said pipe happened to lie directly under *Koru*'s rudder post. As far as I know, that rudder has never been removed. Rebuilding the stern had to be accomplished with the rudder hanging complacently in its rightful place. David received a humble apology from his father.

Another lesson I learned (and I hope I never forget) was not to be too quick to judge other's failures. The graveyard of disaster around us was not really a graveyard at all. It was also a place of re-creation. For the Phoenix did in fact rise from the ashes. I watched in awe as skeletons rose from the dead and developed new flesh, with sparkling new paint and proud stance, to be carried in the strong arms of the ancient Travelift to a life of freedom on the water.

This lesson was both humbling and encouraging, for *Koru*'s wounds were but a gnat compared to some. So it was; at last, the time came to stop the destruction and start rebuilding, to experience the joy of cutting and fitting new wood carefully selected. We received the gift of a laminated timber for the shaft log. Originally conceived for a minesweeper twenty-eight years before, it was now excess from a new shaft log for a forty-foot power cruiser rising from the dead beside us. All the pieces to rebuild the hull structure were cut and fitted like a jigsaw puzzle, because my chosen method of repair required the simultaneous bonding of all the parts, which were then bolted and screwed into place. Therefore, literally overnight, *Koru*'s structure stood complete again.

The most frustrating and tedious of tasks involved removing the deck-caulking compound, which desperately needed replacement. Rainwater leaked through the afterdeck and was trapped at each rib, causing the rot problem in the hull. For some unknown reason, the ship builder failed to leave limber holes in the aft ribs for the water to drain. It was the only error I found that deviated from the design specification. However, it showed the importance of minor details, which can lead eventually to catastrophe.

The frustration of clearing the deck seams for renewal was caused by one of the by-products of the space age. The previous owner caulked the decks seventeen years before, using polysulfide rubber, originally developed as a binding agent for solid rocket motors. The material performed well but, through the years, was sanded and varnished many times and finally started leaking. David had been assigned the task of digging it out of the seams so we could recaulk with the same material. After a couple of days, he rebelled. His hands were blistered and sore from trying to scrape the tough rubbery material out of the seams, and he still had 90 percent of the deck to do. Dad was going to have to try his hand at it. I used a skill saw to cut out the material in the grooves. While I cut, I was greeted with the stench of burning rubber as a cloud of stinking gray fluff shot from under the saw. About twenty-five hours and five saw blades later, the groves were cleared. The next day, David had the privilege of clearing three inches of smelly gray cotton snow from the decks, along with scraping the spots I missed.

Meanwhile, I replaced the rotten hull planks. I reached another milestone when the last new plank was in place. Now it was time to caulk the hull. I read a lot about this process, but just understanding is not enough, for it is an art, which can only be acquired through experience. With this need, the perfect spot again came to the rescue, for I was able to simply wander around one afternoon and watch the masters at work. They were always willing to stop and exchange a few words and point out a few secrets. In the end, it was a young boy, working on his father's boat, who supplied the final touch.

His words were, "It's easy, and I'll show you."

He did too. With a careful explanation and a flick of the wrist, a stream of cotton caulking flowed into the seam. It didn't take long, with his experienced eye watching and making corrections, until I could flip the cotton onto the tool and drive it home with a satisfying thump of my mallet.

I can't fail to mention the pleasant hours spent talking to many visitors, who dropped by to spin a few yarns and pass the time of day, sometimes with a cold beer to make the work lighter. One fellow who stopped by to watch my progress turned out to be a sailmaker on a break from work. We spent a pleasant hour in casual conversation about boats and sails. A year later when *Koru* needed new sails, I gave him the job.

The thirty-day target was rapidly drawing close. My days were filled with eight to nine hours of solving the problems of flying into space and about eight hours of cutting, chiseling, scrapping, fitting, and talking to others rebuilding boats. There was not much time for sleep, but in the excitement and drive to get it done, sleep did not seem that important. I spent the entire month without an out-of-town trip, and of course, I had the weekends, which were the most productive of all.

At last, the end was in sight. The launch date was set for the day before I left for two weeks, and it could not be missed if we were to use *Koru* that summer. The last two days were a frenzy of activity. One thirty in the morning before the final day, we were struggling to finish replacing the rotten deck planks, when I simply could not go on any longer. How were we ever going to finish by the next day with me at work? The entire hull had yet to be painted, the decking completed, the engine realigned, and oh so many other little tasks. The launch was set for six o'clock the following evening as soon as I could get there from work. Again, help came from an unusual source. My nephew, Dirk, was a student at the University of Washington; and a telephone call brought him out the next morning with a friend.

"Would you like to come along to help launch my uncle's boat and go for a little cruise?" Dirk had asked. His friend did not know what he was getting into.

With their help, Phyllis and David accomplished wonders that day. When I arrived at five thirty, still dressed in my business suit, this dirty, sweaty, paint-spattered, greasy-fingered grinning crew waited beside the good ship *Koru*. Proudly she stood like a jewel in shining black, with a crisp white cabin and bright-red bottom. The engine was ready to go, the deck planking finished, the cabin cleared of tools and chips, the forestays were mounted on the fitting Ted welded, the sails were onboard, and Phyllis had supper ready for the fifteen-mile cruise to the marina, where we had arranged a slip. Thirty-one days after being lifted from the sea, our little ship was reborn to float free and dignified again, ready to carry us to adventures unknown.

The evening was beautiful. *Koru* once more parted the water with her proud little stubby bow and let it slip away beneath her graceful counter, this time without the disgraceful diaper. She was whole. She was alive. The big Egyptian cotton genoa (a large headsail) blossomed out, and the main pulled full as we surged across the moonlit water. Oh, but such moments are for a lifetime. The hard work seemed trivial. Mountains can only exist if there are valleys in between.

We would experience one more thrill that day. An omen for good things to come. We arrived at Des Moines Marina late and crept cautiously into *Koru*'s new home, for we had not been there before, the arrangements having been made by telephone and mail. We entered the breakwater and motored slowly past pier after pier to find our own. Dock C deep in the marina with slip number 26 our berth. We glided slowly to a stop. Only after securing bumpers, mooring lines, and preparing to go ashore did we look around. Our hearts skipped a beat, for there in the next berth was a graceful twin dressed in white. *Kilitan* was there to welcome *Koru* to her new home.

Chapter 3

The Beginning of Sailing

Our story of sailing cannot be told without including the tale of how we came to be sailors in the first place. *Bravo* was our first sailboat, and we learned to love sailing with that little vessel . . . but I'm getting ahead of my story. Our boating life really started with a surprise telephone call several years earlier. That innocent call would change our lives.

We were living in New Orleans when friends from my air-force days called from the New Orleans Yacht Harbor. They arrived after a trip down the Mississippi River from Minnesota, where they lived. We hadn't seen them for several years, so we were eagerly looking forward to a visit. We found them aboard a beautiful twin-engine, fifty-foot Chris Craft yacht. They were on their way to the Bahamas in the spring but left their boat in New Orleans for the winter. They offered us the use of the boat through the winter with the invitation to come with them to the Bahamas in the spring.

Unfortunately, we were disappointed not to be able to accept their invitation for a spring cruise to the Bahamas, because my first priority was my job, where I was working on designing the Saturn V rocket, which would eventually fly man to the moon. We did use the yacht throughout the winter as a weekend palace at the dock, but the boat never left the dock that winter. I enjoyed sitting in the wheelhouse, looking at the long flaring bow and the complex chrome-encased control console. I also thought about how much gas two big engines would consume per hour and realized it was way more than our budget could handle while raising three young children. However, just being on the boat was enough to stir hidden dreams and create a deep urge to own and have such a yacht someday.

At that time, a thirteen-foot runabout was the extent of our boating experience, and the glamour of the big Chris Craft triggered a search for a similar boat. Newspaper ads were carefully scanned, marinas were canvassed, and friends were consulted. We even started looking at houses in the bayou country, where we could keep the boat when we found it. Oh, how we dreamed. We discovered plenty of good used candidates, and they were not too expensive to buy. But they still used a lot of fuel. My practical mind could not ignore this reality, even though my heart was filled with desire.

"Why don't you look at sailboats?" some friends persisted in asking.

Sailboats, to my space-aged mind, looked like antiques left over from the past, slow as the sands of time, with little interior space and otherwise without merit.

"Yes, we'll look at sailboats," we responded and looked at a few.

We discovered they did not look so bad. The deep draft allowed more interior room than we expected. They had a pleasant nautical feeling. Then came a surprise. They were not cheap, even used. Many had been owned by one person for a long time, and nobody seemed terribly anxious to sell. The normal reason for selling was to buy a bigger boat, not to get out of boating as had been the case for a discouragingly large number of powerboat owners. Sailboat owners became radiant as they talked about their boats. What was the magic?

We kept looking, intrigued with the yarns we were hearing but were discouraged with the high prices for used sailboats, so we started looking at smaller new boats. A brief demonstration sail, in the beautiful silence of a pleasant warm fall afternoon, hooked us. Added on top as lagniappe (something extra) was the low cost of the wind to feed the lovely white wings of power. Time lost its urgency in the whisper of the wind and the laughter of the bow wake.

The urge for a big fancy power yacht was replaced by the determination to feel the surge of the wind in our own sails. The glitter was forgotten and the magic began. The boat size was scaled down within our smaller budget after buying a beautiful home among the pinewoods and great live oaks in the bayou country near Slidell, Louisiana. With a thirty-four-foot slip in the backyard, we had direct water access to Lake Pontchartrain and the Gulf of Mexico. All this in preparation for the new experience of a waterborne world in our boat.

It was Christmas by the time we found a lovely little lady sitting awkwardly on her shipping cradle in front of a boat dealer's showroom. She was a compromise of size, cost, and draft. We were limited by the depth of our bayou and the slip where she was to reside. However, she was just right as time proved. A twenty-three-foot Ericson, hull number 65, with a fin keel, three-foot-ten draft, and a spade rudder. The cockpit was extra large with a low cabin, which gave the appearance of a flush deck. Inside was room for our family of five to sleep below. Even though the head was between the faces of those sleeping in the V-birth and Phyllis had to cook on her knees in the tiny galley, it would be a fine boat for learning the mysteries of sailing. Her name was to be *Bravo*, because of Phyllis's active participation in the New Orleans opera world and she was a Christmas present to us all.

Commissioning was set for December 28, 1968. We waited impatiently for the great day, only to be disappointed! The dealer couldn't find anyone to put her in the water. He had not sold a 23 before, so it was a first for him also. I'm sure the disappointment came through in my voice.

"I'll find someone before New Year's." He promised.

He did too! I wished later, for my state of mind, that he had not.

The fateful day dawned miserable, cold, and raining. There were better times to launch a new boat than the dead of winter, even in Louisiana. By the time the crane arrived, we were ready to go, but when I took one look at the truck-mounted boom crane, I doubted if he was. I had not written a check for the boat yet, and it still belonged to the dealer. He didn't act worried. My apprehension was based on the observation that the boom on the crane looked more appropriate for hauling roofing material to the top of a four-story building than lifting a three-thousand pound sailboat from under a high-voltage power line with twelve feet of clearance over the deck. Then I found out the truck planned to drive across an open lot with the boat suspended in the air to reach the water. When I checked, it was ankle deep in mud. It didn't look good.

Despair ran high, as I could see my family's disappointment if the New Year came without our boat. The dealer saw his profit washing away in the rain, and the crane operator looked like he needed the money real bad. The solution to a difficult problem is not always fun to behold, and I can tell you I swallowed my heart three times that morning. A conference between the dealer and crane operator soon came up with a plan to hang our dreamboat at the end of the long horizontal crane boom and drive the truck down the highway for a quarter mile to the bridge across the river and lower the boat over the side to the water. It sounded simple enough, but a few complications developed.

Because there was so little room under the power lines, the sling around the hull had to be slipped directly on the crane hook. Andy, the salty old character, who worked for the dealer, boldly climbed onboard to see that she rode all right. As the weight came on the hook and *Bravo* popped clear of the cradle, there was a loud crack, the sound of a hull being crushed like an egg in the pinched slings. The old salt's head disappeared down the hatch. With the crane boom bobbing up and down, inches from the ten-thousand-volt power line, we dragged the cradle from under the hull. With the cradle gone, the boom was gently lowered away from the power line, and we all breathed again. Just for an instant, that is, because as the boom on the back of the truck lowered, the front wheels lifted off the ground. With the keel teetering inches from the earth, the front wheels slowly caressed the turf again.

We were committed. The cradle was gone, the ten-thousand volt lines still loomed overhead, and the truck barely moved toward the muddy driveway. Have you ever watched catastrophe develop in slow motion? It does terrible things to your insides. I watched helpless as the big tandem axle, dual rear wheels of that truck began to sink into the earth. The whole thing was going over in front of my eyes. Finally, the crane operator's sense of balance signaled danger!

Shouting and waving had done nothing to distract him from total concentration on his job. Finally, the macabre dance between the truck, balanced on two wheels and three thousand pounds of boat dangling off the boom forty feet behind, came to an end as the rear wheels settled on solid ground. On we went, up the steep driveway to the highway. There the next exquisite balancing act was about to begin. With all the weight on the back of the truck, the front wheels caressed the ground. A kind state trooper happened by and noticed our dilemma. Instead of arresting us, this understanding soul, with his badge of authority and flashing red lights, brought all traffic to a halt as *Bravo* teetered and staggered drunkenly down the highway at two miles an hour under a ceiling of power lines.

On the bridge over the river at last, the air above was free of obstruction, and the long boom swept high into the air, and with a gentle swish, *Bravo* settled into the water. A dark-blue stocking cap rose tentatively from the hatch to see if the storm was over. I am not sure if the rain soaked my clothes or whether it was the sweat of anguish, but I was wringing wet when it was all over. The only damage was a crushed toe rail, where the sling had bitten in during the first drunken surge off of the cradle. The mast was quickly stepped on a shiny new penny, and with the 9.9 horsepower outboard attached, we motored over to the dock.

We returned the next day, December 31, 1968, the day we took delivery and sailed *Bravo* home. The morning was cold and windy with intermittent showers. We loaded the car with everything we thought we needed, added the kids, and set out for Madisonville, where our boat awaited. The big day was finally here. We were to make our first voyage on our own *yacht*, a small one perhaps, but nevertheless, *our* yacht. Oh, there was also the anticipation of sailing for the first time on our own. Our total sailing experience had been a brief demonstration ride as passengers and a fun two-hour jaunt on a friend's Cal-28, again as passengers.

We arrived in high spirits, only to find the dealer with a long face.

"I don't think you ought to take her today. The winds are pretty high, and there might be rain or fog," were his first words.

"No, we bought a sailboat because of all the great things we have heard about their sea keeping ability. Besides, the wind doesn't seem terribly strong," was my confident reply.

As we lugged stuff onboard, he kept mumbling, "I don't think you ought to go."

"It's only forty miles down the lake to our bayou," I volunteered.

With everything onboard, including two new sails, I walked back to the office to pay for the boat. With all the formalities over, the bill of sale signed, the warranty explained, and an adjustment for the crushed toe rail (I decided to fix it myself), I strolled out to the boat. I was nearly onboard before I realized I had forgotten the most important item of all. I rushed back to the car, pulled a book from the glove compartment and once again prepared to board our yacht. The book was pretty important—*Fundamentals of Sailing*. Actually, by the time I got onboard, I found it really was not necessary, as Andy had already shown Phyllis and David how to raise the sails using the halyard and how to tie a bowline, a most useful knot.

"Oh yes, and don't let go of the halyard," he said. What else did we need to know?

"Don't try to go under the causeway bridge under sail. It's impossible. Use the outboard and crank her up tight," was Andy's last piece of advice.

Wow, it was good he warned us.

"She's a good boat and won't let you down." His parting comment rang in my ear. She never did.

We were aboard, the outboard was started, lines were cast free, and *Bravo* left the little marina. Down the river to the bridge where she had been baptized the day before, we enjoyed our first experience of stopping the world so we could pass by. The lung-power horn (sound range of half a mile is what it said on the box) took a long time to raise the bridge tender, but finally he came. The civilized world, on its rubber tires, stopped; and we experienced the grandeur of proceeding along before the waiting crowd.

Our balloon was burst though, when the bridge tender called down as we passed his miniature castle, "Better get something louder than that tin whistle if you want to go anywhere."

By then, the family adapted to ownership of a yacht. Lisa was happily playing with her Barbie doll in the cozy cabin. Lynn was already curled up on a bunk with a good book. David and Phyllis discussed their important positions as crew and I, as captain and skipper, surveyed my command with a feeling of grand satisfaction. On down the river we went, until it broadened, and there was the lake. Lake Pontchartrain was fifty miles long and twenty-five miles across and does not look like a lake. It is so large you cannot see over the horizon to the opposite shore. On this particular day, we wouldn't have seen it anyway since the horizon was hidden in the murky, low, dense cloud cover.

We were met by a lake scudding white. Our first realization of its roughness when we emerged from the river was the propeller popping clear of the water as the bow disappeared in the next wave. Wow! This is why we bought the boat—to feel the surge of the wind and the water. We brought a bottle of champagne to celebrate the first voyage and to christen *Bravo*. Now was the time to break it out. Her christening was not traditional since she had already been launched, and it seemed a terrible shame to waste a whole bottle of champagne, so her share was half a glass poured on her bow, and the rest went to her crew.

As we plowed through the waves, under power, we looked back to the gradually receding shore and could just make out a car and three figures beside it waving farewell—the dealer, his wife, and Andy was a comforting sight. How could we show our appreciation and understanding? There was only one way—put up the sails.

I knew that by tradition, a captain does not do the work but only directs the efforts of others. Of course, on a small sailing yacht, the captain can handle the helm, but the crew must handle the sails. Fortunately, the captain (me) understood the principles of aerodynamics (water is similar), so I knew which way to turn the rudder, and the crew was trained (Phyllis had a ten-minute lesson on how to put up the sails), so there was nothing to it. I pointed the bow into the wind (it disappeared every few seconds), and the crew waited at the mast (they got a little wet).

"Hoist the mainsail," was my first impressive command.

Nothing very dramatic happened. The sail went up, but it just flapped boisterously in the breeze.

"Hoist the jib," was my next command.

I had been led to believe, by reading my book about sailing, that something more spectacular should happen in that kind of wind. I pushed the tiller over, and *wow*, it happened. The sails filled, the boat healed to forty degrees, and we went tearing off down the lake.

What an exhilarating feeling. With the engine silent, the boat was rising and falling with the waves, sheets of spray flew back from the bow, snowy white sails blossomed above us, and creamy white foam swirled along the lee rail, mixing with the wake. The first few miles slipped by while we simply absorbed the joy of sailing our own boat. A cold wind and occasional rain and driving sheets of spray did little to chill our enthusiasm. In addition, we had a chance to try a few of the maneuvers illustrated in our instruction book. We tacked straight out from shore for eight miles against a strong wind in order to pass under the twenty-four-mile-long Lake Pontchartrain causeway bridge. There were two high-level clearance spans at the eight-mile points from each shore. We tacked more often than required to get the experience and feel of handling the boat. We learned fast in that kind of wind.

Before long, the two girls, turning a decided shade of green, abandoned the pitching cabin. In the cockpit, they huddled in the lee of the cabin, trying to stay warm and dry while they recovered their churning stomachs. At about this time, we saw the first of the two boats we were to see on the water that day. A big coast guard cutter came charging toward us and made a swing around us.

"Is everything all right? Do you need assistance?" a bullhorn boomed out above the howl of the wind.

"Everything is fine," I shouted back with a carefree wave, but it did raise a few doubts. I guess I just expected this was normal sailing with a heel of thirty-five to forty degrees and the bow going underwater on every wave. Anyway, it certainly was exciting, and we were getting our money's worth.

We had lunch, and another hour passed before we finally arrived at the bridge. I felt a little tense when I saw a barge anchored squarely in the center of the bridge opening with about a ten-foot clearance on each side. As we came into the wind to decide our next move, a tugboat cast off of the barge and lumbered out to us. Its low-lying decks were continually washed by the passing waves. Again, the tight circle and the bullhorn inquired if we wanted to go under the bridge? Shouting was to no avail, and finally, arm waving got the message across, and the tug was off.

I remembered Andy's cautious warning, and I started the outboard. With power on and the sails lowered, we felt the true violence of the water. The propeller spent about a third of the time in its natural element and the rest thrashing at unresisting air. Control of the boat was minimal, and I was surprised by the lack of stability without sails. I was nearly tempted to raise them again, but the voice of experience had sounded firm.

After much struggling by the tug and barge crew, a gap appeared at one side of the passage. Shortly, many waving arms signified the time had come to shoot the gap. And a gap it was, not over twenty-five feet wide. Bordered on one side by the repair barge and the other by bridge abutments, the water between was a churning caldron. All wave patterns were gone. The water danced in chaotic abandon with vertical spikes and big holes. The outboard was wound up tight and in we went. One instant, we were looking down on the barge deck, and the next, we were staring up at its rusty side. The mast thrashed from side to side, swinging over the barge and back toward the bridge abutments. My heart pounded during those violent swings until the masthead swished through the open air between the concrete pillars, and then we were through!

The screeching engine was stilled, and once again, silence descended on our bouncing world, except for the screaming wind of a full-blown gale.

Phyllis was scared and shouted above the noise, "I don't think we're going to make it before dark. How will we find the entrance?"

"Don't worry, we'll make it. We just have to find the marker buoy," I replied with more confidence than I felt. With less than four hours of daylight left, it would be close. With sails billowing above, we began the long race down the lake against the dark and the fog. We had to find the buoy; we had no other alternative.

Our world was now only water and wind, with the shore too far away to be seen. On we raced, flying off the wave tops. Remarkably, we sailed thirty miles in three and a half hours in a twenty-three-foot sailboat. With the wind a little aft of the beam, that little boat reverted to her racing pedigree and gave us a thrilling ride. The lake streamed milky white into the mist, and I was sure we had found heaven on earth. With the whistling wind at our backs, water caressing the hull and lapping at the toe rail, and waves slipping underneath as we looked down into the trough six feet below, it was exhilarating beyond description. All I had ever hoped for in sailing was in that boisterous run down the lake. *Bravo* never sailed that fast again.

Darkness was closing in fast, as it does in the south, when out of the mist ahead materialized a red marker buoy; and we were nearly home. A ninety-degree turn to port brought us into the channel leading to the calm broad waterway of Bayou Bonfoucha. Self-confidence is a wonderful thing, and by this time, mine had no bounds. It seemed the only natural thing to do now was exploit our newly polished sailing skills by sailing up the bayou to our house. Four miles of twisting waterway through the salt marsh was just another challenge eagerly met. I don't remember what sail arrangements I called for, but let it suffice to say that Phyllis was yelling, "You'd better turn!" several times before I felt the keel bite deeply into the mud and our bow snuggle comfortably into the marsh grass at the bayou's edge. At the same time, Phyllis, in her hurry to get the sails down, casually let go of the halyard. Our egos were properly deflated, and my hands were covered with sticky black bayou mud by the time we set anchor and winched ourselves off. Another time, it would be a much more experienced sailor who finally accomplished the long twisting channel under sail.

That first night was enthralling as we wound our way home. A wild tempestuous day dissolved in the liquid purity of the night. The clouds parted, the rain stopped, the wind remained only a whisper across the marsh, and the brilliance of the moon splashed through. It was a night of wonder with the dark water of the bayou forming before us, sparkling with diamonds of light and laid out in a silver ribbon of moonlight guarded by shadowy banks of grass standing along the way. It was a beautiful end to a boisterous and remarkable day. Beyond the marsh were the trees, cypress and pines and great live oaks, with moss hanging in ghostly grace. Then there came the lights of man, signals of warmth and life and welcome.

We wound our way the final mile in silence and awe. Even though that first trip home was breathtaking, the real wonder was that every subsequent trip up that bayou produced the same appreciation of a beauty that was at once mysterious and tranquil.

The depth of feeling created that first day of sailing was enough to set the course of our lives, and even though we didn't know it then, we were on a path, which would eventually lead us to the sea and a new life.

When we pulled into our boat slip, the phone was ringing in the house. We rushed to answer.

"Are you all right?" asked the boat dealer. "We worried about you all day in this awful weather."

We were touched. "The boat was wonderful and we had an exciting day."

Launching *Bravo*

Chapter 4

Learning the Joys of Sailing

I had been transferred to New Orleans in 1962 as part of the Boeing team that developed the Saturn V rocket for NASA's Apollo program, and I traveled often on business. But we spent as much time as possible perfecting our sailing skills in all conditions. On a hot summer day, we liked to drop the anchor in four feet of water and jump in for a swim in the lake. We often invited friends to go sailing with us.

One weekend, we invited friends George and Carolyn for a weekend rendezvous in Bayou Lacombe with several other boats from New Orleans. In George's words, everyone had a "fantastic time" at the party Saturday night. The next morning, we were definitely under the weather, and George and I would have preferred to sit in the cockpit with Bloody Marys than head down the bayou on the way home.

We found enough wind to sail, and we were heeled over, going fast, when we came to a sudden stop. Bravo buried her keel in black gooey mud as we sailed onto the mudflat outside the channel. Heroically, George (of the booming operatic bass voice) jumped over the side to the rescue, landing in water just above his knees. It was quite a spectacle as he trudged around in the mud, searching for the channel, hunched over with an anchor over his shoulder, all the while singing bass arias. Oh well, walking the anchor out and sweating over the winches cleared our heads and got us out of the mud and into the deep water of the channel. The music helped. We also learned a big lesson—pay attention to charts.

Sailing on Lake Pontchartrain could be challenging, especially in the summer months. A shallow freshwater lake approximately twelve feet deep at its greatest depth, it became extremely rough during the daily thunderstorms. Howling winds with strong gusts built big waves in just minutes, followed by torrential rain. In the meantime, we cowered in the cabin of the boat, praying that lightning would not find us. Then as fast as it came, it would be gone. The sun left the decks steaming, and the wind tamed to a gentle breeze. We tried hard to dodge thunderstorms.

One day, I wanted to see how well we could tow a dinghy. So on a sunny afternoon, we set out for a sail with our flat-bottomed aluminum jon boat in tow. A jon boat is about eleven feet long with a squared-off bow and is common for fishing in bayou country. To my novice eyes, it looked enough like the common flat-bottomed, square-bow eight-foot pram to be a reasonable substitute for our experiment. Besides, we owned it.

It was a lazy day on Lake Pontchartrain with light winds, the sun hot and the water just right for swimming. Dusk had come and gone when we decided it was time to head for home. About this time, a typical Southern storm came out of nowhere and was suddenly upon us. By now we were experienced enough to handle it without problems, except I forgot about the jon boat tied behind. The girls and Phyllis were below out of the rain, and David and I were in the cockpit enjoying the wild wind and crashing waves. Then I remembered the jon boat some place in the darkness behind us. I quickly dug out our high-powered flashlight, but I was too late by about a second. The light illuminated its path, surging down into the trough of an exceptionally large wave. I hauled on the tiller to bring *Bravo* about but not in time. With a great frothing wave, the jon boat buried its blunt bow and went under. At that moment, David and I were hurled into the cabin bulkhead at the forward end of the cockpit. The jon boat had hydroplaned to the bottom of the lake and brought us to a complete stop. Fortunately, the tow line had not parted. In my typical conservative manner, I used a hefty line, which secured it too well to the boat. Two cleats pulled out, one on each boat, but the tag ends were still attached in backup locations. I had not known what to expect when we began towing in the morning, but this was not it.

We frantically picked ourselves up and somehow got the sail down. With pressure off the sail, the jon boat slowly came to the surface, full of water and barely afloat. So now we were bouncing around at a complete stop in the wild waves with an enormous sea anchor behind us. Someone had to get in the jon boat with a bucket and bail it out. David was elected, in spite of his protests of, "Why me?" With a life jacket on and a bucket in hand, into the swamped boat he went.

Now the tricky part was to get *Bravo* underway again without being able to control her heading. There is one cardinal rule about sailing, which everyone needs to know. An uncontrolled jibe is a bad thing. In the panic of the moment, I made a bad mistake. Normally, the mainsail is raised with the boat headed into the wind and not with a following wind, which is what we had. Phyllis was at the halyard, and I thought I could control the boom by holding it steady as she raised the sail. On a small boat, you get in the bad habit of believing you can manhandle things like a boom. I was holding it steady with my left hand and held the sheet lightly in my right. Then it happened—the wind caught the sail in a particularly violent gust. I flew through the air, launched by the boom as it whipped forward by the suddenly filled sail. With a searing pain in my left shoulder, I came to a shuddering stop at the cabin bulkhead at the forward end of the cockpit again! We were underway with a vengeance with no one at the helm. I now understood why an accidental jibe was to be avoided at all costs. I lay there, completely paralyzed. I could hear and see but could not move. David was shouting that he thought I was dead; Phyllis was in a panic, trying to figure out what to do next; and *Bravo* was surfing down the wave fronts, dead before the wind with the jon boat and David surging behind.

David bailed frantically. Feeling was coming back into my shoulder, and Phyllis helped me regain a more reasonable position in the cockpit. With my returning senses, I was able to grasp the tiller with my right arm. The oars had disappeared in the black night, but David was safely back onboard, and as suddenly as it came, the storm was gone. David was sure we tried to drown him.

Fortunately, I had not broken anything except my pride. I could hardly move my left arm for a week, but it gradually returned to normal. We all learned an important lesson that day about the forces of nature. It was our first experience with problems towing a dinghy. Others would come later. Many cruises go by without incident, and then suddenly we are in trouble. It is most often associated with bad weather as you would expect.

With experience comes confidence, so we decided to venture into the Gulf of Mexico and along the coast of Mississippi to Bay Saint Louis and beyond. We wanted to find out what it was like to sail on the ocean away from land. There were five of us, plus our scraggly dog, Bridgit, on a twenty-three-foot boat. She did not like being on the boat and kept up a constant whine and yip, but we dared not leave her behind because she was in heat. An unexpected complication.

The weather was good as we headed out through the Highway 11 draw span and the railroad bridge. Both opened to our lung-powered, half-mile-range horn (we still had not replaced it). When we passed under the Interstate Highway Bridge, we were on our way into saltwater for the first time. It was a new adventure, even though the gulf looked exactly like the lake. But there we were on the ocean and soon had proof. Alongside came two bottlenose dolphins, each over half the length of *Bravo*. They were close enough to touch as they swam alongside. The kids were beside themselves with excitement to see Flipper in the flesh, swimming with our boat.

We anchored for the night beside a small island in shallow water in calm conditions. With no protective bay or cove or harbor, I figured we would be all right in the lee of the island. It was a typical hot and humid night without even a cooling breeze. David was in the cockpit, and the rest were crowded below—mother, father, two girls, and dog. No one was very comfortable. Phyllis and I were in the V-berth with Bridgit, who was afraid to sleep anywhere but on the pillow between us.

In the middle of the night, the wind came up, and we started to pitch and roll. The poor, miserable dog was whining. David fell off the cockpit seat, and the girls were turning green. Sleeping on the boat at anchor was not as romantic as we expected. At the first glimmer of light, we were up and ready to go someplace more comfortable. We decided to sail a few miles over to Gulfport, Mississippi. We were taking a lot of water over the bow, but at least we were heading for shelter. This had been our first anchoring lesson in a marginal situation. There would be others in our future.

As the sun rose higher, the wind disappeared, and we were soon motoring in the dredged ship channel, which serves Gulfport. The well-marked channel was about three hundred feet wide, with spoils from the dredging piled on each side. In some places, they dry in low mounds above the water level, and in others, you could not see them just below the surface with no way of knowing how deep they were.

A calm anchorage was in sight when David said, "Hey, Dad, isn't that a ship coming in?"

I looked back, and sure enough there was a ship in the channel behind us. Not just any ship but a banana boat, which travels between twenty-two and twenty-four knots, and this one looked like it was going full speed, with a bow wave reaching out from each side like a solid band of silver gleaming in the sunlight. In horror, I watched as this monster chased us like a predator on the hunt.

A vertical wall of breaking water about twenty feet high was fast approaching. We would be capsized or swamped if this mountain of water hit us wrong. I had no choice but to get out of the channel and take this demon on the bow. With no other choice, I turned across the spoil area, fully expecting to hit bottom. We did not. About a hundred feet beyond, I turned to face the enemy.

The girls and Phyllis were in the cabin below with the warning, "Hang on." David and I in the cockpit watched it coming, and I thought we were doomed. Little *Bravo* made a slight dip, and then her bow whipped toward the sky, and we climbed straight up the face of that wave. At the top, we flew through the froth as the wave broke, and we dropped twenty feet through the air to the trough below. I envisioned the fin keel hitting bottom and being driven up through the deck. We smashed down with a gut-wrenching impact through a curtain of spray, but the boat stayed together, and we didn't hit bottom. Without time to even take a breath of relief, we were climbing again. The second smaller wave launched us into the air again as the behemoth swept past in the channel we so recently left.

With a shaken crew and a whimpering dog, we motored into port that morning. That experience planted a fear of freighters in me, which I still have. I don't know if that banana boat did not see us, or why they didn't slow down. I only know we came close to losing our boat and possibly our lives.

A lot happened the year we owned *Bravo*. My job with Boeing was exciting, because we were getting ready to send men to the moon. In 1961, our country appeared to be losing the space race with Russia, so President Kennedy set the goal of landing men on the moon before the end of the decade. NASA and the nation's engineers accepted the challenge and went to work doing what had never been done before. On July 20, 1969, Neil Armstrong and Buzz Aldrin were the first men to set foot on the moon's surface, having arrived on an American-built rocket, which I helped design.

That year, *Bravo* survived a hurricane. In August, Phyllis and David and Lynn left on a trip to North Carolina with a group of teenagers. As they drove along the Mississippi Gulf Coast, the news stations were tracking hurricane Camille. It was expected to come ashore somewhere in the New Orleans area within twenty-four to forty-eight hours. It was a fast-moving category-five hurricane, and when it made its move toward New Orleans, I did not have much time to prepare. I took our youngest daughter, Lisa, to the home of friends in town, who lived on high ground.

I had the afternoon to prepare for the storm. Our home on the bayou was a two-story brick house with a sunken living room. Sitting about three feet above normal high water, it was very likely to be flooded if the hurricane was a direct hit. I made a dam of plastic and sand piled around the base of the lower level, covering the French doors up about two feet and hoped for the best.

A friend had loaned me his MG while Phyllis was in North Carolina with our car, and with the real threat of flooding, I drove the loaned sports car into the living room of my neighbor's half-completed house, which was the highest spot in the subdivision. Now it was time to take care of *Bravo*. I gave her special attention. I moved her into the middle of our small bayou and tied that little boat to trees and the timber supports of the boat slip. I figured the water could raise thirty feet, and she would have plenty of room to move safely up and down. It was the best I could do.

In a race against the approaching storm, I moved all the furniture, except the grand piano, to the second floor and made my emergency-escape route ready. The infamous aluminum jon boat was tied off to an upstairs window with an axe standing by to cut through any obstacles. Many deaths in previous New Orleans hurricanes were caused by people being trapped inside upper floors or attics as the water rose with no way to escape.

Darkness came early and the wind began to howl. This powerful hurricane was expected to come ashore near Bay St Louis, Mississippi, which was about twenty-five miles from our home. The pressure in the eye was the lowest ever recorded of any hurricane to hit the continental United States, and the wind velocity in the northwest quadrant was estimated at 225 miles per hour. This extremely dangerous hurricane would come close to our bayou home!

I waited in the candlelight and wondered what morning would bring. Would I be floating in the jon boat on murky waters surrounding our roof? Would *Bravo* be a smashed pile of fiberglass buried in the muck? Would my body be found covered in snakebites? Would our neighbors be safe?

But now back to the reality of the moment. Throughout the night, the wind was a continuous roar, shrieking and screaming. I opened the front door and stepped out on the porch, which was sheltered from the direct onslaught of the wind, and cringed at what I saw and heard. Live oaks in their writhing cloaks of Spanish Moss appeared as ghostly apparitions straight from hell. Pines—a foot in diameter bent over with their tops horizontal to the ground like an army of bowing soldiers. The constant painful screech of the wind and fear of flying objects drove me back inside as I watched the water rise.

Then the telephone rang. I couldn't believe it was still working. Phyllis called from North Carolina. She was following the continuous weather reports and knew the storm was upon me. She was amazed when I answered.

"We are just about at the height of the storm, and the center is going to pass to the east of us," I told her. "Everything is going just fine, so don't worry." Then the line went dead.

The bayou now covered the ground, and the muddy water came up on the French doors almost two feet. I stood on the flagstone floor of our living room, two feet below the outside water level, wondering when the water would rise above my plastic sheeting and sand dam, which seemed to be holding. I stared out into the inky blackness with my flashlight and could barely see *Bravo* in the ghostly light, but she seemed to be safely riding out the storm. From reports on the battery-powered radio, our location was experiencing winds of over 125 mile per hour.

There was nothing more I could do, so I sat down to rest and have a beer. Bridgit, trembling with fear, jumped onto my lap and buried her head. She had followed me around all day, and I was too busy to pay attention to her cries, but now it was comforting to hug that warm little friend during this nightmare of a storm.

By morning, the wind gradually lost its ear-splitting scream and was back down to a howl, and even that gradually died away. A strange silence settled on the landscape. I was stunned to see the biggest pine in our yard down and lying against the front of the house. I didn't hear it break or hit the house. Other pines were twisted off five feet above the ground as if with vicious gigantic hands. My makeshift dam held; there was no damage to the house or to *Bravo*. The ground was still covered with standing water, and I was stranded for three days after the skies cleared.

Phyllis thought I was dead. The news reports said that Coin de Lestin, where we lived, had been flooded with no reports of survivors! She finally talked the Slidell Police into coming out by boat to see if they could find me. I couldn't believe Phyllis was worried about me since I talked to her at the height of the storm and assured her everything was all right. She obviously didn't believe me. We were surrounded by flood waters and isolated from Slidell but with no serious problems. I just relaxed and moved the furniture back in place. In the meantime, my only problem was I had run out of beer.

I survived but not everyone was so lucky. Many people lost their lives along the Mississippi Gulf Coast. The damage to the coast, where we spent our vacation, was devastating. A ten-mile strip of the coast was hit with a thirty-foot tidal wave, which destroyed all the properties in its path. All that was left of timeless old mansions were concrete walkways and stairs. Huge live oaks hundreds of years old were uprooted. The highway Phyllis and her group of teenagers traveled two days before was stacked up like dominoes as the wind and waves tore it apart. In Gulfport, where we were nearly run down by a banana boat, two huge freighters were sitting in a parking lot surrounded by various fishing boats; and other ships tossed like children's toys helter-skelter in the trees. Private boats like ours, in marinas, simply disappeared, along with the marinas. Camille was the worst hurricane ever to hit the continental United States up until that time.

A side note—our beautiful brick home on the bayou was destroyed by hurricane Katrina in 2005.

After the success of the Apollo program, I was anxious to become part of another exciting space project. In November of 1969, I accepted a transfer back to Seattle to work on the Space Shuttle Definition Studies. It meant we had to sell the house and our beloved boat, *Bravo*. It was a heartbreaking decision, because that brave little boat taught us to sail, survived almost being run down by a banana boat, and went through a terrible hurricane. We vowed we would replace her when we were back in Seattle. The sale of *Bravo* took on a pleasant twist, when our friends George and Carolyn offered to buy her.

We had one last delivery sail from our bayou to the New Orleans Marina and our friends. Phyllis, David, and I embarked on this sad journey. We reminisced about the good times and the exciting ones as we sailed along with a brisk breeze under a cloudy sky. It was another winter day not unlike the day of our first wild sail, which introduced us to sailing. The temperature was warmer, and the wind not as strong, but thunderstorms around kept us on our toes.

Bravo gave us excitement to the very end. We were a couple of miles from the marina when one of the thunder squalls caught us. We surfed down the waves in the strong gusting wind, and rain was a deluge as lightning flashed all around. We left David at the tiller while Phyllis and I sheltered out of the rain below. David was quite an accomplished sailor by now, but he didn't think it was fair for him to be out in the rain and lightning by himself. We entered the breakwater just as the squall passed. Thus ended our adventures with *Bravo*. She taught us many lessons as well as how to sail. Now we looked forward to other adventures with a different boat.

Adventures with *Bravo*

Chapter 5

North for *Koru*'s first Cruise

My return to Seattle was not a repeat of the successful Apollo moon program. Boeing had lost the initial Space Shuttle Definition contract; however, now we were teamed up with Grumman on Long Island, New York, to do an alternate study. I had just spent two weeks in my second home, the Astro Motel, Hicksville, on Long Island; and I had another long flight home from New York. This time there was something special at the end.

It was the summer of 1970, and we were ready to leave for our first vacation on *Koru*, and I could leave the problems of Space Shuttle behind. After my frantic month repairing the dry-rot problems, Phyllis and David finished many tasks while I was gone, and the boat was ready to cast off in the morning.

Seattle weather is gorgeous in the summertime and the first day of our cruise was no exception. The morning was busy with last-minute tasks. At last everybody was onboard, and the captain (me) gave the order, "Cast off." I never cease to be amazed at the joy of simple things, like being the captain of my own ship.

With the breakwater behind us and the sun high in the heavens, we were headed north for the San Juan Islands. The 150 percent Egyptian cotton genoa was up, and the main was pulling full, when *Kilitan* came up beside us. She was lovely. The race was on with a matched pair. It was delightful to sail side by side and then gradually pull ahead. I went below to get the camera to record this momentous event but came to a chilly stop when I stepped into ankle-deep water over the cabin sole. In a panic, I looked for its source, only to be greeted with a virtual wave of water flowing down the inside of the hull by the dinette and in the head. My first thought was, *She's sinking!*

Then logic returned, and I remembered we had a bilge pump and the fact we were heeled over on the port tack. Maybe if we went to the starboard tack, whatever was leaking would be above the waterline. In the meantime, Phyllis was calling for the camera, as *Kilitan* was turning back. Well, first things first, so I took a picture of *Kilitan*, went about, and then started pumping. The problem soon became obvious as we immediately started taking water on the port side through every seam above the normal waterline.

Then I realized the boat had not been sailed for a year, and she had been out of the water for about six weeks that spring. One of the problems with wooden hulls is the seams open as the dry wood shrinks. Our short cruises to the boat yard and marina had not caused any appreciable heeling, and the fresh paint job on the hull disguised the slightly opened seams, so the first time we lay her over, she leaked like a sieve. I pumped her dry and spent an hour stowing wet supplies from the "dry stowage space" to places where they would not get wet if we took a little water. We learned not to assume any place near the sole or hull sides is going to stay dry in a wooden sailboat. Fortunately, wood swells when wet, and the seams were tight with no more leaks a few hours later.

Our first night on the boat was spent anchored in Port Blakely, which was directly across Puget Sound from Elliott Bay and the city of Seattle, yet this little bay was lined with forests, which seemed as old as time. Many years ago, it was a bustling seaport with a lumber mill and filled with square riggers and lumber schooners. Eventually, the mill closed, the ships called at larger ports in Seattle and Tacoma, and Port Blakely returned to its original wooded shores with a few homes nestled among the trees. Now it was quiet and secluded with a few other pleasure boats riding at anchor.

That first night was magical. We were surrounded by a thick forest, alive with birds singing in the ancient firs and cedars. An eagle swept by and picked up a salmon from the depths in its scimitar-shaped talons. The water was alive with waterbirds, squawking and diving. Waves lapped a gentle staccato on the rocky beach, and the glittering lights of a thriving metropolis twinkled across the water a million light-years away. On *Koru*, a soft light glowed in the cabin as steaks sizzled on the hibachi. With sparkling radiance in the burgundy wine, we basked in the wonderful glow of everything being right with our world. These moments were precious and to be savored like fine wine and remembered in times of trial.

Matter of fact, the next night was a time of trial. In the morning, when I started the engine, I thought I should investigate a problem I'd noticed earlier. The amp-meter indicated a discharge whenever the engine was running, so I figured, in my naive way, there was a sure method to check the generator—disconnect the batteries and see if the engine ran on the generator alone. It did, until I reconnected the battery and it quit, never to run again that day. There was no spark, and I could not find what was wrong, so we hoisted anchor and sailed away. The wind was light, and we spent a relaxed day loafing along at two to three knots, rowing around in the dinghy, taking pictures and generally letting the world pass us by. It was a fine day to own a yacht.

That is until dark, when the wind died completely, and there we were in the middle of Puget Sound, with ships and ferries all around and no anchorage close by. We decided to go to the marina at Everett about five miles away, which looked like the only place on the chart to tie up or anchor. All the water around us was a hundred fathoms deep, which was not conducive to effective anchoring with a two-hundred-foot anchor line. Besides, with ferries passing to and fro, who could sleep?

Everett turned out to be an impossible goal with our average speed of a half a knot, so if we were to sleep that night, something closer had to be found. We were neophyte sailors, and the rigors of twenty-four-hours-a-day cruising were not part of our thought processes yet, and besides, we were on vacation. The girls informed us we could stay up and watch the ferries go by, but they were going to bed.

Given the set of circumstances, where could we go? One solution seemed promising—go where the ferries go. But how? We weren't going anywhere as we sat becalmed in their path, shining a flashlight on our sails to make sure they saw us. After awhile, we felt downright friendly because they seemed to remember us and shone their spotlights on us as they detoured around.

About two thirty in the morning, we finally ghosted in toward the ferry dock at Mukilteo. I woke David to help out since I didn't know what our options would be—tie up to a dock or anchor—but one way or another, we were going in. David was half asleep as he crawled out the hatch and picked up the binoculars to look at the shore where we were headed.

"Gee, Dad, there's a square-rigger in there," was the first thing he said.

I really thought I ought to send him back to bed with a delusion like that, but instead, I took the glasses from him and had a look myself. It was not a delusion; there was a two-masted square-rigged boat in amongst the pilings.

As we approached, my anxiety increased, even though we were only doing half a knot. I had never come into a strange place at night with no power and was duly impressed with the inertia of a sixteen-thousand-pound boat. Besides, the tidal current was running close to a knot near the shore. My worries evaporated as we came close enough to see what was actually beside the ferry dock. There was a docking area with floats separating several slips (one of them unoccupied) and a two-masted square-rigged ship only thirty feet long in one of the slips. What more could I ask except for the anchor to hold while I figured how to get into the slip? The anchor did not hold on the steeply shelving gravel bottom, and the current swept us past. I was too tired to give up that easily, so when the brain fails, brawn must take its place. There was no time to lose, so I jumped into the dinghy and started rowing.

Koru made an unladylike entrance to Mukilteo landing, being dragged stern first by her dinghy with me sweating at the oars to overcome the current. We finally made it and had at least a partial night's sleep.

The next morning, the ignition system was reworked with parts from an automotive parts store, which opened that very morning with *Koru* as their first customer. Lucky for them, bad news for me, because all that was wrong was a wiring problem. Oh well, I saved the old parts for spares, and the engine ran nicely.

I must comment on the thirty-foot square-rigged ship. I met the owner before we left and asked him why a square rig on a thirty-foot boat.

"Well," he said, "it's simple. I lost my mast in a race and had always been frustrated by the fact that I was either running before the wind or beating into it on Puget Sound, so I put in a diesel engine for beating and a square rig for running and gave up racing, and I've had a blast ever since." He was right about beating or running if you were going north or south, which was most of the time.

Our next crisis occurred as we approached Deception Pass. Not because of the boat or weather but because Phyllis threatened to divorce me if I took *Koru* through the pass at other than slack water. Deception Pass had a reputation for strong currents, whirlpools, steep waves, and generally unsatisfactory characteristics whenever the tide was running. She knew the sailing directions for Deception Pass said small boats should only enter at slack tide. We arrived at Deception Pass midway in the tide change and would have to wait three hours for slack tide, which seemed unreasonably long to me.

David checked the tide and current tables at the pass and announced, "They aren't big at all today. We shouldn't have any trouble." So with David's encouragement, I overruled Mrs. Chicken and decided there was no point in waiting. On we went.

The pass turned out to be interesting with the currents and standing waves but not particularly difficult for our heavy boat. However, we did split the bottom of our dinghy. For *Koru*, the waves only meant a little green water over the bow, but for the dinghy being towed behind, it was an airborne flight ten feet in the air and a very sudden stop when it crashed into the top of the next wave. Its gallant attempt at flying culminated in a ruptured bottom seam. This was our second bad experience towing dinghies, and we seemed to be establishing a pattern. I guess I am just a slow learner. I understood though the reason for the fear about Deception Pass. A tremendous volume of water must flow through the narrow pass with each tide change, and most people treat it with respect.

Beyond Deception Pass was the eastern end of the Straits of Juan de Fuca and the San Juan Islands. Into the late afternoon sun, we sailed with a half-swamped dinghy behind us and one of the most beautiful island groups in the world before us. The first stop was James Island, a Washington State Park with a nice dock and camping facilities inhabited only by deer and other critters. The dock served as a convenient work space, where I repaired the split seam in our dinghy.

The island sports lovely hills and bluffs overlooking a little harbor. The water was clear, and the view from the bluffs was a tranquil scene of graceful boats floating in liquid space, the glory of a summer sunset bathing the forest around us in its soft radiance, with the magnificent prominence of Mount Baker shimmering across the water accompanied by the laughter of children playing in the distance. It makes one wonder why, with so much beauty around us, we don't stop more often to enjoy it?

The next day, we were sailing north in a light breeze, when Lisa asked, "What kind of boats are those, Dad?" She pointed ahead to a group of dark shapes in the distance.

As we drew closer, they started to take on strange shapes. Then suddenly they were gone! Bewildered, we looked at each other, wondering if it had been our imagination. Doubts soon cleared away when, with a great turmoil, in the water close abeam, the "boats" surfaced with a blow and a swish and became a pod of seven orca whales. Their sleek backs glistened like patent leather in the sun, and towering dorsal fins flashed in the air. What a sight to see for the first time. These gigantic black-and-white bodies leapt nearly out of the water. The leader was as long as our boat and obviously an old veteran of many wars, with a kinked, bent, chewed-up dorsal fin that looked like a plow shear dragged over a field of rocks.

With a wave of farewell, we turned north again. The days slipped by quickly as we wandered our way through the San Juans. We sailed or slowly motored from island to island, stopping each night in another secluded cove. We usually avoided harbors and docks to find a quiet, peaceful anchorage. This first trip through the islands gave us a feeling of serenity that stayed with us through the years.

As we slowly worked our way north into Canada, the islands of civilization became farther and farther apart. Then we experienced entering a foreign port for the first time. It was dusk when we came into Bedwell Harbor, one of the ports of entry into Canada. It certainly was not imposing, with a small office for customs, a small store, a restaurant, a few docks, and not much more. Nevertheless, it was impressive to have the customs official come aboard at the dock, where the signs said, "Only the ship's master may leave the ship until it is cleared." That's me.

Lynn asked, "We can't help tie the ropes to the dock?"

"They probably won't shoot you for that little infraction," I replied. The process was quick and simple, and the official was a model of courtesy.

We spent our days fishing, reading, and lounging on deck. One day, while salmon fishing, we nearly lost the boat. We decided to take a shortcut through one of the narrow passes shown on the chart. With just the engine, we started through. The beginning of the channel was fine, narrow with some current, but not bad. The chart was quite detailed and showed a line of rocks in the pass, some above water and some below, all of undefined depth, all festooned with kelp.

Once I made the decision to attempt the pass, David was on the bow, watching for rocks. The engine was at idle, but a strong current carried us pell-mell for the rocks. "We're going to hit," was the shout from the bow. Into reverse and full throttle went the engine, but all that happened was I lost steerage; the current by now was in complete control. We swept across broadside, and all of us stared at the dreadful image of submerged rocks beneath our keel. It was over in an instant, and we were once again in deep water. I don't know by how much we missed those rocks, but they certainly looked closer than *Koru*'s six-foot draft. This was a good lesson in how hard it is to judge water depth accurately. We experienced this later, sailing among the coral reefs of the South Pacific.

The weather was as perfect as it can possibly be. Without a whisper of wind, the sky was open to the universe without a blemish, the water a mirror reflecting the glory of creation. Then all of a sudden, in a bubble of life, the mass of water danced in delight when in a flash of pure silver, Coho Salmon, creatures of the water, became as one with the air. We waited patiently for one of those great silver flashes to grab our hook and offer nourishment for our bodies, always after a good fight. Our galley soon was well stocked with salmon and one big ugly lingcod.

When at the end of the day the sun dipped into the water and ignited it with sparkling red fire, we waited for the orange and lavender of twilight with the silhouette of purple mountains in the distance behind still coves, the wafting smell of wood smoke from chimneys onshore, and finally, the soft gentle velvet of the night. The anchor went over the side in another quiet cove, and soon, the coals were glowing red in the hibachi. The aroma of cooking salmon only enhanced an already-perfect evening, topped off by eating under the stars with the warm glow of a bottle of good wine. All the dreams of a lifetime cannot envision a finer way to enjoy our world.

Not all days were so nice. The next day was not particularly bad, but it certainly was different. We set out across the Straits of Georgia with a good breeze on a beam reach, with the genoa and main pulling us along in front of a gaily dancing wake. About halfway across the wake was not dancing anymore, it was frothing white and the lee rail was hard down. The wind sang in the rigging and the waves were building. David was on the foredeck, trying to keep dry as the bow dipped deep into the waves. It was not very long until he lost the battle and headed aft, soaking wet. As he passed the mast, he said, "Dad, you ought to see how the mast is bending."

That was not a statement that a structural engineer wants to hear, particularly since this was the first time we were in a strong wind with *Koru*. She had a tall rig for her length, and all kinds of thoughts whizzed through my mind as I ran forward to see how the mast was bending. It was apparent she was greatly overloaded by the big headsail in twenty-five- to thirty-knot winds. We brought her into the wind and lowered the genoa. It was then I learned what the term "in irons" meant. With only the mainsail up, it took us several minutes as we struggled to get the bow off the wind and underway again. We learned that full keel sailboats acted a lot different in some conditions than fin keels and spade rudders.

After exploring a new water world, our two weeks' vacation was over too soon. The many beautiful islands and picturesque passages filled our mind's eye with the image of islands available only to those who set out in small boats.

We checked back into the United States on Sunday, and then it was time to head south and home. By this time, we knew *Koru* and trusted her, so we bravely crossed the fearful Straits of Juan de Fuca. It was not a day of wild wind and waves as it can sometimes be but, rather, a gentle steady west wind and a pleasant afternoon sail. The wakes of many boats and the bloom of spinnakers accented the golden afternoon.

Out of Admiralty Inlet marched a parade of great ships, freighters, tankers, cruise ships, and tramps—all headed for the freedom of the sea. The urge to turn *Koru* to join them on their way was overpowering. The resolve to go someday was born. What did *Koru* need before she could safely go? The dream began to take on substance, and the Straits of Juan de Fuca was the gateway.

We stopped at Kingston Sunday night, unwilling to face the end of an amazing vacation and return to the working world. The next morning, I dressed in the dark, started the old Kermith, slipped the moorage, and headed south in a driving rainstorm. However, I was treated to a glorious end to a perfect vacation. With a magnificent display of phosphorescence, everything that moved in the water was illuminated. The propeller wash looked like a tunnel of fire. The hull was a radiating form, flowing through the water, and the wake was a river of light. The water around me was alive with shooting stars as fish left streaking iridescent trails. This meteoric display more than made up for the early hour and the rain. Five hours later, I was back in my office, worrying about fluid flow at six thousand miles per hour instead of six knots. The wonder of the water world was gone, but the memory lingered on.

Chapter 6

The Next Year

Winter was upon us. Chilling winds blew, and snow flurries fell, but we kept sailing. Occasionally, we left early on Saturday morning with the bow breaking a thin ice crust in the marina as we powered to open water. Sometimes in the evening, we donned long johns, wool turtleneck sweaters, lined boots, stocking caps, and gloves to venture out into the cold. We started the old engine, lit the little Gypsy wood stove and cast off. Into the dark we sailed, to return in the early morning hours, filled and satisfied with the aloneness of a cold winter night's sail and fellowship in the cozy, warm cabin by the glowing coals of the fire.

Many long hours were spent working in my shop. I built a new galley and dinette and installed them in the boat on dark nights at dockside to the cacophony of clanging halyards and howling winds. All through the winter, we alternately sailed *Koru* and rebuilt her insides. In addition to the new galley and dinette, we installed two more water tanks. As the dream of deepwater cruising grew, we prepared our ship and worked on a long list of improvements that needed to be made. In the spring, I cut her open again and completely rebuilt the cockpit. It was much too big to take to sea, so I made it narrower. Now it would hold less water in a breaking sea. In addition, I added hatches with good seals and strong latches. All this was done in preparation for our summer cruise, which would take us far north into Canada and also on a run out the Straits of Juan de Fuca to the Pacific Ocean to test *Koru* and our sea legs.

Spring came and all was made ready. Provisions were bought for a month's cruise, and the boat was loaded. We invited two of my brothers and their wives to join us for a week in the San Juans. With our three kids, we would have nine people, plus two cats in a thirty-five-foot boat that slept five. We arranged to pick everybody up in Anacortes the following week.

The big day finally arrived and we were off. Only Phyllis and I were taking the boat north this time, and we were having a great sail on Puget Sound with a twenty-knot wind dead astern. It was a good time to practice sailing with our new whisker pole, running wing, and wing before the wind as we charged north with a huge bow wave and foaming wake.

Note: Running wing and wing is when the headsail (jib) is held out to one side with a whisker pole and the mainsail is held out on the other side using a foreguy and boom vang. This is used when the wind is behind the boat.

I'd invited a friend of mine, who was fishing that day, to watch for us and join us for a beer. As we came by a large group of fishing boats, one broke out of the pack and came toward us. It was Bill. After some tricky maneuvering, we were able to pick up a line from his bow and bring him alongside. After a pleasant lunch, we reached the area where he wanted to be dropped off.

We were still sailing fast with a poled-out jib and the main tied down with the foreguy and boom vang. Bill's boat was at full plane as we towed it close astern. We brought it up alongside, and I flipped the line around a cleat as he prepared to jump off. At that instant, an exceptionally large wave came up under our stern, causing his boat to surge forward, also throwing him off balance. I watched in horror as a slow-motion catastrophe began to unfold. The heavy runabout jerked the line tight in my hand, and it began to slip through my fingers. The distance between the two boats increased dramatically. Bill couldn't stop himself from falling. He analyzed the situation and then twisted and jumped for his boat as it fell away, landing spread eagle on the foredeck, his boot toes curled around the gunnel on one side and his fingertips on the other. I watched all these things in horror as the nylon line burned through my fingers.

It is true that in times of stress, the senses are greatly enhanced. I had time to think of how stupid it was in those conditions to attempt such a maneuver with *Koru* rigged as she was, unable to stop. The elapsed time had to have been in fractions of a second. In an instant, it was over. Both boats were driving forward under the power of *Koru*'s sails, and my friend regained his composure as it planed boldly in *Koru*'s wake. I nearly learned a tragic lesson from that episode.

The wind moderated as we started across the Straits of Juan de Fuca. We were a little nervous because of approaching darkness, but the wind in the straits was perfect—fifteen knots out of the west—so it was an exhilarating reach into the night. And an extremely dark night it was, with no moon and an overcast sky. This, our second trip to the San Juan Islands, was our first to cross the Straits going north. We searched the chart for the easiest place to stop for the night. The closest anchorage was Mackaye Harbor on Lopez Island, which looked promising with a light on Iceberg Point and easy access from the Straits. We had no modern electronics or even a properly swung compass, so we would have to feel our way in the dark.

We dropped the sails as we idled slowly toward the rocky shore. There were many rocks shown on the chart for us to worry about, but we could not see them. As we came slowly past the point with its welcoming light, we strained our eyes, looking ahead for Iceberg Island. It was there, a black shadow on a black background, but our only guide. We snuck past Outer Bay and crept into the harbor, suspended in inky blackness. When our nerves could stand the agonizing tension no longer, we dropped the anchor. Relieved after our long day, we sat quietly and relaxed in the quiet cove, no longer worried about rocks. We sailed over seventy-five miles that day, had a near-disastrous experience, successfully entered a strange harbor in the dark of night, and now could savor the lessons of the day. Morning light revealed the rockbound shore less than fifty feet away.

The next day, we picked up our passengers for the week. We planned to stop each night at locations where part of our group could sleep onshore and the rest on the boat. The first night worked out that way as we stopped at James Island again. The weather was glorious, with brilliant sunshine and mild temperatures. Everyone was in high spirits when we tied *Koru* to the dock and set up the campsite. The evening was a wonderful beginning, with steaks and a glowing campfire, a gentle wind in the pines, an occasional deer wandering through the woods, and the joy of a family together in lovely surroundings.

In the morning, Loretta, my sister-in-law, said, "Let's go fishing." That sounded like a good idea, so the two of us set out in the rowing dinghy to go salmon fishing off the island, where hordes of birds were gathered. We assumed if there were all those birds, there must also be small fish. If there were small fish, there would also be big fish, our logic went; and they must be salmon. Well, we did not catch anything, but we had fun trying. When we started rowing back to the boat, we weren't making any headway at all against the current. Before long, I was wringing wet and not a foot closer to the dock and our boat. Finally, with a great surge of energy, I rounded the point and entered the cove where *Koru* waited. It was good training for me, considering what happened the next week at Bedwell Harbor. It also reminded me that tidal currents should not be ignored.

After the first night camping ashore, we never seemed to find the right place again, so *Koru* became a regular dormitory. All the bunks were full, the cockpit slept two, and two more were on the forward deck. We were amazed at how well we all got along, except our cats, Rosa and Sam, weren't sure who they should sleep with. Our biggest problem was the wood-burning Gypsy cook stove. Its heat was usually welcome in the cool Pacific Northwest, but we were having an unusual heat wave, and it made the cabin miserable when trying to cook anything. Finally, Phyllis rebelled and refused to cook any more for a crowd of nine. We found many charming places to eat ashore. The heat plagued Phyllis for our entire month's vacation, and I promised to find a better solution in the future.

My brother, Earl, had been the captain of a U.S. Navy minesweeper during World War II, and a couple of times, I think he wondered about my seamanship. We were sailing north on our way to Sucia Island, close on a port tack in a good stiff breeze. Coming up behind us was a very large tug with an enormous barge in tow. He was closing the gap rapidly, with relentless speed and a huge bow wave. We have been in this situation before! I had to get out of his way. With a rocky reef on our port side, I turned to starboard, heading ninety degrees across his bow. Not a good decision as we were now broadside to him, and it looked as if we would be cut in half until the sails filled, and we slowly gathered way as he passed behind us. The captain must have wondered what kind of fool was at the wheel, and I think my passengers thought the end was near. I learned another lesson that day about how long it takes a long keel sailboat under sail to come about. It was reminiscent of *Bravo* and the banana boat in the pass to Gulfport. It was the second time I looked at imminent disaster. Will I never learn?

Our guests would leave us in Victoria, British Columbia. Coming into Victoria Harbor was a treat for the eyes. The small boat dock was in the middle of the city, with the Empress Hotel and the parliament buildings across the street from the harbor. Many beautiful yachts were at the dock, and a couple of festive cruise ships were docked on the quay. Victoria, known as the city of flowers, was ablaze with reds, yellows, blues, golds, oranges, and greens, hanging from baskets everywhere.

As we slowly motored toward the dock, it was apparent they were filled to capacity. We made a couple of slow circles, trying to decide what to do. Idle passersby on the sidewalk above stopped to watch. As we edged in closer, a man waved from one of the boats.

"There's room on the inside of the dock, behind me," he shouted. "Me," in this case, referred to his thirty-eight-foot powerboat.

So I yelled back, "Thanks, we'll come right in."

Earl, the navy captain, was quietly saying, "It doesn't look deep enough."

We did not have a fathometer, but regardless, I was going in anyway. Those other big boats were there, so why not us? Well it was soon clear "why not us," when we were stuck in the mud in front of the sidewalk gallery of onlookers. Our exit was accomplished by having our whole boatload of nine people run back and forth from bow to stern to rock the boat while little old Kermith labored in reverse. Our landside audience was laughing and applauding the good show while my brother just scratched his head. I was suitably humiliated. We eventually found a slip, checked though customs, and spent an enjoyable two days in historic Victoria before our passengers had to leave.

It was from Victoria we planned to make our big oceangoing experiment. During all the past year, we had upgraded *Koru* for this adventure. Now was the time to see if we were ready. Our plan for this test was fairly simple. We would leave Victoria in the evening on an outgoing tide and then sail out the Straits of Juan de Fuca though the night, reaching the Pacific Ocean at dawn. After sailing straight west until noon, we would then turn around and come back in the straits before dark.

After our passengers left, we were busy preparing the boat and ourselves to go. All loose articles were stowed, the forward hatch closed and latched; the sails were rigged and the dinghy lashed down on deck. We learned our lesson about dinghies under tow in rough conditions.

As the afternoon slipped away, we motored out of the harbor on the ebb tide and set sail as we passed the end of the breakwater. We headed out into the teeth of a stiff breeze. As we cleared the last headland, the wind was building out of the west, right on our nose. Large steep waves were rolling in from the Pacific Ocean. *Koru* pounded and fell off each wave that swept relentlessly across the slippery varnished deck, sending gallons of salty ocean water down below. Working the foredeck was dangerous. We had no lifelines, and the dinghy took up most of the work space. I soon realized we were not ready for sea conditions like these. When a thick fog bank rolled in and a ship's horn sounded close off our bow, we turned tail and returned to the safety of the harbor.

Down below everything was wet—the bunks, galley, Phyllis, Lynn, and Lisa, plus the two hapless cats. It was with deep regret and disappointment that we failed in our first attempt to sail on the ocean. It was well after midnight when we quietly tied up to the dock and went below to contemplate our failure over a glass of scotch. The sting of failure seeped away in the glass, and a new deeper resolve started to take its place. We would not give up. We were naïve to think *Koru* and we were ready for such a challenge. We simply needed more experience and a boat better equipped to handle the unforgiving environment of the ocean.

We faced the realization that *Koru* was not the boat to upgrade for ocean cruising after all. She was thirty-one years old, and nearly everything in her was original, except the rigging and sails. We didn't have proper safety equipment or even knew what we needed. Most important, we were not experienced enough sailors for ocean passages. We needed to better prepare ourselves. We talked late into the night as we lay snug against a solid dock, instead of beating down the wild and wave-swept Straits of Juan de Fuca.

A pivotal decision for our lives was made that night. We were set on a new course, even though we dared not speak it out loud. We both knew we needed a different boat to do what formed in our minds as our dream of the future. We did not know at the time, but it would be sixteen years before we would once again point our bow westward toward the Pacific Ocean and sail out the Straits of Juan de Fuca to fulfill the dream of sailing the oceans of the world. We would not turn back the second time.

The morning dawned bright and warm with a fresh breeze. It was a time to put aside the disappointment of the previous night and strike out anew. So we headed north toward the Canadian Gulf islands, Princess Louisa Inlet, and Desolation Sound. The trip north was stunning in its beauty and enjoyment. We stopped at several of the places we visited the year before, including Bedwell Harbor. This time we did not have to check through customs, as we had already done that in Victoria, but we needed ice. As we came up to the visitor's dock, a couple of attractive college girls came out to help with our lines.

As they tied us up, they asked, "Are you going to join our dinghy race?"

"What dinghy race?" I responded.

"Oh, the one we have at noontime. You will get some free beer too." That got my attention. "Come on and enter, we need some more boats and you could win a free dinner at the restaurant." Now the promise of a free dinner upped my interest.

"Yeah, Dad, you can win. Remember when you rowed us into Mukelteo?" Lisa added.

Well, free beer and the kids' enthusiasm were too much of an enticement, so I was soon entered in the dinghy race. At noon, we all gathered for the event. It turned out to be a little different than I expected. The rules went like this: The start was at the main dock onshore, where you were given a can of beer. This had to be fully consumed before you could leave the starting line. Then you rowed around the dock and out to the end of the log boom, where you were given another beer to be consumed before you could proceed to the gas dock to get another beer that was to be chugalugged down before floundering on to, I think another place, where they stuck something cold in my hand to get rid of and give back. Well, so it went.

When we started, a giant of a man was among us mere mortals, who were lined up to start. The gun sounded and there was the beer in our hands. I watched in awe as this huge character breathed deep and the beer was gone while I was choking through the first swallow. Onto the oars, he leaned, and with an explosive crash, he landed in the bow of his miniature dinghy with his head in the water, his feet in the air, and the two splintered pieces of wood that used to be oars in his hands. Now that taught me something—do not try to go the full distance on the first stroke. Taking my lesson to heart, I slowly eased away from the dock in a trail behind the dozen boats ahead of me. It soon became evident that I was too quick a study, as I was falling far behind. Recovery tactics must be implemented soon, or I was going to look awful silly since there were two members of the fairer sex among the pack ahead of me. With studied intensity, I increased the pressure, and sure enough, the oars held. On to the log boom we went, thrashing across the then-still water with me next to last. The indestructible giant was close astern, beating the water into froth with the stub end of an oar. I was sure he could never keep up the frantic pace. As I reached the log boom, I was ready for that nice cold beer. I was sweating freely by now in the hot sun, and the beer slid down cool and easy.

Boy! I was in great shape. Now there was more than one boat behind me. This leg was a breeze. My eight-foot wooden pram was starting to pay dividends over the little six-foot plastic Sportyaks. The gas dock was ahead and things were looking up. I still had a little thirst and more boats were behind me. There was a problem with the can of beer they gave me though. The last half of it held a lot more than the first half, but then you can't be too sure of true measurements nowadays, so I wasn't going to object. There were even fewer boats ahead of me by now, so I was feeling pretty good. I'm not sure where we went next, but there was a pretty face behind that cold thing that appeared in my hand. I didn't really think I wanted another beer. I'm sure I didn't order it; somebody must have felt generous. You can't insult someone who buys you beer, so I forced it down under difficult circumstances. I thought I'd better leave before someone else felt similarly inclined. Shore and the finish line were over there someplace, and I thought it would be very nice to rest and have a little nap. The only problem was this crazy guy in front of me didn't seem to know where he was going and was slowing me down. After awhile, he stopped for a rest, so I slipped by and crashed into the beach.

A tiny bikini, with a cute girl inside, came over to help me ashore and told me I had won. It took a little while to understand what I'd won, and I'm still not sure if I was the winner or the restaurant, as the two prize dinners forced me into buying three more for the rest of the family. At least Phyllis had another escape from the Gypsy in the galley.

In the morning, fully recovered from my triumphant victory of the day before and having proven that an eight-foot pram had some redeeming virtues as a dinghy, we headed north again. We were on our way to Princess Louisa Inlet. Along the way, we were graced with the sight of one of man's most elegant masterpieces, when a stately two-masted schooner under full sail came whispering by under a billow of white wings. After seeing such a vision as that, one wonders why man didn't stop inventing while he was still ahead. The lines of a well-designed schooner must be the height of artistry on the sea.

A beautiful lodge at Malibu Rapids guards the only entrance to the inlet. Our passage through the rapids was smooth and uneventful at slack tide. Inside, the wind was calm, the sky faultless blue, and the water as clear as the air. Even the gentle throb of the engine was subdued by the grandeur. The mountains marched into the sky and down into the water with equal boldness. Through the midday, we glided along, hardly daring to speak, for fear we would spoil the perfection of this place. We were alone, intruders where man must not desecrate. The splendor increased as we went further into the inlet. Great rock walls told the story of the world, of the winds, the rains, the snow, and ice—the sculptors of stone, God's true builders of the earth. We were in a gigantic bowl of stone with thin feathers of white water plummeting to the bosom of the basin below and from there to the sea. Upon arriving at the end of the inlet, we found a great cataract of water spewing forth between towering ancient cedars, across great rocks, to come to rest at last, in the crystal clear bay below Chatterbox Falls.

Here we found more of our kind, some anchored precariously on the steeply shelving bottom, some tied to mooring buoys secured to the giant cedars onshore, and some resting on a dock near the shore. We reluctantly tied to the dock, as it was the only safe place open. Here in this most beautiful place, tying to the dock turned out to be a big mistake.

In spite of being surrounded by mountains and cold water, the weather was unexpectedly hot, so we had all the hatches and ports open. The long eventful night began with David leaning over the rail after eating too many oysters. He then announced that Rosa had just gone ashore. A few moments later, Sam followed. Knowing they would be back by morning, we rolled over and went back to sleep. I soon wished they had waited that long. They returned in a few minutes and bounded through the forward hatch over Lynn and Lisa's bunk. Unfortunately, they did not come back alone. They each brought a friend—no, not another cat but a mouse, as the screams from the forward cabin attested.

Our daughters now had new bedfellows instead of the cats who normally slept there. Things were not going well when two healthy mice-loving cats left two very lively mice behind as they scurried ashore again. Sure enough, soon the cats returned, proudly bearing more gifts. We now had four live mice and off they went again. Before the night was over and after waging a mouse war, we had a pile of dead mice on the cabin sole, two hysterical daughters, a woefully sick son, and two cats trying to scratch their way through the glass in the now-closed portholes. In desperation, we were trying to sleep in a stifling hot cabin with no ventilation and an indeterminate number of live mice in the bilge.

Our family still remembers that miserable night at Chatterbox Falls in stunning Princess Louisa Inlet as the place where no person or cat slept aboard *Koru* that night. I finally gave up trying to sleep and was steering a course down the inlet in the small hours of the morning. By dawn, we ran the rapids with the tide and were again under full sail. My crew was below in exhausted slumber, while I sat in the cockpit and glared at two luxuriously satisfied felines stretched out on the deck, nonchalantly taking a bath in the sun.

The bow pointed north once more as we headed for Desolation Sound. We heard many stories about the beauty of Desolation Sound, and we looked forward, in expectant anticipation, to seeing it for the first time. We weren't quite sure what to expect. The name did not sound like the incredible place people described, but we would soon know for ourselves.

We rounded Sarah Point and caught our breaths at our first sight of Desolation Sound. Silence enveloped the boat, with the noisy engine stilled, and we uttered not a sound, as we were absorbed in the panorama before us. The sea stretched into the distance, shimmering with bright flashes of reflected sunlight and then turned slate gray as it flowed between the islands and land, finally becoming a soft purple as it merged with the forest and mountains. In the foreground stood Mink Island, tree shrouded, thrust out of the glittering water, its shores rising steeply from the water's edge.

In the background, East Redondo Island emerged from the sea and reached for the heavens as a great hulking mass of deep emerald green guarding the eastern end of the sound—indistinct in its outline that flowed into the deep purple of the rugged mountains towering into the clouds behind. To the north, vertical rock walls of West Redondo Island jutted skyward in an endless search for infinity. Because of the magnitude of its size, we began to understand why its discoverer, Captain Vancouver, named it Desolation Sound.

Dark shadows and haze stretched away in endless grandeur. It felt as old as the beginnings of time and appeared that there could not possibly be life there, even though it was there in lush abundance and in an exuberance of animals, birds, and creatures of the sea. Mere words cannot describe the emotional impact of this spectacular place.

We motored deeper into the sound and made our way to Roscoe Cove. Our chart showed a rocky reef across the entrance to the cove, and since we were nervous about crossing shallow rocks again, we anchored in the channel leading to the entrance. We dropped an anchor off the stern in ninety feet of water and tied a line to a tree onshore. We were floating on dark waters close to a rocky wall, where we could literally pick oysters from the bow of the boat. With words of caution, David avoided the delicacy.

We stayed at nature's oyster bar for several days, swimming, eating, reading, and exploring by dinghy; but finally, the time came for me to return to designing rockets and Phyllis to return to her students and singing career. We left Desolation Sound with great reluctance, vowing to return. We had no idea our return would be delayed for nine years, and it would not be with *Koru*.

We headed south down the Straits of Georgia, and before the day was over, we would learn another lesson. The day was overcast, and visibility was low, but we had a good wind for sailing. At that time, my navigation skills were pretty rudimentary and were basically local piloting from visual observation of the shoreline that was now invisible. We had a compass, but it was not very accurate, and I didn't trust it. So basically, now I was lost and nervous. The chart showed several small islands and rocky reefs in front of us. I knew where they were, but I didn't know where we were. My gut didn't feel good.

By now, the waves picked up as the wind increased out of the west, and we were on a broad reach at hull speed, racing toward the known but unseen hazards ahead. It was time to reduce sail. Dropping the large mainsail would slow us down considerably. We came about into the wind, and when I released the halyard, the main started down and then stopped. I looked up to see what was wrong. I knew in an instant that I had made another stupid mistake. I had tied a tagline on the head of the main to help pull the sail down, and this line was now wrapped around a stay and jammed solid. In the meantime while I struggled with the main, the backed jib brought our bow around, and we were now heading east, with the loose main flapping wildly. Lynn left her normal hideaway, where she usually curled up with a book, to see what all the commotion was about. Phyllis was at the tiller, and Lisa and David were standing by as I tried to free the main. Lynn casually asked, "Oh Dad, aren't those rocks?"

Directly ahead of us, a reef of drying rocks emerged from the haze. Phyllis immediately turned away, but we were moving too slowly under the tangled-up sail for *Koru* to respond to the helm and steer us clear. And now current and wind were pushing us toward the rocks. All of us were struggling to get her underway in time to miss. I hauled on the halyard with all my strength and raised the main high enough to give it some shape. *Koru* slowly gathered speed and finally responded to the helm. We missed the rocks, but the episode was not quite over yet. The good news was at least I knew where we were. The bad news was the problem of lowering the main still existed. As our nerves settled down, David and I worked at it, and with some help from the wind, the line broke free. In a violent gust, the mainsail flapped in wild abandon as it came down. In its joyous burst of freedom, it also freed the stainless-steel chimney from its perch on top the stovepipe. Phyllis's Gypsy nemesis lost its Charlie Noble hat when, with a loud clatter and a splash, it flew overboard. There were several lessons to be learned that day, and it pains me to put in writing how dangerous it was.

The next day, we raced a forty-four-foot ketch from the San Juans back to Seattle and won! A fitting ending to an adventure-filled vacation.

Desolation Sound courtesy of Doug Cram.

Chapter 7

The Time to Decide

Our vacation was over and I was back at work. In the back of our minds was the burning question about what to do. To be honest with ourselves, we already knew. It was only a question of how, what, and when. A simple question, but the answers were not simple at all. We knew it would mean a dramatic change in the direction of our lives. We did not earn enough money to be able to do it any other way, except a total commitment to a new way of life. We talked around the question for months. We could not seem to come to grips with an issue of such magnitude. We took *Koru* on many winter sails.

One cold morning as we backed out of slip C-26, the decision seemed to come as crisply as the ice fracturing under *Koru*'s hull. If we were to venture out beyond the confined inland waters of the Pacific Northwest, we needed a boat designed for the sea. We could not afford one the size we wanted without selling our home and *Koru*. Even then we probably did not have enough money for the boat we had in mind. At least the decision was out in the open, so we could talk about it and discuss the options. With the barriers down, our minds ran wild!

We dreamed of the exotic islands of the South Pacific, the canals of Europe, the Greek Isles, the Fjords of Norway, and the freedom of being on our own, away from the everyday grind of civilization. Our desire was not to make a quick commitment to sail around the world but, rather, to convert to a seagoing life and sail to interesting parts of the world. As a result, we wanted a boat that could be our future home for many years.

So now we were again looking for the right boat. We decided it must be larger than *Koru*, but it had to be small enough that Phyllis and I could handle it by ourselves. Phyllis did most of the research through the literature available. It encompassed a very large array of books, magazines, and articles.

I concentrated on boat brochures and boats for sale. We concluded that the size range to consider was a minimum of forty feet and a maximum of fifty feet. The larger size received most of our attention. We also felt it should be a ketch rig to keep the sail size down, but I must admit we had never sailed a ketch, so we relied on others' opinions.

We went to the boat show in Seattle and were staggered by the prices. An advertisement for the Whidby 42 intrigued us, and we made a trip to Canada to see one, only to find the ad preceded actual construction. All we saw were larger illustrations of the advertisement. The trip was not a total loss since we stopped off at Samson Marine in Vancouver, British Columbia, on the way home. We had been reading about ferro-cement boat construction, and Samson Marine seemed to be the leader in our part of the world. We stopped by to take a look. The brochures in the lobby were interesting. The gentleman, who came forward to offer his help, listened politely as we described what we thought we wanted.

When we stopped for a breath, he said, "We have a forty-five-foot ketch being built for a customer. You can see it if you like. It's out back in our shop."

As we made our way to the shop area, he explained that the boat was their Sea Deuce design, a ketch with a midship cockpit. It was being built for a well-known musician and had several extra luxury features. This was our first contact with a ferro-cement boat, and it was impressive. It was not so much that the hull material was ferro-cement but, rather, the total package. The design was classic with a clipper bow and full keel, the interior was roomy, the finish was beautiful, and the layout close to what we were looking for. As we left, we stopped in the lobby to pick up more brochures and to buy John Samson's book, *A New Way of Life*. We drove back to Seattle with stars in our eyes. Now we knew there were boats available to satisfy our dreams. The problem was to convert our dreams to practical reality.

As we added together our biases, our wishes, and our roughly outlined plan for the future, the requirements became more focused in our minds. We wanted a boat with minimal maintenance and a long life. We were looking for a boat where we could live aboard and use for ocean cruising. Since the children would be grown and on their own before that could happen, we only needed space for two people.

The problem we faced was common to many. Our wishes were larger than our pocketbooks. The cost of a boat like the one Samson was building was beyond our realistic reach, but it was what we wanted. How could we manage? One way was to build a boat. This thought kept coming back each time we tried to determine how we could afford the boat we wanted. At the same time, we also realized the magnitude of the job of building a forty-five-foot boat. A compromise that started to emerge would be to buy a hull and complete it ourselves. With this thought in mind, we began to search for a hull to buy.

At about the same time, Phyllis came across a small ad in the newspaper, which said, "For a dollar, you can tour the construction of the largest ferro-cement yacht being built." It was a sixty-foot ketch being fabricated in Port Angeles and a clever way to make a little money.

Since we were thinking about a ferro-cement boat, it sounded interesting, so off we went on a Sunday drive. When we arrived and paid our dollar apiece, we signed the guest log and were ushered into a huge old shed that held what looked like somebody's art project gone wild.

Before us stood a huge boat-shaped wire basket, fully framed with steel pipe frames bent to shape and quarter-inch steel rods at two-inch intervals running horizontally from bow to stern and vertically from the keel to the deck. This basic framework was covered inside and out with a half-inch galvanized wire mesh that filled out the form. All of this was tied together with wire ties at each intersection, creating the steel armature of a ferro-cement boat. The entire hull, deck, and deckhouse sides would be plastered with cement, filling the entire sandwich of steel and wire, resulting in a solid cement hull with an embedded steel frame about three-fourths to seven-eighths of an inch thick.

For us, it was an inspiring experience. It gave me a detailed understanding of ferro-cement construction, and Phyllis was able to inspect the roomy interior and was sold when she was shown where the piano would be located. We went home with more dreams. We returned several more times as the construction progressed, and David and I volunteered to help on cementing day. That was quite an experience as nearly a hundred people mixed cement, carried it up into the boat, plastered cement into the mesh, and checked for full penetration; and then finally, the professionals trawled it smooth. The whole sixty-foot hull of *Haramby* was cemented in one day.

I began to believe that ferro-cement would be good hull material. This was particularly true since we could not find a fiberglass hull of the size or design we wanted. We returned to Vancouver again to visit Samson. I had scaled up the drawings in their book to one inch to the foot and built a model of the Sea Deuce hull with some modifications in the aft deck level, which would allow us to have an aft cabin starting at the transom. With my model in hand, we talked to Cecil Norris, the designer of the Samson boats. Our query was to determine the problems of raising the aft deck level and a few other minor rearrangements. He was very patient with us and pointed out the variety of configurations that he had developed for the same basic hull, which was about forty-six feet on deck. His latest was the Sea Strutter design that had been developed and built for John Samson as his own home and cruising boat. This configuration was perfect for our modifications and layout, and we particularly liked the added advantage of an enclosed wheelhouse.

We discussed the possibility of having them build a hull for us and asked for a cost estimate. They were reluctant to commit to a price without having all the details pinned down, but they thought it would be about twenty thousand dollars. I was to write up a specification with what we wanted, and they would give me a firm price. We went home with a pretty solid idea of what we were going to do. The Samson Sea Strutter design, with some modifications, was what we wanted. It meant we would have to sell *Koru* and our home in order to buy just the hull and some of the materials for finishing it.

The first and most traumatic decisions were to put *Koru* and our home up for sale. When we signed the listing agreement with the real estate company to sell the house, we were committed. There would be no turning back. We kept looking at boats for sale and hulls for sale as we waited for the house and boat to sell. I worked up the specification for Samson, and we agreed on a price. All we needed to do was place the order.

An earnest money offer was presented on the house, and we accepted. Now it would only be a matter of weeks until we had enough cash to place the order for a hull. That was when Phyllis, who is a voracious newspaper reader, including the classifieds, looked up from the paper one Sunday morning, saying, "Hey, there's a fifty-foot ferro-cement hull for sale." A phone call gave us directions and some basic data, so after lunch, we started out on yet another trip to look at a boat.

The location was not very promising. It was an industrial area in just about the bottom rung on the ladder of Seattle neighborhoods. When we got there, we found a dismaying array of black plastic-covered sheds of different sizes and shapes, huddled together and filled with ferro-cement boats of all sizes under construction and in all states of progress—except finished. A query pointed us toward the largest and best constructed shed. That was promising. When we opened the door, all we could see was the graceful clipper bow of the Cecil Norris-designed Samson hull. It was a mosaic of wire and steel with a shadow inside. We saw fingers projecting from the darkness, holding pliers and wire.

The shadow said, "Hi, are you the people that called?"

The voice was light and bouncy and coming from a petite young woman, who materialized from the darkness as our eyes became accustomed to the dim light. She was dressed in an oversized fatigue jacket, sitting cross-legged with her long blonde hair hanging straight in front of her shoulders as she leaned forward with pliers in hand, tying the wire mesh together.

"Thom's back there some place. You need to talk to him," she commented.

As we walked back through the shed alongside the hull and under the graceful transom with its three stern windows, we knew this was it. We looked at each other and did not have to say a word.

Thom turned out to be a wiry young man with long wavy blond hair and a red beard. He told us the hull was a Samson Sea Strutter with a few of his own modifications, specifically in the bow, where he added to the length to make it more graceful. Hence, the fifty feet versus forty-five on the Samson drawings (actually, neither was correct). The Samson design measured considerably over forty-five feet, and the boat Thom was building was forty-eight feet, six and a half inches overall, excluding bowsprit. He also modified the transom to incorporate windows for an enlarged aft cabin similar to our ideas. As we looked at the hull and construction, it became apparent we were seeing the work of a craftsman with careful attention to detail. Thom had no previous boat building experience but had done a considerable amount of research, and his workmanship was superb. Besides, he was building the boat for himself, which he told us when I asked why he was selling.

"Well, I've run out of money, and either I sell this hull and start over with the proceeds or I can go back to work. I've decided to sell and start over, as I have another set of frames already formed," he explained.

Thom showed us around the hull, pointing out its features and all the things he had done to improve on the original design. As we looked it over and crawled around the scaffolding, inspecting its cavernous interior, our feeling of satisfaction increased. There was no question we were looking at the yacht of our dreams. Thom told us the price would include cementing, with finishing to be done by a professional crew from Canada. He had already contracted with Bernie, the same plastering crew that did sixty-foot *Haramby*. It also included the bronze hardware he already had for the boat, including the portholes. Thom was a clever negotiator and casually asked me what Samson's offer had been. With that information, he set the price in his mind as we looked and talked. By the time I asked his price, it was less than Samson's at $16,500, and "no other offer will be considered." He knew we were hooked.

We talked late into the night, reassuring ourselves that we were making the right decision. So we bought a hull that, at that moment, was only a wire basket. If I had known how much work was ahead, I am not sure I would have made that commitment, but in my mind, the wire basket was a fifty-foot yacht.

With the agreement to buy Thom's boat, we not only bought our dream boat, but we also formed a close friendship that endures to this day.

With our home sold and the hull purchased, we had to find two new homes: one for ourselves and one for our new boat—and we still had to find a buyer for *Koru*. The home problem was easy, as we rented a house only two blocks from the one we sold. Selling the boat took more time.

Our last cruise on *Koru* took us to Harstene Island in South Puget Sound. After a great weekend camping with a bunch of teenagers, including three of our own, Phyllis and I left to sail the forty-five miles back to our marina. The morning dawned cold and windy. As we pulled away from the dock with the jib alone, the kids waved good-bye and cheered us on our way. We were soon romping along at hull speed until we started up the channel past the Federal Penitentiary on McNeil Island and into the narrows near Tacoma. We beat into a strong wind toward the narrows' bridge, when we saw we weren't getting any closer. A check of the tide tables confirmed our fears. We were entering the narrows on an incoming tide, and the current was running against us as fast as we could sail.

With five hours to go until the next tidal change, it was time to get some help from Kermith. Unfortunately, it was not in the mood to cooperate. The batteries were well charged, but the engine made not even a hiccup as it turned over. I knew the valves were getting bad, and apparently, there was not enough compression to draw the fuel from the old-fashioned updraft carburetor. I quit trying before I wore the batteries down, and we worked harder at getting more speed from the sails.

With the current running strong in mid channel, we were able to ride the back eddies near the shore. Courageously, we held our tack until we saw the bottom close to the bank and eventually made it through the channel. By dusk we were only five miles from home. Then the wind died. It was time to try and breathe some life into the Kermith.

I haven't told you much about the old Kermith gas engine. It was a battle between me and this ancient relic for all the time we owned *Koru*. It just did not want to run, particularly when we were in greatest need of its services. It seemed like no matter what I did, it stubbornly refused all my attempts to coax it back to life. This time I checked the carburetor and then the ignition. Everything checked out okay, but that cranky old engine just would not run. By this time, it was dark, and we were becalmed, sitting on a large opaque mirror reflecting a starry sky. I had one more desperate option left. The way things were going, we were not going to make it home that night, so I gave it a try.

Since *Koru* and the Kermith were both built in 1940, the electrical system was six volts. I simply rearranged the electrical system so it was twelve volts. When Phyllis turned on the switch, the starter twirled like a sewing machine; the valves did not have time to leak, gas was sucked into its tired old lungs, and the spark was irresistible. Phyllis thrust the throttle forward, and the result was a great surging roar as the engine came to life. The plan worked perfectly. In the meantime, I was below desperately trying to switch the battery leads back to six volts. I was about a half second too late. The old six-volt coil could not take twelve volts any longer, and it blinked out in a flash of glory. Scratch the last option. Kermith was done for the day.

Now we had to sail but there was no wind. We worked at it though. Over the next five hours, about all we were able to do was keep the bow pointed in the right direction while the current carried us along at about a half knot. By two in the morning, we were off Robinson Point, looking at the lights of our marina a mile away. At last, a cat's-paw of breeze was visible in the reflection of the stars, and soon the genoa stirred slightly. We finally had steerageway. As we ghosted toward the breakwater, the problem now became one of making our way through the narrow entrance channel and down the length of the marina to our slip on C dock near the far end. As we approached, the wind picked up, and by now a good breeze was blowing out of the east.

It was going to be another first for us to sail into a very tight marina. The entrance is from west to east, with the breakwater running north and south. To the north of the entrance was a shallow mud bank and to the south the rock breakwater. This meant that we had to approach from the south, round up into the wind, and carry through on the boat's inertia as we rounded the breakwater on the opposite tack. On the first try, I didn't come close enough to the breakwater, and it was only when I was into the turn that it became obvious we were not going to make it. I had to decide whether to hit the rocks or run up on the mud bank. I thought the mud would be softer. Luck returned to my corner at last. The wind caught the sail and swung us around at the last instant before we touched the mud. We were away and ready for a second try. This time, I hugged in close to the breakwater and, with a clean sweep, rounded the entrance and we were on the port tack down the length of the marina. As we approached C dock, we dropped the sail and glided neatly into our slip. It was 3:00 a.m. Easter morning, and Phyllis would be able to fulfill her commitments (although a little bleary-eyed) as choir director and soloist at our church. We learned a sailboat can be sailed nearly anywhere. This was a good lesson in how to sail in an impossible situation. We would later use it many times, usually under difficult circumstances

Our last cruise with *Koru* had been a mixture of emotions—sadness at leaving a heart's love, joyful anticipation of our next larger boat, as well as anxiety, frustration, and the annoyance at an unreliable engine. We had to find a buyer, and overhauling the engine was imperative. It was thirty-two years old and saltwater cooled, so I was nervous about what I would find when I opened it up. Having the valves ground was easy, but in the repair process, a corner of the block broke off along with a stud. No more Kermith engine. That was not a fun day.

We simply could not afford a new engine for *Koru*. What were we to do? Since we had time, the best thing to do was think. Time and thought often result in innovation. Innovation means to do something different. Since a new engine was not practical and a used one probably would not be much better than the one we had, it seemed the only thing to do was find some way to repair Kermith. Technology helped repair *Koru*'s stern, it ought to help with the engine. Why not bond the missing piece in place with epoxy along with a stud, and reinforce it with fiberglass? The repair was fairly simple. I bonded in the missing corner and stud with Marine Tex, followed with laminates of glass cloth and resin for reinforcement. Heat lamps helped the cure, and the new stud held to full torque. Old Kermith purred like a kitten. Selling *Koru* involved taking her out several times to show her off before she left us. That ancient engine never missed a beat.

An offer came quickly from one of the first people who looked at her. The offer was contingent on a marine survey by a surveyor of the buyer's choice. I arranged to have her hauled out at Vic Frank's, where she had been built thirty-two years before. The surveyor spent nearly a whole day going over her inch by inch. The list of items he compiled covered pages. During the day, I made a few inquires and found that the surveyor and the prospective buyer were close personal friends. He was giving *Koru* the full treatment, and I was being set up!

When it was over, the buyer said if I repaired all the noted defects, he would go through with the purchase. The situation looked discouraging, but the first thing I had to do was determine the magnitude of the problem. So the three of us started through the list and looked at each item on the boat as we came to it. After the first few, it became obvious that the vast majority were minor maintenance items. The surveyor was becoming embarrassed as we went along. When we were through the list, it boiled down to two soft hull planks about eight feet long, three small soft spots on the rudder, and one deck plank. These, the surveyor felt, were legitimate items that had to be fixed. The rest, he agreed, were incidental; and the buyer should accept it as is at the agreed price. He never mentioned the repaired engine block.

Next we had an estimate on the cost of repairs from Vic Frank. They estimated the hull, and rudder repair would be about $750 and the deck plank about $2,000. I came unglued! Seven hundred fifty dollars for the hull sounded high but acceptable, but $2000 for one piece of fir deck planking eight feet long was ridiculous. It took the foreman about ten minutes to calm me down. Then he explained: the bad plank ran from the cockpit seat under the cockpit coaming and forward beside the deckhouse. He said there was no way they could get the coaming off in one piece, so it would also have to be replaced. I calmed down, but my anger was not gone.

"Why don't you chisel out the old piece, slide a new one in, and not disturb the coaming?" I asked the foreman.

His reaction was a haughty, "We don't do things like that. Besides, it's curved and it can't be done." That was the wrong thing for him to say to me.

I turned to the prospective buyer and said, "It's your boat at the offer price if you do the minor maintenance items. I pay Vic Frank for the hull and rudder work, and I will do the deck plank myself."

The buyer looked at the surveyor, who had seen my workmanship in rebuilding the stern, and he nodded. "Okay, when will you do the deck?"

I told him, "If Vic Frank can be finished by Friday and have her back in the water, I will do the deck on Saturday."

"One day?" he asked.

"One day is all I need," was my cocky reply as I looked at the foreman, who just shook his head and walked away.

By Friday, everything was concluded except my part. The Vic Frank bill came to a little over a thousand dollars. I think I paid an extra $250 for insulting them, but it was done. I had the necessary clear fir replacement plank ready, the fasteners, caulking materials, and my tools. The new owner had moved *Koru* to Port Madison to her new moorage, and that was where I was to work on her.

Saturday morning dawned cold and overcast, and I felt terrible. My head ached, my muscles ached, and my throat was sore. Not an auspicious beginning of a day to accomplish one of the toughest jobs I ever attempted. However, I made my own challenge, so I could not back out now. I didn't tell Phyllis how I felt but just picked up a bottle of aspirin from the medicine cabinet and headed for Port Madison. I also grabbed a tarpaulin to keep off the rain. It was a couple of hours, including the ferry ride by the time I found *Koru*. The aspirin helped, so I felt nearly normal by the time I started.

It took hours of chiseling to dig the hard cured fir from under the coaming and around each fastener. Then I had to use a wrecking bar to pull the galvanized nails from the oak frames. I only found a few areas of rot. It was late in the afternoon, with the wind and rain whipping the tarpaulin when finally the entire old plank was removed. I carefully cut the length and beveled the upper edges of the new two-inch-wide plank. I slid it in place under the coaming behind the cockpit seat and into a graceful curve, matching the hull shape. "Simple"—that is what I told the foreman at Vic Franks.

By this time I was really sick. The aspirin no longer kept my fever down, and I knew I wouldn't be able to go on much longer. A two-inch-wide fir plank is mighty stiff, and the curve I had to match seemed impossibly severe. Fortunately, I brought my ten-pound sledgehammer, and there was plenty of line onboard, so with the plank started into the slot under the coaming, I bowed it with a block and tackle secured to the far side. Using the sledge and a block of wood, I started driving it further into the slot. This worked fine until it came to a deck beam, and then it had to bend in two directions. I was finally able to block up a support underneath and drive in a wedge. It forced the forward tip of the plank upward just enough to clear the beam.

It was back to the sledgehammer and another ten inches to the next frame. Each frame required a repeat of the blocking procedure, and each was more difficult than the last.

I alternated between sieges of profuse sweating and teeth-chattering chills by the time the forward end of the plank finally thumped home in its correct position. Now I had to remove the lines from the aft end without letting it spring free so it could be lowered into place. It took every ounce of strength I had left, prying with the wrecking bar as I loosened the lines and worked them free. As the last one came out, there was a loud bang, and I fell across the cockpit as the wrecking bar slapped against my shin. The plank had snapped neatly into its slot.

Drilling the screw holes and countersinks went quickly, and the bronze screws were driven in by electric drill. I had just finished pounding in the wood plugs on top of the screws when the new owner walked down the dock.

"How's it going?" he asked.

"Fine," I said, "I'm nearly finished."

He watched as I put in the caulking compound, and I told him it would need to set for a few days before it could be sanded. "I think you can do that yourself. It's not much area."

I couldn't even think of doing any more. I had reached the end of my strength. He helped me take down the tarpaulin, and I gathered my tools together. I asked him if he would help me carry them to the car since I didn't think I could manage two trips. I did not look back as we walked up the dock. I didn't want to remember *Koru* that way, not after one of the hardest days of my life. It was dark as I drove away. I don't remember the trip home. The ferry ride revived me enough to make the drive from Seattle to our house. My fever was 103 degrees when I arrived home, but I had installed that plank in one day. It was a hard way to save $2,000.

Part II

Building the Dream

The Stone Boat's steel armature

Chapter 8

The Stone Boat Begins

The plan was progressing. Our home was sold, and we were living in a rental house. *Koru* was sold and delivered. We were ready to focus our full attention on our new boat. The purchase agreement with Thom included the cementing process, with the finishing to be done by a professional boat-plastering crew from Canada. Bernie's crew had finished a great number of boats, including *Heramby*, the one where David and I helped. Thom was anxious to have the cementing done so he could get our hull out of the way and start his new one.

We scurried to finish last-minute tasks before the big day. Thom lined up a crew of his friends and acquaintances. Several of our friends were fascinated with the thought of a concrete boat and could not believe it would work but were willing to help. Thom had all the materials on hand, the cement mixer was ready, tools were laid out, and the weather forecast for plastering day was good. We expected a volunteer crew of more than fifty people in addition to the six professional finishers.

Everything was set to start at 7:00 a.m. the next day. Then Bernie and his crew from Canada walked in with long faces. They drove down that afternoon from Vancouver, British Columbia, in anticipation of an early morning start the next day.

Bernie walked over to us and said, "Thom, I'm sorry, but we can't do the job."

We were dumbfounded. All we could say was, "Why?"

"We were stopped at the border and warned not to perform any work in the United States, as we did not have work permits and wouldn't be granted any."

The problem was generated by the swimming pool plasterers union in the U.S., who were trying to break into the boat-plastering business but could

77

not compete with the quality work of Bernie and his Canadian crew. Their latest action was to stop the Canadians from working in the U.S. The union had been watching the progress on our hull and knew when we planned to cement. They also knew Thom had contracted with Bernie for the finishing work. In fact, I made it part of our purchase agreement.

What were we to do? I certainly did not want the cementing done without expert professional guidance and finishing. I had seen too many disasters that resulted from when that happened. We were not about to hire the swimming pool plasterers, particularly after the stunt they pulled. Bernie took his crew off to the side, where they carried on an animated discussion for several minutes.

Bernie came back to us and said, "Thom, I know I promised you we would do the hull. My crew and I have agreed we will make this our last job in the U.S. under one condition—you wait several weeks and then do it at night, without anyone knowing the date beforehand."

We did not have much choice but to accept the condition. After a little plotting and scheming, the plan evolved. The date was set for Saturday night of Seafair Weekend, with the Gold Cup Hydroplane Race taking place the next day. Attendance at the race usually exceeded a half-million people. Nobody in his right mind would dream of cementing a boat in Seattle on a night like that. In addition, we would spread the word that the plastering was rescheduled for the following week, using a crew of the more-experienced amateurs building boats in the conclave clustered near Thom's shed. Bernie and his crew headed back to Canada, and Thom and I hustled to notify everyone the plastering was off for tomorrow.

The delay was disappointing to say the least, but it did give us time to do a few more things on the armature before cementing. It also gave Phyllis and I time to sit and look at the wire basket that would soon be our responsibility. The magnitude of what we were undertaking was daunting. We crawled over the hull, planning what to do first and how the layout would be developed. It was so much larger than *Koru* we had trouble adjusting our thoughts.

We decided the only logical place to take her, after plastering, was to Hylebos Boat Haven, where we rebuilt *Koru*. They could lift her as long as she weighed less than twenty tons. The problem was how to get her there. The shed where she began life was about 150 yards from the Duwamish Waterway with some obstructions in the path to her natural element. Oh well, first things first. We had to get her plastered so she could float. We also needed to decide on a name. Talking about the hull or the wire basket or the boat or the armature just did not seem dignified enough for a beauty such as she.

We thought of many romantic-sounding names, but they did not seem to fit us. One name, with some historical and personal significance, was the name we finally selected. We named our new boat *Fram*. The original *Fram* was built for the Norwegian explorer, Fridtjof Nansen and his expedition to the North Pole in 1893. It means "forward" in Norwegian and is pronounced "frahm." Since our name is Nansen, was there any other choice?

She was a three-masted sailing vessel with an auxiliary engine and a massively built wood hull. She was locked into the ice pack north of Siberia, near the Bering Sea, on September 22, 1893. He theorized it would drift in the ice to the North Pole and back to open water.

After a year and a half, *Fram* was three hundred miles from the pole, and it was clear they would not be successful. Nansen and Hjalmar Johansen left the ship on March 14, 1895, in an attempt to reach the pole on foot. They were within two hundred miles but were forced to turn back when their dogs died and their provisions were gone. After wintering in an ice cave on Franz Josef Land, they stumbled across an English scientific expedition in June and were returned to Vardo, Norway, on August 13, 1896. This same day, *Fram* broke out of the ice into open water and set sail for home. She arrived August 20, with all aboard alive and well.

Fram was given to Roald Amundsen in 1910 for his expedition to the South Pole. Today, the original *Fram* resides in her own museum near Oslo, Norway. She is an impressive namesake after which to name a boat.

After the first aborted try at cementing the hull, I was not able to convince quite as many of my friends to help. They had better things to do on the Saturday night of Seafair Weekend. Besides, they thought we were nuts! I tried to convince them that by working at night, it would not be as hot, because the second week of August is usually the hottest time of the year in Seattle. I felt that was a better story than telling them we were bringing in illegal aliens to do the finishing, and it was the only time we could slip them across the border unnoticed. Our friends might not understand. The people Thom had to draw from were a different proposition. A part of the hippy community, they did not care at all. Many were building their own boats in the same enclave.

During the weeks of waiting, we learned more about this tight little community living on the fringes of society. Few worked at normal jobs. They were heavily oriented toward a bartering society, where work, material, and favors served in place of money. In appearance and lifestyle, they certainly weren't like the engineers I worked with at Boeing. When we got to know them, we realized that when they worked, they worked hard, and when they played, they played hard. They were the perfect group for *Fram*'s cementing night.

During the day that Saturday, Thom was preparing for the night's activity with the least possible visible fuss. The cement mixer would not be picked up until just before closing time at the equipment rental outlet. The electrician would appear around 5:00 p.m. to string lights. Others were bringing the beer keg for the postcementing party. When the cement mixer arrived at around four thirty, towed behind a battered old pickup, I began to believe maybe the plastering was going to happen. That feeling was short-lived when the cement mixer would not start.

Thom's reaction was swift. "Don't fool with it. Go get another one before they close."

So off the old pickup rattled to return a half hour later with another mixer. While they were gone, someone fixed the first mixer, which was a good thing since we were able to mix with both machines during that long night.

When the electrician showed up in an old Ford Econovan with coils of heavy two-strand wire and boxes of clip-on light sockets, I began to wonder what kind of crew we had. Jerry stepped out of the van wearing a pair of leather leggings and moccasins, with a sheath knife at his belt with about a ten-inch blade. He wore a fringed leather vest that could not begin to cover his massive furry chest and shoulders. His hair was braided into a single braid that hung down his back like a ship's hawser. He shouldered the coils of wire and headed for the shed.

"Hey, Thom, where's the juice box?" he called.

When he found it, I tagged along to watch what was going to happen. He threw the coils down, whipped out the sheath knife, cut off a twisted end, stripped the insulation, and turned to hook it up to the power outlet.

"Aren't you going to turn off the power first?" was my surprised question.

"How would I know if it was working if I did that?" was his casual answer.

He proceeded to string wires and lights for the next hour. He hooked up the power end first, and as he added each additional coil, he stripped the insulation with his knife, twisted the bare ends together, and went on to the next coil, with a string of bright lights glowing behind. I didn't even see him blink, as he must have received repeated shocks. This was just the beginning of his performance that night.

By 6:30 p.m., a good-sized crew had gathered, which included both guys and gals and some little ones. The finishing crew arrived from Canada without incident.

Thom split up the crew and assigned their jobs. The mixing crew was preselected based on experience, as it was a critical part of the job, getting the material proportions right and particularly the right amount of water. If too much water is added, the excess drains out of the cement during the setup period, leaving capillary paths that later allow water to reenter the cement and corrode the wire and reinforcement bars.

The plastering crew would do the plastering from the inside and smooth the hull on the outside. It consisted of the pros from Canada and a small group of experienced amateurs. The remaining jobs were the cement carriers and the checkers. The checkers (including Phyllis) watched from the outside to be sure the cement penetrated completely through the wire mesh as the plasterers troweled it into the armature from the inside.

The first mixer load was ready by 7:30 p.m. It was an exciting moment. The mixers were set up beside the shed near the pile of fine-graded sand and a big stack of cement sacks. A small cache of pozzolan, to increase the strength of the cement, was close by. After the cement was mixed, it was dumped into buckets that were hauled fifteen feet in the air, to the upper level of the shed. It was then distributed throughout the hull. All of the cement was forced through the armature from the inside, with the boat in the upright position. The keel sat on a large timber, but the rest of the steel armature—made of pipe frames, small-diameter steel rods, and wire mesh—hung from the roof of the construction shed. The keel was cemented first, using vibrators to make sure the cement penetrate the mesh. All the rest had to be done by hand without the vibrators.

Cementing started in various areas all over the hull. It did not matter about joints, because the whole thing would be done before any of the cement could set up. My job was to watch and make sure everything was going all right, but Thom was in charge. That gave me an opportunity to get acquainted with many of the people.

Inside the chain locker, which is a fairly large compartment but only accessible through a sixteen-inch-diameter hole that would someday be filled with a bronze port, I ran across a small fellow curled up in the very forepeak, troweling away like mad.

When I asked him his name, his reply was, "Oh, I'm Rat. I'm the smallest, so I have to do these tight spots."

I made many tours around the boat that night, and Rat was working in the chain locker the whole time. When he finally crawled out, it looked like he had fallen into a cement mixer. His jeans were threads hanging down his legs, his shoes were worn through the toes, and his knees, elbows, and knuckles were a bleeding mess. Even with all that, his eyes were twinkling, and he was grinning though the caked gray mass that had formerly been his beard.

Up on the top level, where the cement buckets arrived after being hauled up from below by a rotating crew, I found Jerry, the master electrician. His job for this part of the night was to reach out and pick up the cement buckets as they came up on the pulley. Then he would swing them inboard to be handed to the carriers, who took them to the various plasterers. He had to reach far out from the platform to grasp the sixty-pound buckets, lift them clear of the hook, and hand them off.

Throughout the night, he kept it up, never missing a bucket. Every ounce of the fifteen thousand pounds or so of cement that went into *Fram*'s hull that night was lifted by Jerry. It was an amazing feat of strength and endurance. His sustaining fuel seemed to be beer. He had an Igloo cooler full of beer in his van, and when a thirst came on him, he would slide down the ladder, run flat out to his van, grab a beer can, race back to the ladder, scramble up the fifteen feet, and be waiting for the next bucket. It appeared from the accumulated pile of cans that the thirst was self-priming. In any event, I was impressed. He was a different breed of man than I had run across in my engineering profession. It was very refreshing.

As the plastering progressed and the workers became tired, it was apparent that they had ways to stimulate themselves to keep going. I think some of our friends that came to help that night not only experienced the new phenomenon of concrete boats, but also worked shoulder to shoulder with a culture they had only heard or read about. I know it was the first time we had seen it in full bloom.

By midnight, the primary cementing was about done. There were some areas that had not been back-plastered or smoothed, but we were concerned that the main hull cement was setting up in the warm August night, and workers inside might cause cracks in the green cement. The areas that had not been back-plastered and smoothed were the inside of the integral water and fuel tanks and the inner facing of the cabin-side coaming. Thom called a council of the pros and me to decide what to do. They recommended we stop work inside the hull. It meant I would have to back-plaster the insides of the tanks and the coaming after the hull was cured. It was my decision to make. It did not seem like too big a job, and I did not want any cracking, so I said, "Let's stop." I later wished we had finished the tanks, because that turned out to be the most miserable job I had to do in finishing *Fram*. My six-foot-two body was definitely not Rat.

With the main plastering completed, the work was finished for all the general helpers, so it was time to start the party. The beer keg was sprung and the food laid out. That's when the pros went to work finishing the exterior. First they plastered on a thin layer of cement about an eighth of an inch thick. Next they went over the hull with long flexible steel splines, scraping the cement off the high spots and fairing the surface. Then another check to add small amounts of cement to the low spots, followed by another scraping of the surface with the splines, to bring it to its final faired condition. Now she was ready for the finish troweling.

I think I counted six times that they troweled the outer surface with various types of trowels to bring the surface to a glassy smooth finish. I said I think it was six times, because by then it was 6:00 a.m. on a bright sunny Sunday morning, and I had been inspecting the beer keg and food tables as diligently as I had been checking on the finishers during the last half of the night. I didn't think there was much I could tell them anyway. Someone recorded my careful inspection technique on film, and I was caught checking the insides of my eyelids while sitting on the ground, leaning back against the construction shed.

The party was breaking up. Empty food dishes were disappearing, the beer keg ran just foam, most of the people were gone, and a few stragglers were roaming around, picking things up or just staring at the completed hull. She was beautiful in the morning light. The plasters were gathering their tools, obviously bone tired. Thom produced a new bottle of Glenfiddich single-malt whiskey, chipped some ice from the remains around the beer keg, and poured Bernie and his crew hefty portions as they sat down to relax and contemplate the fruits of their labors. They had done an outstanding job. The hull was as smooth as glass and fairer than any ferro-cement hull I have ever seen. There would be no filler on *Fram*. Years later, coated with high-gloss polyurethane paint, people would walk by us on the dock, knock on the hull, and ask if she was fiberglass. They had trouble believing she was cement. The last job for Bernie and his crew in the U.S. was a beauty.

Their job was done, but Thom and I still had work to do. The curing process was next on the agenda. Around 9:00 a.m. Sunday morning, we started to build a plastic liner inside the construction shed. We had to completely encase the hull with as tight a seal as possible, because we were going to steam-cure the cement. By noon, the cocoon was finished. Thom had three big steam generators ready to go and extra fuel standing by. One by one, the generators were started, and *Fram* disappeared in a cloud of steam. The intent was to bring the entire hull up to 160 degrees and keep it there for at least forty-eight hours, with no air present, only steam.

The mass of steel and cement was huge, so we figured it would take at least twelve hours and maybe twenty-four just to bring it up to temperature, so we planned to keep the steam going for seventy-two hours. The hot August weather was a big help. After a couple of hours, to be sure everything was working, we could leave the steam to do its job. Now it was time to sleep and wait. With one last look at our new baby inside her womb of steam, Phyllis and I walked out to our car. We could hear the roar of the unlimited hydros on Lake Washington a few miles away as they vied for the Gold Cup Trophy. It was a day to remember.

Wednesday evening, we came back for the birth. The steam generators were stopped and the plastic cocoon opened to allow in fresh air. As we stripped away the plastic, sweating in the radiating heat from the hull, I realized she was now truly ours. Thom's job was finished. The cement was a light gray, fully cured, and bone dry. She was still too hot to touch, or board, but we stood and admired the first concrete evidence of our dream.

Chapter 9

Moving Day

We decided to move *Fram* by water from the Duwamish Waterway to Hylebos in Tacoma. My nephew Dirk was working as the engineer on the tug, *Langston Hughes*, which belonged to an organization called North by Northwest, directed by Paul Bellson, who worked with underprivileged kids. Paul thought it would be a great outing for the kids to make the run from the Duwamish to Tacoma, so we had an eighty-five-foot tug available to move forty-nine-foot *Fram*.

First, I needed to add the heavy weight of ballast to the keel to keep her floating upright. I had been playing with my model of the Sea Deuce hull in our bathtub and found that without ballast, it floated on its side—a disastrous condition for *Fram*. I could just see us launching her in the Duwamish Waterway and having her turn turtle and sink to the bottom. A home-built steel boat launched nearby had done just that. I told Thom about my concern, and he graciously offered me a couple thousand pounds of boiler punching he had accumulated. So up the ladder I trudged with buckets full of iron cubes to dump into the water tanks in the keel. I discovered I was no Jerry!

It was time to prepare for moving day. Our experience with moving our two previous boats on land had been nerve-racking. I was feeling anxious about this one because of the confined space around the shed. Thom was now the consultant and I was in charge. The preparations were extensive. First, we needed to move *Fram* out of the construction shed. I had agreed with Thom not to disturb the structure of the shed, which meant that I had only six inches of clearance above the hull and under the massive beam at the rear wall. By the time we removed the supporting timber under the keel, there would still only be twelve inches of clearance to work with. Given the problem, the options were limited. I finally located a house-moving company to move the hull out of the shed and another seventy-five yards to an open area, where a crane could pick her up and lift her into the water of the Duwamish at high tide. It was just as well that I did not know what was in store for me, or I might have developed ulcers in advance.

Moving day arrived quickly. Several of my friends from work came to help. The house movers arrived early with their six-by-six tow truck, low-wheeled dollies, and a truckload of massive timbers and equipment. The estimator for the moving company exuded confidence, but the crew that came to do the job was clearly worried when they saw what needed to be done. They sketched out their plans to me, and it did not sound easy at all. Because of the low clearance, they would have to dig trenches for the main longitudinal beams in order to have room for the transverse support beams. It was a mixed crew that started digging, some of the house movers, and some of my engineering friends. A few of us worked with hacksaws to cut the overhead support rods that supported the framework of the vessel during the construction and cementing process. Now that the hull was cured, it only needed enough support for balance until the support beams and braces were in place.

By noon, the trenches were complete, and the massive fore and aft timbers were manhandled into place. It took a couple of hours to wrestle the transverse beams in place and build the cradle. The last rods were cut, and the hull settled onto her cradle with an audible groan.

Big hydraulic jacks were moved into place to raise *Fram* in her cradle above the ground. So far, the work progressed smoothly but slowly. Now, however, we found there was not enough room under the cradle for the many-wheeled dollies. The shovels began digging furiously again. Slowly we gained the additional inches, and dollies were slipped into place. Meanwhile, a great parade of vehicles began to arrive. First, a huge crane lumbered into place, followed by a smaller crane and then three trucks carrying all the parts to assemble the enormous boom. What had I contracted for? My heart skipped a beat or two since we had not yet solved the problem of moving out of the shed. Looking at that great gathering of cranes and trucks, my mind flashed back to the launching of *Bravo*, only this time I would be paying the bill. Back to the shed to drive the crew faster.

Finally, *Fram* was ready and the move began. I was inside the shed to check the clearance of the overhead beam. With a slight lurch, she moved and then progressed steadily. As we approached the overhead shed timber, I realized she would not clear. My shouts were drowned out by the roar of the diesel-truck engine, so I ran, ducking under the large support beam, waving my arms. Then everything went black.

When I came to, I was flat on my back and felt someone wiping my face. The truck was stopped, and I looked up at a crowd of worried faces around me. In my panic, I had not seen a large bolt sticking through the beam and ran right into it with my bald head. Blood was gushing from my head, and everyone thought I had been killed. A few minutes later, they had me patched and taped back together. So with my head covered in gauze and tape and bloodstains all over my shirt, I continued directing the exodus.

Fram was finally clear of the construction shed, but progress came to another halt. A tree was standing in the way, and our huge load could not turn around it. There simply was not enough room to get by. A quick council was held with Thom. He said the owner of the property would kill him if he cut down the tree.

After chewing on the subject for a while, one of Thom's friends said, "Thom, why don't you go find a brew somewhere."

Thom glanced at the waiting crane, hesitated a minute, and replied, "That sounds like a good idea." And then he was gone.

The friend said, "I'll be back in a minute."

He returned with a chainsaw in his hand and made short work of the tree. With that obstacle gone, the truck started moving again, turning to clear the building. As it turned, the truck and dollies had to leave the hardened driveway, and a horrible vision flashed through my mind as I saw the wheels of the tow tractor sink into the soft sandy soil, along with one set of moving dollies. The whole rig came to an abrupt stop with the truck and its load leaning at a sickening angle. For the second time in my life, I was having a heart-stopping experience launching a new boat.

To add to my dilemma, the crane foreman walked up and said, "I hate to add to your problems, but we have been here two hours, and that is the maximum on our quote, and it's after quitting time. If you want us to wait, I'll have to charge you overtime for the standby time."

"How much is that?" I gulped.

"It's $540 per hour," he replied. I guess I must have turned white, because he added, "I'm sorry, if it wasn't for the power lines, we could pick it up from here."

Overhead power lines again! There was not much I could do about them, so I told him to stand by for another half hour. I was going to have to pay whether they lifted *Fram* or not. I was in so deep now, what was another half hour?

It was time for another council of war. This time the foreman of the moving company came up with a suggestion. He thought if we jacked up the cradle, he could get the tractor truck out, reposition it back on the driveway at a new angle, and put planks under the dollies. The problem then was that he would not be able to clear a small building. It was not much of a building and was only used for storage, but it was not ours. Thom was back by this time, and we looked at each other for a while.

Finally he said, "What the hell? We've come this far. You guys start jacking, and I'll take care of the building."

He grabbed the chain saw and we set the jacks. Inside of ten minutes, he had cut the end off the building, starting at the base of a wall, up to the roof, across the top, and down the other side. A half-dozen pairs of hands picked it up and carried it away.

In the meantime, we were jacking on the four corners of the cradle. In our haste, we made a fundamental error that I recognized an instant too late. My shout of warning was interrupted by a loud cracking sound, followed by a stunned silence as all activity stopped. We had been jacking all four corners at the same time, but one crew was much faster than the rest. In the process, it twisted the cradle, with the hull trying to resist. The result was an incredibly high load on the forward port strut as it pushed against the hull, deflecting it three to four inches into a large bowl shape. The cement had finally broken at the instant I shouted. I was sick at heart as I gazed at my wounded boat, but we had to carry on, as the clock was running.

After leveling the cradle, we resumed with the task at hand, this time being sure to keep it from twisting. When we had it high enough, the tractor easily extracted itself from the soft earth. The ruts were filled and planks laid in place as it was backed into position again, this time pointing in a new direction and with most of its wheels on the hard driveway. More planks were laid under the aft dolly wheels, and the rest was easy. The whole rig moved smoothly the next fifty yards into the street, where the crane sat with its engine idling and at the ready.

Twenty-five minutes had elapsed since I gave the crane a half-hour target. The slings were slipped around *Fram*'s belly, and she was lifted clear of the cradle. Now we could inspect the damage in the bow. There was a six-by-six-inch dimple with the cement crazed over the area. I was not sure if it would be above or below the waterline, but just in case, I borrowed a hand bilge pump for the journey to Tacoma. We did add one precautionary measure. We carefully covered the area with the ultimate stop-gap, boat-repair material—duct tape. History was repeating itself. This was the second time we would be taking a boat into Hylebos Boat Haven with a diaper on her bottom.

The big diesel roared, and our future yacht was swept effortlessly into the air and swung out over the river. When she came to rest in the water, floating high on her lines, she was a wonderful sight. The crane foreman came over and winked as he said, "I think you made it in a half hour." I felt like I was walking on air.

One of my friends with a large runabout was on the river to keep *Fram* under control until the *Langston Hughes* arrived, so that gave us a little time to get organized for the trip to Tacoma. We gathered up the worst of the mess and started a shuttle service from the shore to *Fram*, using a small rowboat someone had brought along. We loaded up with beer, food, and miscellaneous stuff. Several of the volunteer helpers were coming with us for the ride, so we were going to have a party on the way. It was nearly seven in the evening but still light on this clear summer evening. I realized how hungry I was as we loaded the food aboard. In all the excitement, I had not eaten all day.

I was on the bow, rigging the towing harness, when I heard an anguished shout. "Ralph!" I looked back and could not help but laugh. The fellow with the oars in his hands was looking in dismay as Phyllis hung halfway between *Fram* and his rowboat. Otis, one of my engineers, was desperately holding her by the arms as he hung over the side. Her toes were curled over the bulwark of the rowboat with her knees just touching the water. She was hanging betwixt and between, not knowing whether to laugh or cry. It was such an impossible situation she couldn't help but laugh. That didn't help matters at all. The only one that could not see anything funny in the situation was Otis, whose eyes were popping with the strain, trying to keep her from falling in the river. I finally gathered myself together and ran aft to help. Before I got there, he gritted his teeth and, with a last mighty heave, pulled her up. When she climbed onboard, still weak from laughter, I complimented Otis on his magnificent effort.

His reply was, "I couldn't drop the boss's wife in the river, could I?"

By this time, the *Langston Hughes* was in sight. After a little maneuvering with the old direct-drive tug, which required stopping the engine and shifting the camshaft in order to restart it in reverse, we were ready. Paul, the captain, was nervous about a tow with people aboard but finally agreed it was all right if all the children rode on the tug and we had enough life jackets onboard for everyone.

We were underway at last. Paul started slowly and gradually picked up speed since everything seemed to be going smoothly. As we left the entrance of the Duwamish Waterway and headed out into Elliott Bay and Puget Sound, the sun was setting behind the Olympic Mountains, and the strain of the day washed away. Phyllis and I stood on the bow, trying to comprehend the hectic effort of the day and what lay ahead. Everything happened too fast for any full sensation to develop, except a strong sense of déjà vu.

It was overwhelming. Our new ship was certainly big—a giant cavern as we looked back at the empty hull, vastly different now that she was out of the confining shed and in the water. The bow wave was huge and the wake impressive as she squatted low in the stern, being towed faster than her natural hull speed. We stayed there for a long time as the day became night, just trying to absorb the moment. We knew it would be a long time before *Fram*'s bow would be parting the waters again.

Then it was back to the stern to join the party and ease our growling stomachs. Quite a group was gathered there, sharing *Fram*'s first cruise. Thom and Karen were thinking their thoughts and probably wondering how their creation would fare in our hands. With *Fram* out of the shed, they would soon begin construction of her sister ship.

We sat relaxing and chatting about the drama of the day, when there was a sudden decrease in our speed. Looking ahead in the dark at the tug, all we could see was a great white cloud where the tug should be. Was it on fire? The parents of young children on the tug were frantic. Thom was ready to swim over to help, but I discouraged him, saying we should wait until we saw flames. After a few minutes, an outline of the tug began to materialize. About then, we could see the faint outline of someone coming to the rail. The outline shouted across to us saying, "Sorry about the stop, but our engine cooling system pressure-relief valve popped. It does that if we push it too hard. We'll be underway in a minute." It was Dirk, matter-of-factly reporting a little mechanical problem. The cloud was steam condensing in the cool night air. The tug's passengers were in no danger, only those of us in the tow behind had a fright.

The rest of the trip went smoothly. When we reached Hylebos, there were a few tense moments as we maneuvered our new boat into a dock for the night, but it was successfully accomplished, and the long day was over. *Fram* had her baptism but not her official launching, for she was scheduled to come out of the water the next day to sit on dry land for a long, long time. She had but a very brief taste of what was to come.

Chapter 10

The Aborted Start

We were safely tucked away in a far corner of Hylebos Boat Haven—that "land-locked graveyard for boats," with their weathered rotting skeletons. It was with a sense of irony that work was about to begin on this our new treasure. Number one on my list was to repair the damage to the bow. That proved to be relatively easy, except for the five hours it took David and me to break out the cracked cement. We filled the hole with cement after coating the edges with epoxy and allowing it to cure. The repair proved, through the years, to be as strong as the original hull.

With the hull patched, construction could begin. The floor frames and stringers came first, and a temporary plywood floor was in place. The work was moving right along when once again I received discouraging news at work. Our project was being transferred to New Orleans.

We were in a quandary. I could refuse to go, but it was for a good position working on the proposal to build the external tank for Space Shuttle, so the decision was made. We would just have to find a way to move the hull to New Orleans. Boeing had a home-sale plan for employees who were being transferred, and since we already sold our home to buy the boat, I felt they should be willing to negotiate a deal on moving it to New Orleans in place of paying my home-sale expenses. With that position in mind, I broached the idea with my boss. It was received with laughter, but I persisted. After many sessions and referrals to senior management, they agreed to pay for shipment by rail. It cost less than by truck, and it looked like the best I could get, so I said okay.

They wanted me in New Orleans right away, with the family to follow later. I scurried around and found timbers to lie over the open hull and covered her with plastic to keep the rain out. Phyllis was left to take care of our affairs and get our household ready to move while I went on to New Orleans to work and find a place for us and the boat.

Remembering our last bayou home, I hoped to find such a place again, where we could finish *Fram*. It didn't take long to find a spectacular place. It was more expensive than we planned, but I could not resist, so I signed a purchase agreement and called Phyllis.

Located on Bayou Liberty outside of Slidell, the property was on two and a half acres of grass and trees, with a football-field-sized front yard fringed with pines and cypress at the edge of the bayou. At the side of the property was a boat slip, forty feet wide and four hundred feet long and twelve feet deep. At the end was a covered boathouse, thirty-five feet long with a dock alongside with plenty of room for a forty-nine-foot sailboat. Behind the boathouse was a two-bedroom guesthouse with bath and a large storage area that would be ideal as a workshop. The approach to the house was a circular drive through a grove of live oaks and pines. Even though the price was high, it was an ideal situation for finishing the boat. I never before bought a house that Phyllis had not seen, so I was worried if she would like it.

After making a commitment to buy the house, I now had another problem. The maximum width the railroads could haul between Seattle and Slidell was thirteen feet six inches due to bridge clearance over the Mississippi River and our hull was thirteen feet nine inches at her maximum beam. Because of three inches, she could not come by rail. I bought a beautiful home for her, and after stretching our budget to the limit, we could not afford to move *Fram*. We decided to leave her at Hylebos for the winter and see what spring would bring. This latest setback seemed to set the tone for other changes in our lives.

We spent Christmas in a tiny apartment, waiting for the house sale to close. Phyllis was enthusiastic about our new home, and she was most impatient to move in. David was enrolled at LSU in Baton Rouge, and Lynn and Lisa were waiting to start school in Slidell. We were waiting for our lives to become normal again.

Meanwhile, Dirk was watching over *Fram* and reported that the plastic covering was in tatters, and the hull was filling with water to a worrisome level. I managed a business trip back to Seattle with my toolbox checked as baggage. She was a lonely sight, sitting gray and abandoned in the far corner of "the graveyard for boats," dressed in a shredded plastic shroud hanging from her deck.

Heartsick, I climbed the ladder and looked inside. The new plywood floorboards, stained with rust from the boiler punchings in her open water tanks, were floating in water. I was dismayed.

What could I do? I only had two days and spent most of them trying to overcome the feeling of despair that immobilized me. Our beautiful yacht was experiencing the fate of so many others left abandoned to rot or rust away. This time we were the guilty ones. Would this be her grave? I managed to gather more timbers to hold down a new plastic tarp, but I knew it was a futile effort. The final disgrace came when I had to drill a hole through her bottom to drain the water. Now she could not even float. With a heavy heart, I returned to New Orleans.

We finally moved into our bayou home and began one of the most turbulent periods of our life. We had a beautiful home in an exquisite location and were delighted to renew old friendships, but it was not a happy time, with nearly every other aspect of our lives in turmoil. Our children were all having difficulties of one sort or another. David returned from an unsuccessful first semester in college and did not know what he wanted to do. Our teenage daughters were in new schools at a time in their lives when it was not easy to adjust to new friends.

The management of my project at work changed, and an atmosphere of conflict became routine. While we tried to figure out how we could afford to move *Fram,* there were signs that we might lose the contract I was working on. If that happened, my job in New Orleans would disappear.

To try and cheer ourselves up, we bought a used runabout for water skiing, but even that did not help much. To give me a new project, we became part owners of a Dragon racing sailboat in need of repair. Unfortunately, its wooden hull was in such bad condition we only sailed it a few times. I started the repair work but with only half a heart since my real heart's desire sat forsaken three thousand miles away. I was working long hours on our space project, and in the hot humid summer weather, it was nearly impossible to work on the Dragon. I soon realized that even if *Fram* sat in our slip, I would not be able to do much with her in this heat and humidity.

In this state of mind, Phyllis and I debated about what we should do. When I received a notice that the storage costs for *Fram* would more than double, we made a tough decision—sell her and start over again somehow when our situation was different. We could not admit, even to ourselves, that we were losing focus on our dream. Our lives were adrift without a goal. I asked Dirk to put a For Sale sign on the hull and run some ads, but there was not much response. Who could blame people when they gazed into the rust-filled tanks of a lonely bare hulk abandoned like a great beached whale?

In the meantime, the situation at work continued to deteriorate, and it was apparent to me that we were likely to lose the competition for the contract. Phyllis and I started looking seriously at alternate directions for our lives. I was discouraged with Boeing and my job, and we looked for a way to stay in Louisiana. We even considered starting a boatyard and marina that included an exclusive restaurant. We kept our eyes open for likely sites as other events fell upon us.

We took a vacation trip to Pensacola, Florida, where we spent many happy times in past years. The beach was beautiful. We had a good time, but even there, we were unhappy. Phyllis and I got into a bitter argument over something I cannot even remember. I was so uptight about events I could not control that I was lashing out in frustration at everyone around me. It was a hard time for all of us.

Then the hurricane season started. That year, we were not hit with a full-blown hurricane like Camille, but throughout the season, we had several hurricane warnings, and the Mississippi River had the worst flooding in decades. The emergency spillway from the Mississippi was opened into Lake Pontchartrain for the first time in recent memory, causing the lake to rise, which in turn caused our bayou to rise. In the event of a flood, the house was surrounded by a three-foot dike. As our football-field yard became a lake, water lapped at the base of the dike. Then it started to rain. The area between the house and the dike began to fill. Fortunately, we acquired a large gasoline-powered pump when we bought the house, and now was the time to use it. The pump engine started on the first try, spraying a three-inch diameter stream of water over the dike.

By now all we could see in every direction was water. The bayou was gone, and the road was gone; only the small patch of yard inside the dike showed evidence of land. When darkness came, the rain came down harder. I did not dare let the pump engine stop for fear I might not be able to start it again in the torrential rain, so we just kept adding gasoline through the night. It was eerie outside with the red glow of eyes staring at us from the dark when we flashed the light around. The nutria (large rat-like animals) were looking for high ground. We knew the water moccasins were there too.

Water was creeping higher and higher on the dike as the storm raged on. Inside the dike, the last patch of land also began to flood as the pump was slowly losing ground. Phyllis worried our house would become the higher ground the nutria and snakes were looking for. When the rain finally abated after thirty-six hours, the water was at the threshold of the doors to the house. It rained seventeen inches in those thirty-six hours. In the next four months, we would run that pump during three more storms. Fortunately, it always worked, and we were not flooded, but even the weather seemed to be conspiring against us.

In the late summer, David joined the navy and was accepted into their nuclear program, so just Lynn and Lisa were left at home. Phyllis and I located an ideal spot for a marina and restaurant, but we would have a problem raising the money to start a business.

Fram didn't attract any buyers, even though we dropped the price a couple of times. Boeing submitted their proposal on the Space Shuttle External Tank project, and we waited for the announcement of the winner. At last I was not working such long hours, and some of the stress was gone from our lives. The house was great for parties, and there was always a bunch of teenagers around, and we also gave parties for people from work and our Slidell friends. Phyllis was painting again and busy with music activities. The girls were feeling accepted in their schools and had a growing circle of friends. At last our lives were beginning to feel normal again.

Our day of decision came at 12:30 p.m. one fall day in 1973, when the call came informing my boss that we had lost the Space Shuttle competition. My job in New Orleans was over! Now what? Should I stay in Slidell and change professions or return to Seattle and stay with Boeing. I was unhappy with our management, but it would be a big financial gamble to start a restaurant and marina. We knew that if we stayed and changed professions, it probably would mean forsaking our dream of ocean cruising. We had to get our lives back on track. In the meantime, *Fram* sat abandoned and unwanted at Hylebos, tugging at our conscience.

We made a decision. I went to Seattle the next day to talk to the president of the company and lay my concerns on the line. If the management situation improved, I would return to Seattle; if not, we would stay in Slidell and take our chances at something new. Within a half hour, I was being paged by our division manager. He assured me that steps would be taken to change the situation and asked me to please come back to Seattle and participate in planning the changes.

The die was cast. We would return to *Fram*. Our lives had been sidetracked and blurred when we strayed from our dream and lost focus. But out of the troubled time, we emerged with a new resolve to follow our vision with purpose and a clear goal.

Chapter 11

A New Start

We had been gone one year, nearly to the day. *Fram* looked right at home with the other neglected and forgotten derelicts surrounding her. The new plastic tarp was now tattered ribbons hanging over the bulwarks and into the hull. The steel cabin side stubs protruded through the plastic, like rotting teeth in an old hag's mouth. Weeds and brush had grown up around the blocks, making her look like part of the earth. Rust streaks ran down her hull from the steel cap strip on top her bulwarks. We nearly sat down and cried at our lost dream. Then I walked over and tore off the faded For Sale sign. She was no longer on the market.

This time Phyllis picked out the house. It was in our old neighborhood, near the home we sold to buy *Fram*. The girls were back in their same schools, and much of the tension of the last year was eased. Phyllis renewed her singing activity and was again working with her teenage singing group. I started work on *Fram* with renewed energy and purpose. The first thing I did this time was build a sturdy plastic shed on top, over the open area of the hull. It wasn't going to come off this time. I also bought an old pickup to haul materials and tools.

We quickly settled into a routine of working on the boat as much as possible in the evenings and weekends. When winter came, I added a little Gypsy wood-burning stove, just like the one we had on *Koru*. On that boat, the little stove could drive us out of the salon with the heat, but inside this greater space, it was a losing battle. The plastic shed was too big and drafty to be heated by the Gypsy.

It was spooky late at night, working alone, with no one else in the boatyard and with the wind and rain beating a staccato on the plastic. There were no lights except mine inside the boat. Every night when I finished, I had to pick up all my tools and power cord and everything, load them in the pickup, and take them home. I had no way to lock the boat, and things disappeared if I left them. I also found that when the temperature was below forty degrees, my hands were too cold to do anything effectively, and I might as well go home.

Fortunately, there were many jobs I could do in the comfort of the workshop in my heated garage. One of these was bending the frames for the cabin top. They were fabricated out of one-and-a-quarter-inch square steel tubes on eleven-inch centers. It was fun building a jig to shape them, using a hydraulic jack for the bending force. I also made a form to check the contour. The shape had a large radius in the center that became increasingly smaller at the edges of the cabin.

The shape of the cabin top grew before my eyes. I was anxious to get it installed so I could cut down the volume of space to heat. It was a happy day when I started welding the frames to the sidewall stubs that Thom had welded into the armature of the hull. I bolted wood-furring strips to each side of the frames so I could screw on the plywood sheathing.

Some days I drove around in my old truck to service stations and bought old batteries. My intent was to melt the batteries down to lead for ballast. When I started, they cost me 25¢ to 50¢ apiece, but after awhile, the price went up to 75¢ due to the Arab oil embargo of 1973-74 that caused the price of most raw materials to rise. When the price hit $1 a battery, I decided to use iron boiler punchings instead. But I had a stack of batteries by that time. Our home was in a nice residential area, and somehow I knew it would not be acceptable to have a lead-smelting operation on our patio. Besides, I was not quite sure how to go about it.

Luckily, Paul Bellson was in the lead-casting business, and his primary source of material was batteries. He agreed to smelt my batteries for one-third of the lead. It sounded like a good deal to me, so in my groaning three-fourths-ton pickup, I drove up to Paul's furnace. A week later, I went back and picked up 1,200 pounds of lead in thirty-pound ingots.

As spring of 1974 turned into summer, we made yet another major change in our lives. The home we bought in Marine Hills was large and beautiful. It was perfect, but we were not enjoying it, and it cost money that needed to go into the boat. It was twenty miles round-trip to Hylebos, and I was spending too much of my time driving back and forth. Packing up my tools and equipment each night was also a waste of time and energy. We needed to find a different home, where we could have the boat in our own backyard.

Finding the right place took awhile. Our requirements were unique, particularly because we were hoping to find a bargain as well as a large yard and workshop. We looked at several potential houses, but none of them were quite right. Then one night I came home from work, and Phyllis was beside herself with enthusiasm.

"I've found it! It's got everything and it's cheap."

I started to get a funny feeling in my stomach, which was reinforced as Lynn, who had been with her the day of the great find, piped up with, "Dad, you can't buy it. It's horrible. I'd be ashamed to let anyone know we lived there."

"Well it could use a little work," Phyllis admitted, "but it has a garage with an oil stove for heat and a big backyard with a huge garden and room for the boat beside the garage," she continued. "Besides, it's in a rural area, where no one will care if we built a boat in our yard." Then she added, "It's across the road from a beautiful lake."

She really had my attention with, "And the price is under $20,000."

We went to see it later that evening (it is impossible to stall Phyllis, when she is on the trail toward a goal). They were both right. It had everything we needed, and it was horrible, except it had a large living room, with a fireplace and a huge window overlooking the lake. The colors made me a little sick, and the thread-bare carpets looked like they had been installed at the turn of the century.

The kitchen was out of the Stone Age; the master bedroom was the access hall to the bathroom and other bedrooms. One bedroom was so tiny it could only hold a single bed. Except for the big old oil furnace in the middle of the house looking like an overweight monster, with heat pipes going every which way, it was perfect. Oh yes, it had a separate dining room. And the price was right.

Our offer was accepted, and when the real estate agent came to our home with the final paperwork, she looked around our living room and asked why on earth we were buying that place by the lake to live in? At that point, we swallowed hard and silently asked ourselves the same question. However, when we make a major decision, we just keep our eye on the goal and go forward.

Work stopped on *Fram* for two months while I did a major remodeling job on our new old home. Phyllis and Lynn and Lisa pitched in as we all worked to make this dump into a charming cottage by the lake.

Painting the exterior was an experience. Phyllis had this bright idea of inviting her singing group over for a house-painting and barbecue party. Twenty party-minded teenagers do not make the ideal house-painting crew. There was some paint on the house and a lot on the ground and on the shrubs and on the windows and on the kids. The next day, I finished up with a spray gun.

We moved in August 1, 1974. David came home for the weekend from San Francisco, where he was stationed in the navy, to help us. The airline ticket was his birthday present, but we forgot to mention he was going to have to work for it.

Now it was time to bring *Fram* home. I dug out a level spot next to the garage/workshop as her dwelling place, and everything was ready. It was two years since she became ours, and I knew by now the magnitude of the job before us. I originally thought we would be ready to launch her by now. I prepared her home well, because I realized she would be there for a long time. I put down a layer of black vinyl plastic and then a layer of gravel. Her cradle was composed of old railroad ties that would be cut to size when she arrived.

We all bid farewell to her miserable-looking companions as the Travelift picked her up and set her on a lowboy boat-moving trailer. Simple. The only difficulty was making the turn into our driveway and her spot by the garage. A crane was standing by to unload her, and everything went smoothly, a far cry from her last move on land. Now the work could begin in earnest.

After all the movers were gone and *Fram* stood immobile beside the garage, with her bow pointing at the treetops and her stern high in the air only four feet from our living room window, Phyllis and I sat and stared at her, wondering what the future would bring now. Could we really finish her or would we face more unexpected changes to keep us from realizing our dream? So many others started projects of this magnitude and failed. We already missed two years of sailing. How many more would it be before *Fram* could spread her wings and fly before the wind? She looked so much bigger now as she hovered over the vegetable garden. She took possession of her resting space with her decks towering high above the rooftop, dominating the yard with her awkward presence.

As we tried to digest the reality of our new situation and what we must do, we talked about where to start. The first item was so obvious that we did not even have to discuss it. If we were to build a boat in our yard, even in a semirural area, it had to look less like a dull, mottled, rust-stained cement septic tank. We prepared her for painting. Within a week, she looked ready to launch. What an improvement for the neighborhood and our morale to have a glistening white boat sitting in our yard. With that done, we were ready to get down to the serious business of boat building. This time the environment was right, and we let the vision of the shining white yacht sitting in our yard blot from our minds the trials and failures of the proceeding two years.

Fram in our yard

Chapter 12

The Long Grind

Now that we had a yacht that looked like a yacht, the natural next step was to buy an engine. We probably would not need it for a while, but it would determine the size and location of the engine beds and where much of the equipment would go. We selected a Ford Lehman 254-cubic-inch displacement, four-cylinder diesel and bought it or, I should say, ordered it at the Seattle Boat Show. The price was a boat-show-special $2,700. There was only one problem. The dealer sold more engines than he had in stock, so ours was placed on order. We were in no hurry and could wait.

The basic engine was built by Ford in England with the marine conversion and transmission added by Lehman in New Jersey. By the time our order was sent out, the Ford workers in England were on strike and stayed out for months and months. By the time they built our engine, a year had gone by, and the price had gone up a $1,000. Fortunately for us, our purchase price was firm.

In the meantime, I could not put on the wheelhouse roof until the engine was installed in the engine room underneath it. This delay of a year was frustrating, but I did not lack for tasks to do while we waited for the engine.

When it finally arrived, Phyllis, Lisa, and I made a holiday of driving our old pickup truck to Poulsbo to pick up the engine from the dealer.

As the 1,100-pound engine was being loaded, Lisa said, "Hey, Dad, how did they know our boat's name was *Fram*?"

I didn't know what she was talking about until I realized the fuel filters and the oil filters were all labeled FRAM.

When it came time to put the engine in place a few days later, I was glad I waited to put on the wheelhouse roof. A very large auto wrecker, hired for

$25, took about three minutes to swing the engine up over the side and down into place on the galvanized steel bed I had built.

Soon the wheelhouse framing was finished, and I could close off the inside, so my little Gypsy wood stove had a chance to warm up the interior. The big plastic house was placed back on deck, and in spite of the sparkling white hull, *Fram* once again took on the ugly look she had at Hylebos. It was a necessity, however, to keep out the rain so I could work on the hatches, wheelhouse windows, and cockpit area. A large stairway led from the deck down to the heated shop in my garage.

With all the basic framing done, I planned to start at the bow and work my way to the stern, finishing each cabin as I went. The primary interior material was mahogany, and the exterior and wheelhouse would be teak. Since, as Phyllis often said, "we are building the boat out of the grocery budget," economics dictated the selection of mahogany for us.

Thom called one day and asked if I would be interested in buying some mahogany. He and a friend had just bought ten thousand board feet for their boats, but that was more than they needed, and he would sell me all I wanted for 30¢ a board foot. The price was right, and with careful selection, it looked just fine. I ended up with about one thousand board feet that turned out to be enough for the entire project. Judicious use of teak as trim throughout the interior added a touch of class befitting her station in life as an oceangoing yacht.

The teak also came through Thom. A group of his ferro-cement-boat-builder friends pooled their resources and sent one member to Hong Kong to buy a large quantity of teak to be shipped to the States. They sold the excess for a small profit to help cover expenses. I bought enough to do most of the teak work at about half the retail price. My garage was full of lumber and equipment, with the boat alongside and our home ten feet away. All I had to do was work and work and work and then work a little more.

Phyllis and I agreed on the basic interior layout, and it followed the Samson arrangement for the forward half of the boat, but from the wheelhouse aft, it was quite different. Now that I was starting the detail cabinet work, we had to make some final decisions. Phyllis bought dishes and pots and pans so that all lockers could be made to fit. Every little area received constant revision to make the best use of space. Ultimately this attention to detail resulted in an efficient galley with maximum usable space in minimum available space. We worked together, and the process turned out to be one of the most enjoyable aspects of building our own boat. There was plenty of time to sketch out new ideas, think about them for a while, maybe throw them out, or if they were good, adapt them into the design. As a result, we were able to utilize every cubic inch of space and ended up with a practical and satisfying layout.

We searched everywhere for ideas. We went to all the boat shows, crawling over the boats to see how they were designed and built. We talked to anyone that was building a boat to exchange ideas. We even went to see boats for sale (if they sounded like they had unique features we could use). We were pests with our questions at the marine hardware stores. We haunted the library and bought all the boating magazines and sailing books, looking for ideas to apply to *Fram*. We joined the Puget Sound Cruising Club with their many experienced blue-water sailors, and they proved to be a treasure trove of useful information.

The aft cabin and wheelhouse received a great deal of attention and generated the most arguments. We both agreed on the basic idea that the aft cabin was to be our stateroom and had to be comfortable while living onboard at a dock as well as safe and comfortable at sea. Many ideas were explored in sketches and layouts. Through most of the construction years, the aft cabin was simply a dark cave that served as a storeroom for materials and assorted junk

Enough decisions were made, however, to be able to put in the aft wheelhouse bulkheads. The wheelhouse would be the heart of the boat at sea and was home to all the various operating systems involved in a forty-nine-foot boat. The engine was there under the floor and, eventually, an auxiliary generator. It was the center for all the electronics as well. It was finished in teak and equipped with all the mechanical and electrical equipment we could afford to buy which would make her more comfortable, safer, and easier to operate.

With the boat in our yard, I came home from work and changed into my boat-building clothes and started to work. After taking a break for dinner, I went back to work. When I was not traveling, I would work until about 11:00 p.m. or sometimes until one in the morning if things were going well. The weekends were particularly productive because I could usually get in twelve to fourteen hours a day. It was a labor of love.

Before I began to work on *Fram*, Phyllis and I went shopping for warm work clothes at the Salvation Army store. We bought wool pants and sweaters at low costs. I bought a heavy red wool sweater with a high semi-turtle neck for a dollar, and it came to be the symbol of my work building *Fram*. I soon found that with a T-shirt and sweatshirt, plus my special sweater, I was plenty warm in any weather that my hands could tolerate. So the red sweater became my work uniform, and in addition to being warm, it turned out to be extremely durable. It lasted through all the construction years, with only one small problem. Shortly after I bought it, I was welding the wheelhouse frames and a globule of molten steel burned a hole, right in the middle of the front. Even though I sewed it together, it forever after was known as "Dad's belly-button sweater." They knew that when I put on my belly-button sweater, I was going to work on the boat.

Sometimes the work became drudgery, and I simply had to stop for a week or so. When this happened, it would take some time to psyche myself back into the state of mind necessary to work the long hours required to keep a full-time job and build a large boat at the same time. My business trips helped. They gave me a break without the psychological feeling of deserting the boat. They also gave me time to sketch new ideas without taking time away from construction. A five-hour flight from the East Coast gave me a lot of design time.

Music was my constant companion and was another great aid. I had a portable radio that played for weeks on a set of batteries, and it was going all of the time I worked, but it was stolen about a year before we launched. A sad loss. After the radio was taken, I wired a set of speakers from our stereo in the house. When Phyllis was not using the stereo to study her music, I put on a stack of my favorite records and switched on the boat speakers. It took the drudgery out of the work.

Finishing the forward cabin took all of the first year. In the summer, I worked on the outside as much as possible. The second winter was spent working on the wheelhouse and building all nine windows accounted for a major portion of it. The windows were done in an old-fashioned, classic yacht design that required many frames to make each window, and of course, none of them were square. I made them all in teak, and with my small six-and-a-half-inch table saw, it took a long time. They were made in my warm shop in the garage, so I suppose I stretched that job out as long as I could.

Many nights after I quit working, I went out into the yard and stared at *Fram* in the moonlight, wondering if she would ever be complete. Would the bow ever crash through the waves of an ocean storm? Would her stern trail the bubbling wake of a trade-wind passage? Or were we fighting a losing battle we could never win?

One particular day during this long building process stands out clearly in my mind. It was the Fourth of July 1976. Our nation's bicentennial. It was a long weekend, so I made good progress. The weather was glorious. My radio was tuned to all the bicentennial festivities, and suddenly, I couldn't work anymore. I sat down on the aft deck as if in a trance. There were fireworks going off all over the neighborhood. I could hear Phyllis playing the piano and singing.

I looked out over the garden, the strawberry patch, and the fruit trees basking in the sunshine, and time seemed to stop. I tried to visualize *Fram*, not landlocked with her deck twelve feet off the ground but, rather, running before the wind on a surging sea, with sails billowing out and her stern rising to the ocean waves. But the vision would not come clear and I was scared. It had been four years since our last sail on *Koru*.

We could not go on much longer or we would burn out. Many people who attempt building their own boat fail for that reason. Sitting there that day made me realize we had to push on as rapidly as possible, or we too might fail. Time was running out for us! So that date was a crisis day for me. From then on, I redoubled my effort and worked with the haunting image of failure slithering along behind me.

I moved my shop from the garage into the main salon to save the time and energy of going up and down the stairs. The salon only had a roughed-in floor and a table for a workbench and my little six-and-a-half-inch table saw, which was my primary tool. I also had a skill saw, a saber saw, three electric drills, a belt sander, an orbital sander, a borrowed body grinder, and, my prized possession, a large hand plane. I planed all the wood that went into the boat by hand.

After I shifted my shop into the salon, I discarded my plan of building from bow to stern because the salon was between the forward cabin and the wheelhouse and made a good shop. I already made appreciable progress in the wheelhouse, so it was now time to switch ends of the boat. It was time to work on the aft cabin.

We shortened the wheelhouse in order to leave more room in the aft cabin. This left enough space for a large chart table, a small second head, and a large hanging locker. The major decision was the bed. I wanted it to be queen-size and athwartship. This would allow fairly decent clearance to the overhead, so we could sit up in bed. The problem was it would not go all the way to the stern, leaving a large unreachable shelf aft. Phyllis wanted a king-size bed running fore and aft, starting at the transom under the three windows. This meant that the level would have to be raised to provide enough room underneath to clear the hydraulic steering installation. It would be too close to the overhead to sit up comfortably.

We could not make up our minds, so we decided to have a test. I built a temporary frame at the proposed level of a king-size bed and spread out some lawn-chair cushions to simulate the mattress. It was a chilly fall night when we climbed into our makeshift bed. There was not enough headroom to sit up, but we did not feel at all claustrophobic. In all other aspects, it was perfect. We built the king-size bed, and it was one of the best decisions we made. It was wonderful to lie in our bed and look out the stern windows. We also had room for sea bunks on each side, and they could also be used for storage when not needed for rough weather. I built bookshelves to hold our many pocketbooks.

During the third summer, the cockpit was built, the hatches were added, the ports were installed, and the windows were mounted. The wheelhouse and stern windows were made up with three-eighths-inch-thick tempered glass in teak frames. It seemed like a miracle when the stern windows and portholes were installed in the aft cabin. With the bed and interior finishing done, I could hardly believe it was the same dark, junk-filled cave lurking back there each time I climbed the wheelhouse ladder.

The worst job on the whole boat was finishing the integral tanks. These tanks had been left unfinished the night the boat was cemented. Now it was time to back-plaster the insides of three water tanks in the keel area under the main salon and the two fuel tanks on either side of the hull in the wheelhouse. The only way to reach the insides was to climb down through the manholes and work from the inside. I was too tall to fit comfortably, but there was no alternative, so I folded myself into a pretzel and suffered the misery of cramped legs and wet cement smeared from head to foot. If I only had to plaster, it would not have been so bad, but after they cured, I had to climb back inside to coat them with either fiberglass or epoxy resin. After all five tanks were plastered, I filled them with water to cure the cement and forgot about them for a few months.

When the time came to finish the job, I pumped out the water, and they were left to dry. That allowed me to procrastinate a few more months. Finishing the water tanks under the main salon was not too bad, for first, we added several thousand pounds of steel boiler punchings and cement for ballast and, after they were cured, a coat of epoxy resin. This was a job for Phyllis, and she grumbled about being twisted into a pretzel as she managed to get a little more epoxy in the tank than in her hair.

The fuel tanks were another story. They needed to be fiberglassed inside, and Phyllis just plain refused that job. The starboard tank holds about 230 gallons and the port tank about 215 gallons. There was nothing to do but climb in and start. We set up a large vacuum cleaner to pump in fresh air as I worked with the polyester resin. Phyllis and Lisa were standing by in case I passed out from the toxic fumes and had to be pulled out. I don't know what they would have been able to do though, as I could just barely worm my way into the port tank between the deck and the tank manhole. I wished I was Rat!

I could only work on part of the tank at a time, because my body took up most of the space. The sticky dripping resin was on my clothes and in my beard, and if I bumped the wet fiberglass cloth, it would fall loose and drape around my head. The liner was a layer of mat and then a layer of cloth. I lost count of how many days it took me to smear it all in place. I had been folded up inside those tanks for so long and had so much resin on me, I thought I would never stand up straight again. I am prone to claustrophobia, so it was a constant struggle to stay calm and under control. I was extraordinarily happy when the job was done.

During the winter of 1977-78, David was out of the navy and came home for a while. We put him to work doing the wiring while I installed the engine systems. As the spring of 1978 approached, Phyllis and I decided we would launch the boat that summer come hell or high water. We were about at the end of our rope. The long hard grind now had a finite end. The magnitude of work to do seemed impossible with only three months to go. We would launch in August, which was becoming a very big month for us since it seems many major changes in our lives occurred in that, my birth month.

Now when I walked around *Fram* in the moonlight, I could hear the rustle of the palms, listen to the lap of the surf on the beach, hear the songs of the natives in the distance, and feel the gentle rocking of the ocean swells. I looked up at the bow and knew it would soon be cutting through the waters of the sea. I continued the task with renewed vision and vigor.

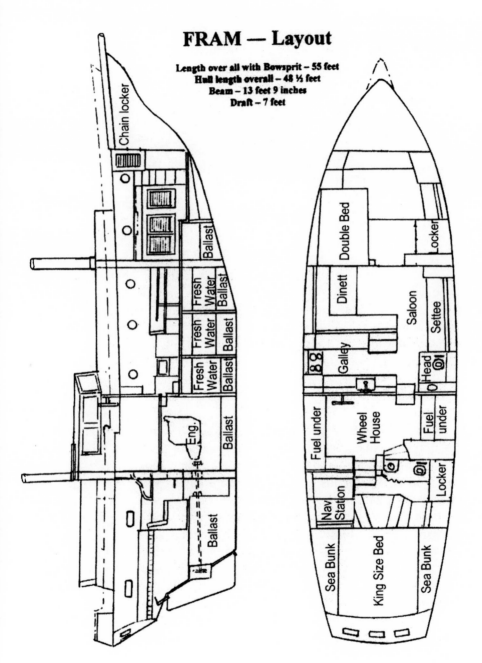

FRAM — Layout

Length over all with Bowsprit – 55 feet
Hull length overall – 48 ½ feet
Beam – 13 feet 9 inches
Draft – 7 feet

Chain locker

Ballast

Ballast

Fresh Water / Ballast

Fresh Water / Ballast

Fresh Water / Ballast

Fresh Water / Ballast

Eng.

Ballast

Ballast

Double Bed

Dinett

Locker

Saloon

Settee

Galley

Head

Fuel under

Wheel House

Fuel under

Nav Station

Locker

Sea Bunk

King Size Bed

Sea Bunk

Interior layout plan

Chapter 13

The Frantic Time

Now with the decision to launch, we took stock of what remained to be done. The list was incredibly long. I looked around the boat, and it did not seem much different than when I started; the change had been so slow. The finished work was mainly in the ends of the boat, where it did not show very much. I had the hull liner in the main salon, but it still featured a Gypsy wood-burning stove, and that was about all. The main bulkheads were in, but I did not have the teak paneling on yet. Up until now, most of the work was building, but now there was finishing work to do, and Phyllis was up to her elbows in it.

She finally settled on the galley and salon design, so I went to work on them. It was much easier than anything I had done before. In this, the middle of the boat, most of the contours were straight, and it went very fast. I framed in the head and Phyllis laid tile. We were having fun since everything we did changed the appearance. The salon wasn't a big empty shell anymore. I hardly had room for my saw. The settee was built, and the dinette seats were in place. The faithful little Gypsy had to go, and it was a red-letter day when there was no longer a stove pipe sticking out a porthole, making *Fram* look like a nautical version of the Toonerville Trolley, the way it had to cant and bend its way above the plastic shed with guy-wires adding to its ludicrous appearance. I imagined the neighborhood would miss it.

Phyllis was having a great time staining the mahogany to match the teak and then adding coats of teak oil until the wood took on a deep glow. We spent one day bonding the teak panels to the bulkheads with contact cement. All the hatches were open, and everything was turned off to ensure there were no sparks. At the end of the day, we were lightheaded and staggering in a crazy, hazy daze after sniffing so much solvent.

When some of our friends came by to check our progress, they cast furtive glances at each other as they asked, "Are you really going to launch this year?" Were we just fooling ourselves?

It was like Christmas as I unpacked boxes of hardware that had been stored since we bought the hull from Thom. Bronze cleats and hawsehole liners went into the bulwarks. Bronze ports were mounted in the hull. When we sail healed over, the hull ports will be underwater, so I drilled holes through the cement to through-bolt and screw them in place. All were then countersunk and filled with epoxy so the outside of the hull was as smooth as Bernie's crew left it. It was just another long complicated process as had been so many before.

It was now time to install the propeller and shaft. I made very careful measurements and sent Phyllis to buy a propeller and have a shaft made to size. I made one mistake. I told her the prop should be right-handed for clockwise rotation, because that was how I remembered the rotation arrow on the transmission when we installed it in place years before. It was hidden in the bilge ever since, and I did not bother to check.

It was not until David and I were lining up the engine to the shaft that I saw the arrow on the transmission showing it rotated counterclockwise. Oops! I was too embarrassed to take the prop back myself, and it took all kinds of sweet promises to talk Phyllis into going back and exchanging it. The sales outlet did not cut the taper in the prop until they sold it, so it was a little more complicated than you would think.

She wasn't happy but returned later in the day with a left-hand propeller. "You're lucky it's a common size," was her caustic remark. "They didn't want to exchange it, but I think they felt sorry for me. It's a good thing since they are expensive!"

I was beginning to believe we actually would be ready to launch. We checked the tide charts and found that on August 18, there was an extra-high tide late in the afternoon. It was just what we needed. *Fram* could be loaded on a lowboy trailer in the morning, hauled to Des Moines Marina, unloaded there for the day so we could apply a coat of bottom paint, and launched on the high tide.

I was nervous, because a heavy ferro-cement boat with over fourteen-thousand-pounds of ballast would be close to the capacity of the Travelift. That particular Travelift dropped a fifty-foot sailboat two years before at low tide. A sling broke, and the boat fell stern first, smashing into the rocks near the bank. The damage was devastating. The mast was broken in three locations and splintered into many pieces. The hull had to be totally rebuilt. I wanted lots of water under *Fram* and not far to fall.

I arranged with a crane company for a forty-five-ton hydraulic boom crane to lift her on the morning of the eighteenth and for Associated Transfer to haul her to Des Moines. The Travelift at Des Moines was available, so everything was set. We scheduled an open-boat party for the Saturday before and invited the world. We were committed.

Phyllis rented a commercial sewing machine and made cushions while I plumbed the water and fuel tanks. I also had to buy batteries. Now the expenses were piling up as we bought and installed all the equipment necessary to put a forty-nine-foot boat in the water. With the batteries installed and all the instruments wired, it was time to find out if the engine would actually run. We bought a five-gallon can of diesel for one tank. I filled a bucket with water and dropped in the raw water suction hose. David was working for a boat dealer at this time, so he was experienced in getting everything ready. When I hit the starter switch, the engine was running on the first revolution. It sat in the engine compartment on its bed for over three years without moving and started on the first turn. I was ecstatic.

As the big day approached, the pace became frantic. Dirk came and helped install the pressure water pump. The outside hatches for the cockpit and deck lazarette were finished. I began installing the head liner in the main salon one night and worked nearly until dawn to complete it. When I finished, the joy in my heart washed away my weariness. *Fram* looked finished.

We needed some sort of dinette table, so one day near the end, I took a piece of scrap plywood and a three-sixteenths-inch piece of cheap mahogany plywood and bonded them together with contact cement. I added a fiddle and mounted it on a couple of pieces of two-inch pipe, and we had an instant temporary table. After Phyllis applied stain and several coats of oil, it looked pretty good, but even today, Phyllis complains about our ugly temporary table. After years of promises, some day I must get around to replacing it with something more attractive. Twelve years later, it has held untold numbers of meals and has been the gathering place for family and friends from around the world.

Phyllis located and purchased a used propane cooking stove that came with two rusty horizontal tanks. The stove had been sitting on our porch for months. Now it was time to install it in its new home. However, the tanks looked pretty grim, covered with rust and flaking paint.

"Phyl, those tanks look pretty bad. We can't put them in their new compartment looking like that. Why don't you see if you can get them sandblasted. We can spray paint them later."

She came back all bubbly with two crisp, bright, clean tanks. "We don't have to do anything to them. I had them sandblasted and metalized, and they will never rust," she announced.

That earned a big kiss from me, and she was right. They never did rust in twelve years of sailing.

In our race against time, more equipment was installed, the galley was finished, and one head had been installed. The last day before the open-boat party, I took the day off from work to finish up last-minute details. When I walked out of the house to begin this day, I was greeted by a glorious, brilliant sunny morning. Not a cloud in the sky, no haze, the temperature still moderate, the wind calm, the time about 6:30 a.m. I wandered out to the boat to take stock of what had to be done that day.

It gave me great satisfaction to dismantle the ugly plastic house that covered *Fram*'s deck for five years. The last floor boards were fitted and installed. All the junk and tools accumulated over the years were removed. She had to be vacuumed and cleaned. The cockpit hatches had to be sanded and another coat of gel coat applied. The dinette table had to be installed. The carpeting had to be cut and installed in the entire boat. The cushions and mattresses had to be put in place. The beer keg and champagne for the party had to be picked up and cooled, and the food had to be prepared. How could it possibly be done by the next day?

One thing is for certain—if you do not start, you cannot finish. I started working on my list, and Phyllis started on hers. She concentrated on the party items and the cushions. I would work on the boat. David and Lisa would lay the carpet later that evening.

That morning, as Phyllis and I stopped to look at *Fram* without that ugly plastic shed on top, our hearts swelled with pride. This sight was our reward for all the late hours, aching muscles, and despairing moments; the delays and setbacks and; the money spent and vacations untaken. She wasn't finished yet, but she was beautiful to us. Her paint sparkled and the varnish gleamed. My fear of her never making it into the water was gone. She was on her way. Now my worry was us. Would we be worthy? Could we handle her? I wasted a lot of time that morning just letting the realization sink in that *the day* was almost at hand. We had not been on a boat—other than our fourteen-foot runabout and a couple of brief sails in the Dragon while in New Orleans—for six years!

Was our dream still alive after all this time and work? How would we feel with a moving deck under us again? These questions were there, but seeing *Fram* sitting unveiled and ready to go overcame all the questions with excitement and anticipation of things to come.

When I went below, I was not so sure she would be ready by tomorrow. The day progressed with unrelenting determination, and we just kept working through the endless lists. By the time I had the floor boards down and the sawdust vacuumed, Phyllis came aboard with a load of cushions. Then the kids arrived and the carpet work started. While they laid the carpet, I applied another coat of gel coat to the cockpit hatches and prepared the dinette table for installation.

We took a brief break for dinner, and then back to work we went. By midnight, the end was in sight. David was laying the last piece of carpet in the aft cabin. Lisa was vacuuming the stray threads in the salon. The beds were covered with bright new comforters, and Phyllis and I could only stare in awe at what we had wrought. *Fram* was beautiful in her yachty grandeur.

What had been sawdust, bare wood, and confusion just a few hours ago was complete; and the beautiful yacht of our dreams was now before our eyes. The salon was stunning with the soft glow of oiled wood and its cushioned settee, dinette, and carpeting, all highlighted with matching wallpaper. And for a final touch, dishes were in the dish racks and cups in the cupboards. Phyllis brought some books from the house for the bookshelves and set a vase of flowers on the table. We were ready for a party.

Chapter 14

Fram is Launched

Saturday morning dawned bright and clear. A few tasks were left to do, but now it was time to party. We weren't sure how many people we invited, but we expected a crowd. The icebox in the galley was full if ice and bottles of champagne. David was assigned the job of serving it. A large keg of beer was set up on the patio. Phyllis had the food all ready, and the party started early as people started showing up. All through the day, people came, some for a short time and some stayed for hours.

Many who helped us on cementing day were there. Some people were seeing *Fram* for the first time, and others had followed our slow progress through the years, watching as each step was achieved. Most of those who had seen the boat only a few weeks before were amazed that we were ready to launch. Others were surprised that we had stuck with the project through all the years in order to reach this day, when we could proclaim, "We did it!"

We were touched as our friends came to see the results of our labor. It was strange to show people through the boat with everything in place. My eyes could hardly accept the reality of cushions and carpet and tile and soft, glowing wood. In my mind's eye, I still saw what had filled my sight for so many years. Everyone's reaction finally convinced me it was done.

When our guests climbed the stairs to the deck and then down through the wheelhouse to the galley, David was ready with the champagne, happily popping the corks through the open hatch over the finished galley. We found corks all over the yard for weeks afterward. Our guest book had about three hundred names by the end of the day. Many brought lovely gifts for the boat to celebrate its launching.

Late in the evening, our neighbor Dan from across the street came over with a couple of bottles of fine wine. The day was about finished, and I sat in the corner of the dinette for the first time and relaxed over one more glass of wine. I looked around at my surroundings, where I had toiled for so many years, which now was unrecognizable. Phyllis joined me, and together, we gazed in awe at our splendid yacht. My gift-bearing neighbor told me that whenever I ran my power tools, it would cause interference on his TV. Through all those years of late-night work, he never once mentioned it.

His comment was, "It wasn't any problem. I just told our friends it was only Noah building his ark."

I would have been a lot better off without the last glass of wine, but it had been a wonderful day, one we will never forget. Major transitions in our lives need to be marked by ceremonies in order to allow our minds to adjust to new circumstances of life. Birthdays and weddings to mark happy beginnings, funerals for sad endings, and parties to mark the good times in between. The prelaunching party of *Fram* was our time of transition. We had embarked on a huge task with setbacks and discouragement along the way, but we stayed focused on our dream, and together, we accomplished it. We had been builders; now we were boaters. The transition was nearly complete. Only one step remained. The launch was set for next Friday, August 18.

The next day, I was off on another business trip but scheduled to return on Wednesday night. Everything seemed to be in order, so I left on Sunday, feeling the aftereffects of our big party the day before. Thursday, after I returned, I checked to see if everything was still on schedule with our movers. The Travelift at Des Moines was ready for us and would have a cradle available. Associated would be at the house bright and early.

Then I called the crane company, and a lady answered with, "Oh didn't you get our message? We won't be there on Friday. Maybe we can make it sometime next week."

My heart sank, and then I exploded.

No, she said, there was nothing they could do about it. They picked up a big new job and had moved all their cranes to it. Yes, they had my reservation, but no, that didn't mean too much. They just slip in the little jobs when they have some spare time.

I talked to the dispatcher, her supervisor, and the manager. By late afternoon, I was really furious and asked to speak to the owner of the company. About six o'clock in the evening, I finally reached him and laid out the situation. I reminded him that I had contracted with them weeks before, just to be sure this very thing would not happen, and they assured me there would be no problems and had confirmed the date and price by letter. The owner gave me the same runaround as the previous people.

I finally interrupted and said, "I can't schedule the tide, and I have a written contract with your company for eight in the morning, and if they aren't here, I will sue!"

Silence. Then he asked, "You're serious?"

"I'm damn serious," was my reply.

"I'll call you back in fifteen minutes." When he called back, he said, "We'll be there at eight, and you better have our money ready." And then he hung up.

We were up at six in the morning. Phyllis had not slept all night. She was nervous worrying about the move. Since we brought *Fram* to our house, we added nearly two feet to her height with the wheelhouse and a great deal to her weight. The ballast alone was over fourteen thousand pounds. The engine was 1,100, and all of the interior cabinets and equipment did not make her any lighter.

We cleared everything away except the basic cradle, and now we waited to see if everyone showed up. I added some long wood runners from the bow to the stern over the cabin and wheelhouse to help deflect any low-hanging wires. The height above the ground would be about fifteen feet with a lowboy boat-moving trailer. Associated Transfer assured me they could get to Des Moines Marina, about fifteen miles away, with that height.

When the Associated truck turned into our street at 7:45 a.m., I breathed a sigh of relief. I don't know what I would have done if they had not shown up after threatening the owner of the crane company the day before.

At eight forty-five, a forty-five-ton boom crane rumbled into the yard. They had not been there more than ten minutes by the time they had the stabilizers down and the sling rigged. With a surge of diesel exhaust, *Fram* was lifted free from her cradle of four years. A few swings of my ten-pound sledgehammer, and the pieces were small enough to drag free and out of the way. With the boat hanging free and clear, the Associated driver, who happened to be the same one who had brought her in four years ago, jockeyed his long triple-axle lowboy trailer into place with only inches to spare. She fit snugly in place in the center slot. As soon as the side stabilizers were in place, the sling was lowered, and the crane was free to go. They had only been there a half hour, so the $550 it cost me seemed a fair trade for the hour they lost on the big job.

With the crane gone, the driver walked around for a final check, and looking at the bulging trailer tires, he said, "Wow, she's heavy. We could never pass a load limit test." That sure gave me a lot of confidence! "Don't worry, we won't pass a scale on the way to Des Moines," he added. "It looks like we're ready to go."

"Aren't you going to strap her down?" I asked.

He just laughed. "She will never move with all that weight. You ride in the boat and take this walkie-talkie. If there are any wires we won't clear, let me know."

Phyllis blanched white. "You're not going to ride in it, are you?"

"Why not?" I asked.

"I've had nightmares for years about *Fram* falling off the truck and being smashed to bits," she answered.

The driver looked at her and at me and shrugged his shoulders. "It would be best if someone was up there to check. It could be awfully expensive if we tore down some wires, even though they are supposed to be a minimum of eighteen feet high over the roads."

"Why don't you just follow us in the car?" I suggested to Phyllis.

"Ralph, please don't ride on the boat," she begged. "I can't stand to watch." I could see she was unhappy with me when she added, "I'll just go another way and meet you later!"

So I took the radio and climbed aboard my ship, saying, "I'll see you in Des Moines."

With radio communication established, the driver started out. We had barely gone forty feet when I thought we lost her. The right-side wheels sank deep into a shallow ditch beside the road, and the whole rig lurched violently, only to right itself at the last instant as it reached firm ground. Would I ever move a boat again? I hope not! I was properly scared. Phyllis drove away in the opposite direction, her face a pale shadow through the windshield.

When the rig reached the roadway, it settled down to a more sedate ride, and we progressed slowly along the back roads, slowing to a crawl as we approached overhead wires. Only once did my runners brush an overhanging telephone line. We swung onto a main arterial highway for a half mile and then northbound on I-5. In seconds, we were doing fifty-five miles per hour down the interstate highway. Lynn was driving the lead car with flashing yellow lights, trying to stay ahead, and David, in the rear escort, was trying to catch up.

I was caught between being scared to death and the exhilaration of sitting in the cockpit of my own boat, fourteen feet off the ground, with a fifty-five-mile-per-hour wind whipping through the few fringes of hair I had left. I began to panic as we approached the next overpass and knew it probably wasn't high enough for us to pass under.

I got on the radio in a hurry. "What are you going to do about the overpass?" I asked.

"Don't worry," a calm voice responded, "we'll take the off-ramp, go up, cross the street, and down the other side. I do it all the time."

It definitely pays to hire professionals.

We received some surprised stares as we cruised up the off-ramp and down the other side. Lynn missed it, but David only had to follow. Lynn slowed down when we disappeared from her rearview mirror, but a blast on the air horn soon caught her attention. We were going fifty-five again soon after reentering the interstate. By this time, my confidence was back, and I was having a ball, waving to the passing motorists. They were in quite a state of shock to see a forty-nine-foot sailboat cruising down the interstate with some crazy nut sitting in the cockpit, grinning and waving.

We arrived at the Des Moines exit sooner than I expected and slowed to a more acceptable speed. As we made our way toward the marina, the overhead wires became a forest, and our speed dropped to a crawl before we swung into the boat-launching area. Phyllis hadn't arrived yet. She said she was going to buy groceries, but I think the truth was she couldn't stand the thought of arriving before us and waiting to see if we made it.

The Travelift operator came over with a ladder so I could disembark from my ship. When he brought the lift over and straddled *Fram*, I suggested that he ought to move the lift a little farther forward in order to balance the load, but he would have none of my suggestions—he knew his business.

"The center of gravity is farther forward than you think," I told him. "I know, because I put in the ballast, and you are too far aft with the straps."

"No," he said, "it's just right."

"Okay, if you have insurance, go ahead and lift," was my reply.

He did and *Fram* lifted clear of the truck cradle by about three inches with the Travelift grunting and groaning. The truck driver lowered his stabilizing struts and gingerly pulled his rig from underneath. *Fram* hung free.

"I think we will move into the yard now," commented the lift operator.

His cocky confidence evaporated, and his jaw was clenched tight as he maneuvered the lift into the yard with difficulty. Once inside the yard entrance, he stopped.

"The cradle I'd planned to put you in is a little small, so I'll put you down here while I figure out what to do," was his shouted statement.

He jumped down to set some blocks under the keel and then climbed back up to lower the boat onto the blocks. As he moved some levers, there was a terrible screech, and the bow dropped with a sickening crunch onto the forward block! Fortunately, it was only an inch or two but, nevertheless, heartrending. The stern came down slowly, so now the weight of the boat rested on the ground with the slings holding her upright. As the operator climbed down, he did an excellent impression of Phyllis. His tanned face had turned white.

"You might as well go ahead and paint the bottom while I hold you in the straps," he suggested. "I need to check on what is wrong with the brakes."

Phyllis chose this time to arrive. Everything seemed in order. *Fram* was sitting safely on blocks and held securely in the Travelift slings. All her loved ones were chattering with the story of our successful journey to the marina.

It was time to get on with the bottom painting. The lift operator had decided it was easier to just hold us in the slings than put *Fram* in a cradle since he did not dare lift us again.

I'm not sure when Phyllis found out that everything was not quite what it should be. It was probably when several other boaters complained bitterly that they were scheduled to be hauled that day, and the lift operator told them that he could not move his lift—it was broken. I thought I might be broken too before Phyllis calmed down.

There was little I could do but paint *Fram*'s bottom and hope they could fix the brakes on the lift. If the operator had listened to me, he would not have this problem. I wondered if it crossed his mind as mechanics came and worked and clucked over the brakes and a bunch of boat owners continued to rant and rave.

The day was nearly gone when the lift operator said he thought they could lift us again. The bottom was painted a dull red, the tide was as high as it would be for a long time, and there was no reason not to commit *Fram* to the water, where she was meant to abide. Our dream was about to make its grand entrance.

The crowd that gathered was bigger than expected as the Travelift once more groaned under the load as the boat was barely lifted free from the blocks. With *Fram* in its clutches, the precarious machine waddled the hundred feet to the water and straddled the open slip. There she was held as Leon Thompson, our pastor and friend, gave thanks and blessed our vessel. She certainly needed it right then. With no brakes, the lift operator gritted his teeth and powered *Fram* rapidly down toward the water. As her keel touched, Phyllis christened her with a bottle of champagne. It was August 18, 1978, and our ship had been properly launched.

It was six years since we bought the hull and more than seven from the time Thom first laid her keel. She was now a creature of the sea. We had made the commitment to our dream and molded it with our own hands into solid reality.

Fram sat in the water before us, and I was shocked at how big she looked. It made no difference that I knew her every nook and cranny. She was a ship now and different—positively intimidating as she sat in the slip. As expected, she was heavier than her design waterline indicated she should be, but that was typical of the design. However, we couldn't just stand around and admire her, for it was time to see how *Fram* would perform.

We needed to get away from the launching slip and over to the fuel dock. The five gallons of diesel I had put in the tanks would not get us very far. I was still intimidated by her size and asked David to drive her over to the fuel dock since he was used to handling boats of her size in his job with a boat dealer. Besides, he had his own thirty-foot sailboat by this time, and I had not handled a boat for six years. The engine started without a hiccup, and the propulsion system worked fine. It was a thrill to feel our new yacht moving under her own power.

We had been deeply moved, when Thom and Karen pulled into Des Moines Marina with *Aura*, *Fram*'s sister ship, which they finished during the years we had been working on our own boat. They came to participate in the launching of this, their first creation. They were waiting on the dock to take our lines, and the two boats were together at last. This special couple was going to accompany us to an anchorage for the night, where we could celebrate this momentous occasion together.

After so many years, I was overwhelmed with emotion, when I backed *Fram* away from the dock and took her out the channel into open water. It was as if a great weight had been lifted from my shoulders. The long late nights working in the cold with numb fingers were over, and it was time to enjoy the fruits of our labor. Phyllis and I sat in the cockpit in a state of euphoria, trying to absorb the fact that we were really underway at last. Our dream was another milestone closer to reality—a giant leap on our path to the sea.

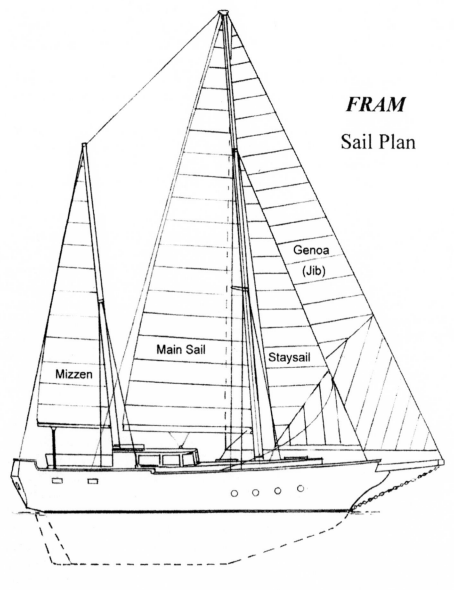

FRAM

Sail Plan

Genoa
(Jib)

Main Sail

Staysail

Mizzen

Sail plan

Chapter 15

Back on the Water Again

Now that *Fram* had been launched, it was time to learn to handle her. We had a lot of work to do to outfit and prepare her for ocean cruising.

It was time to take *Fram* to her new home on the Duwamish Waterway. We brought *Fram* into slip B-14 at the new Duwamish Yacht Club that was to be her home for the next eight years. Strong river currents made docking an exciting sport. It was nerve-racking to have the helm of a thirty-ton sailboat caught in a two-knot crosscurrent as we turned and tried to maintain control and dock her without wiping out either the dock or our neighbor. Phyllis refused to learn this maneuver. She claimed it took nerves of steel that she didn't have. Besides, when we leave to sail the oceans, it wouldn't be a needed skill anyway.

Fram did not spend much time at the dock, and Phyllis insisted on learning how to handle this bigger boat. After our thirty-five-foot, eight-ton gas-screw *Koru*, this thirty-ton fifty-five-foot (including the bowsprit) ship was intimidating. Looking out over the bow required careful judgment of distance and understanding of how far all that weight will travel before coming to a stop. Even though she refused to dock *Fram* in our slip, eventually she could back out, open three bridges on the way down the Duwamish Waterway, raise the sails, sail to an anchorage, drop the sails, and anchor—all while I changed out of my business suit and relaxed with a drink after a long day at work. She could also navigate a narrow channel in a marina and bring *Fram* into a fuel dock.

Installation of a forced-air diesel furnace with a thermostat control made the boat comfortable in all weather. We were shirtsleeve sailors as we steered from inside the wheelhouse during cold, rainy weather. I had holidays between Christmas and New Years, so we began our tradition of a Christmas cruise that year. The family came to *Fram* wherever she was, each year a different place.

December of 1978 was colder than normal with brisk days and clear skies. It was pretty chilly for the Pacific Northwest at eight degrees Fahrenheit. After the family left, Phyllis and I decided to spend New Year's Eve at Coupville, a charming little town that retained many of its early settlement characteristics. We were the only boat tied up at the small municipal dock and went into town to celebrate. The faded sign on the pier was barely legible, but I could make out the notice that said Depth 5' at Low Tide (we drew seven feet). We ended up at an old-fashioned tavern for a hamburger and a beer. The place was jumping. One beer led to another, the jukebox was going full blast, and people were dancing. We were swept into the spirit of the evening and forgot all about the boat until late in the evening.

It was dark, dark, dark as we made our way out the long pier to the dock. The wind had freshened, blowing hard from the east, and we could hear waves slapping against the pilings. When we got to the ramp, the waves were washing over the old wooden dock. *Fram* was rocking and surging against her mooring lines. We had an hour to go before low tide, and we had a problem.

It was so cold the waves froze as they washed over the dock, and in the dim reflected light from the town, we could see that the dock and the lower part of the frightening steep ramp was a glistening sheet of ice. The small ice-covered floating dock was gyrating and bucking wildly and would be impossible to walk on. We faced a hazardous situation, but we had no choice.

Phyllis looked at me and at the dock and asked, "How in the world are we going to get to the boat?"

"We're just going to turn around and back down the ramp. You know, like rappelling down the face of a glacier," was my response.

Then on hands and knees, we searched for a crack in the galloping dock to catch a finger or a toe so we would not be pitched into the freezing, cold water. We were soaked in seconds from the splashing waves, but the adrenaline rush of fear kept us from feeling the bitter cold. By the time we scrambled aboard and had the engine running, we could feel the keel bumping bottom as we bounced in the waves. I used a hammer to break the ice from the cleats and dock lines to free us. With a shaking sigh of relief, we pulled away from that dangerous trap of a dock just before midnight.

After a sleepless night anchored in the bouncy bay, it was long before dawn when we were up and headed back to Seattle. We learned an important lesson. We should have checked the tide charts before placing *Fram* in such a vulnerable situation.

Soon the wind died, and morning brought a ghostly subdued light in the heavy overcast, revealing an incredible sight. The surface of the water was covered with ice as far into the distance as we could see. I slowed *Fram*, and as the bow pushed through the ice, a tinkling song began. The ice broke in large sheets that went sliding out ahead and to the sides, sending radiating cracks from our bow for hundreds of feet, each crack sounding its own unique tone. They were the brass section of the orchestra that accompanied us that morning with the sliding ice being the strings and tinkling bells coming from the small pieces rippling along the hull. This symphony of sight and sound welcomed in the New Year.

Our encounter with ice was not over yet. Coming up the Duwamish Waterway, we could see a lot of ice along the shores. The main waterway was clear because of the barge traffic and river flow, but when we arrived at the marina, it was a different story. Most of the marina was frozen solid, and now we had to break ice to get into our slip. We named *Fram* after an arctic exploration ship but never intended for our ship to go anywhere near ice. Anyway, I started maneuvering *Fram* into her slip, using the standard ice-breaking technique, I think. I had *Fram* nudge the ice gently and ride up on it, using her weight to break the ice under the bow as she settled back down. I slowly repeated this over and over, being careful not to damage the hull. I broke open a pathway through the three-inch-thick ice, and eventually we worked our way into the slip. Later when I checked the hull, there was no paint left at the waterline.

Phyllis often had rehearsals in Seattle until late at night, so it was convenient to stay overnight on the boat. In my job as Boeing's Solar Power Satellites program manager, I was either traveling or working in my office, not far from the marina, so we both found it convenient to stay on the boat instead of the long drive back to our house. She became a comfortable apartment in the city.

In 1979, we decided to sell the house and move onto the boat. No sooner said than it was done . . . well not quite. What were we going to do with twenty-seven years of accumulated furniture, keepsakes, junk, and memories? More important, what would I do for a shop?

Phyllis went looking again and found a small commercial building about three blocks from the marina for sale at a reasonable price. In addition to storage and shop space for me, it made a convenient music studio for Phyllis and her students. As a bonus, it also had a small apartment with a tenant already in place. Our house was on the market and sold very quickly. So just like that, we became liveaboards. Time proved it was the wisest decision we could have made. When the time came to cut our ties with the land and go to sea, *Fram* was already our home.

With our personal things aboard, books in place and pictures hung, we were comfortable in our cozy home. Almost. Phyllis, the cat lover, had been without a fuzzy friend for several years. One day I came home from work, and she greeted me with, "Surprise!" It seems our liveaboard neighbor Don invited Phyllis over to see his boat and just happened to have four adorable part-Siamese kittens ready for new homes. So it was that a little ball of energy with lynx-point markings and blue eyes came to be a part of our new life.

We named her Katisha after the Gilbert and Sullivan character Phyllis was playing in *The Mikado*. Her character and the cat had similar ornery personalities. Imagine our surprise when the veterinarian informed us she was a he. In time he was no longer a he but still Katisha, ornery guard kitty.

Living aboard full time allowed me to get quite a few little jobs done while Phyllis prepared for a three-week summer cruise to Desolation Sound. It had been eight years since we were there in *Koru*. I purchased a new electric anchor winch and four hundred feet of three-eighths-inch chain that I planned to install along the way on our new sixty-six-pound Bruce anchor.

My brother Earl and his wife, Loretta, joined us for a week. One day started out innocently enough. We were running out of beer and ice, and the closest likely spot to find a store was Big Bay on Stuart Island just beyond Whirlpool Point and close to Yuculta Rapids. We checked the current tables, and it looked like we had just enough time for a quick run into Big Bay before the rapids began. We tied up to a rickety old dock, only to discover that there was no beer or ice in Big Bay, so we cast off and headed out.

All of a sudden, with an ear-splitting honk, the engine alarm sounded; and on the control panel, the engine overheat light was glowing red. I hit the engine-stop switch and dropped the anchor. In the engine room, I discovered the alternator was hanging loose by a couple of wires in front of the engine. The alternator support bracket that was part of the forward engine mount casting had broken off. Without the alternator, the freshwater cooling pump would not work, and we could not run the engine. We were not going anywhere.

We drifted slowly in the current, but our new Bruce anchor was well set. Using the fittings I welded to the steel beams in the wheelhouse ceiling for just such an emergency, I lifted the engine and removed the forward mount. With both parts in hand, Earl and I set off, rowing the dinghy toward the dock we so recently left. But the news was not good. The nearest welder was five miles away and reachable only by water.

The fellow who gave us this discouraging news asked, "Why don't you just glue it together with epoxy?"

I thought the guy was nuts but kept my mouth shut, as we were back in the dinghy to return to the boat. We were not far from the dock when I knew we were in trouble. The current from the rapids began to swirl inside the bay faster than I could row. At least it was taking us toward *Fram*, and while Earl gave me instructions, I struggled to get lined up with the boat as we were being carried swiftly in her direction. We had only one chance to grab on to something before being swept into the maelstrom outside.

By now we could hear the rapids as they thundered outside the bay. We both grabbed the anchor line as if our lives depended on it and slowly eased our way back alongside as the water surged past. The anchor line was tight as a fiddle string and humming like a swarm of bees. I wished I had taken time to install the chain that lay useless in the bilge. Back onboard, we looked at the nearby rapids and worried as the sound increased to a roar. We could now see overfalls and whirlpools.

Here we were with the engine hanging free of its bed, too small an anchor line stretched bar tight by the raging current, a literal waterfall a couple hundred yards away, and I wondered how to get out of our predicament. Then I thought about the old fellow on the dock and his suggestion to glue it together with epoxy. It was our only alternative.

Fortunately, I carried Marine Tex epoxy aboard and simply glued the two pieces together and set it in the sun to harden while I dug out some fiberglass cloth and resin. The sound of the rapids was deafening by now as the current approached maximum flow and *Fram* danced wildly back and forth on the anchor that was still holding. With nothing else to do, Earl had a fishing pole out and was trolling astern in the current while I worked. By the time I had the first wrap of fiberglass cloth around the broken mount, he had a salmon on the line. By the time I built up several reinforcing layers of resin soaked glass cloth, he had it alongside. By the time the resin was setting, he netted a twenty-pound salmon.

The engine now sported a big messy cast, and by the time everything was back together, Earl caught two nice cod, and the rapids were no longer roaring. I flipped the switch and the engine started immediately and the bracket held. It seems ironic that some of our more awkward boating experiences happened when the retired navy captain was aboard.

We celebrated my birthday the next day in a quiet anchorage with a salmon dinner, cake, and the works. Yesterday's excitement was just a memory but a lesson well learned about taking strong currents and rapids seriously.

Phyllis and I spent the next week exploring favorite coves and bays. I was on the bow, installing the anchor winch and chain, while Phyllis ran the boat. She was quite competent by now but always complained about poor depth perception and was not able to judge distances very well. I did not realize how serious her problem was until we were approaching the entrance to Prideaux Haven just as I was finishing my project. The entrance was a narrow cut in the rock-lined hills with large underwater rocks that require a zigzag course just inside the entrance. Remembering the rocks in the entrance, Phyllis asked me to come and steer the boat in through the pass.

"Go ahead and take her in. Just take it slow. You can do it," I told her.

"I'd really rather not," she said, "but okay, if you think I can." But she did not sound confident.

I was on the bow tightening the shackle to the anchor as we started through the entrance and everything was going fine. She lined up just right for the entrance, and I was busy doing the final turns on the shackle, when a huge rock filled my vision right under my nose. I yelled at Phyllis, "TURN RIGHT!" Which she did instantly, and the bow swung away, but now the stern and rudder were pivoting into the rock. As we came past, I yelled, "TURN LEFT!" Again she responded immediately, and the stern swung away, missing the lurking underwater dangers, and we were into the bay. Phyllis had nightmares about the near miss long afterward. It was really my fault for not believing her when she told me she could not judge where she was in tight places. It was a scary lesson for both of us.

After a couple days, we reluctantly headed south. We were anchored in Boot Cove, trying to catch some bottom fish for crab bait, when a nine-year-old boy rowed out in a dilapidated wooden boat to say hello. He also showed us how to catch bottom fish for our crab ring. Phyllis poured some M&M candies into his hand while we tried the crab ring. After a few minutes, we had a couple crabs, and the boy had another handful of M&Ms. He seemed disappointed that we hadn't caught more crabs.

"Just a minute, I'll be right back," he said as he jumped back in his rowboat and went charging off across the cove to a float a short distance away.

He hauled a heavily loaded crab trap to the surface and reached in for a couple of crabs and dropped them into his boat. He was back in a minute, tossing two big Dungeness crabs on the deck as he came alongside.

"There, those are better," he said. We tried to refuse them, but he said, "We have lots of crabs, but I don't get many M&Ms."

With the rest of the bag of M&Ms clutched in his hand, he waved good-bye, and we thought we made a great trade.

The next day, we cleared United States Customs at Friday Harbor. It was August 18, and *Fram* was one year old.

The white *Fram*

Chapter 16

The Searching Times

In the spring of 1980, I took a leave of absence from my job at Boeing. For the last five years, I was the Boeing Solar Power Satellite program manager, and we had just completed a three-year System Definition Study for NASA and the Department of Energy. My team included General Electric, Raytheon, and Grumman, and many other subcontractors. This major effort involved most of the aerospace companies in the country. Solar Power Satellites was an energy system that generated electric energy in space with solar cells on giant satellites. The abundant, nonpolluting low-cost energy would be available twenty-four hours a day any place on Earth. The final reports presented to NASA and the Department of Energy recommended that they go forward immediately. However, the Department of Energy cancelled the program, and we were not allowed to release any information to the public. This was a huge loss for mankind and a gut-wrenching decision for me.

My project was gone, and I needed time to put myself back together again. I resolved to write an advocacy book about this energy system for the future of the world in order to acquaint the public with the advantages of space solar power. My leave began in May, and I was free to do as I pleased. We often anchored in a quiet place, and I wrote. One of our favorite places was Blake Island, a state park near Seattle. It was a peaceful time to lick my wounds. I enjoyed writing and the freedom of not having to go to work.

Our list was long and our budget short to complete outfitting *Fram,* so we were always watching for bargains on needed hardware. The bowsprit was a major project. I was looking for a large clear fir timber at a reasonable price and found it just down the road from the marina in a salvage yard. I wandered in one day, and back in a corner, I found a whole pile of various-sized timbers out of some old building. Except for a few nail holes and some surface checking, I could see that they were marvelous pieces of fir. I pawed though the stack and came across one that was fifteen feet long and ten by twelve inches in cross section. When the yardman told me it would be $27, I could hardly contain my excitement. It took a few days to carve the bowsprit out of that piece of wood that was so hard and well cured.

When we moved back from Louisiana the last time, one of the items on the moving van was ten feet of rusty three-fourths-inch chain. Phyllis thought I was crazy and could not understand why I wanted that chain. I told her, "Just wait, you'll see." Now it was time to show her. After being cleaned and galvanized, and with a three-fourths-inch galvanized turnbuckle from another salvage yard added, we had a perfect bobstay (connects the bowsprit to the hull). She could hardly believe how good it looked when it was installed.

It was an exciting day when we stepped the masts at the boatyard next door. We found two used wooden masts that were perfect for the boat. Both masts were deck mounted with silver dollars underneath for good luck.

The stainless steel rigging was fabricated in Seattle, and David and Phyllis helped me install it. When we were finished, I could not stop admiring her. *Fram* looked so different and majestic with her tall masts and jaunty bowsprit. I always wanted another black boat, so we painted her hull black, and the cabin and wheelhouse were painted white. With gleaming teak rails, hatches, wheelhouse windows, and trim, along with her new rigging, she was a classic beauty.

Katisha was a great ship's companion, except when he brought mice and live baby rabbits home as gifts. Even worse was when he left little ears and a pile of innards at the foot of our bed after a midnight snack. It was a shock to my bare feet first thing in the morning. He also endeared himself to our neighbors, who were used to watching out for him as he crouched in wait on the bowsprit, ready to leap on an unsuspecting passerby. Siamese are not only good hunters but were also trained as attack cats.

He often added drama to life on *Fram*. One evening as we were waiting to go through the locks in Seattle's ship canal, he decided to go exploring, and when it was our turn to move into the locks, he was far away, walking on the edge of the wall where we had tied up. No sweet talk or cajoling could coax him back until we rattled his box of cat food and he came running back just in time. Meow, meow, meow, meow. We barely kept our place in line for the locks.

Katisha

One time we were anchored in a quiet cove and had all the hatches open on a warm spring night. I lay half asleep in the middle of the night, when I heard Katisha's claws as he raced around the deck at full speed, sliding and scratching to stop and reverse directions. I also heard birds chirping in the rigging. The next thing I remembered was Phyllis poking me in the ribs.

"Ralph, Ralph, Katisha is in the water. You've got to go get him. Hurry!"

I struggled to wake up and stumbled out the hatch buck naked with Phyllis right behind me. We were greeted with the panic-stricken, blood-curdling yowls of Katisha, swimming around the boat, looking for a place to climb out. I was still thinking of how to rescue him when Phyllis grabbed the big fish net and stuck it over the side. He flew at it like iron filings to a magnet, wrapping his claws in the web so tight we had to pry him loose after he was back onboard. He was mad and pouted in his hidey-hole under the chart table the rest of the day. I wanted to feed him to the fishes.

A new twelve-and-a-half-foot Callegari inflatable dinghy and a used fifteen-horsepower Evinrude outboard replaced the venerable eight-foot pram. I had been caught too many times in situations when the current or waves made rowing a small dinghy impractical and was looking forward to having some power to replace my muscles. Later we had to buy a new fifteen-horsepower Evinrude, because I really screwed up the old one! I planned to have it worked on and put it in the trunk of our '73 Chevy Impala. A couple of months went by before I took it to a repair shop.

The guy called me later. "Come pick up your rusted piece of junk." He sounded disgusted.

A leaking trunk in the Seattle rain—good-bye, engine. The new one was always reliable for many years to come. At the time, I had no idea how important the Callegari and a fifteen-horsepower outboard would be for ocean cruising.

I continued working on the book and thought about my future. When the Solar Power Satellite Program was cancelled, I was devastated, and my heart just was not into starting a new program. I wanted to consider not going back to Boeing and hoped that my writing might produce some income. I also wanted to explore the possibility of working with boats in some way.

By the last week in July, we managed to borrow a couple of mismatched sails that didn't fit, but at least they were sails when the wind blew—although to the yachting crowd, it must have looked like we raided the ragbag. Phyllis stocked the boat for at least two months of cruising in remote areas. This would be good practice in provisioning for extended ocean cruising in the future.

We were going back to Canada, where I would continue writing as we contemplated the future. When we left our slip for the first time as a sailboat in July, we scurried around at the last minute to find someone who knew the horn signals for the bridges. We had replaced our lung-power horn with a handheld air horn much more appropriate for *Fram*. I was worried that after operating as a powerboat for so long, I might forget that we needed to watch out for bridges. It was a wonderful feeling as we headed down the river with masts towering over our heads to watch three bridges open in our path. We headed north to Canada with light joyous spirits.

We were on our way across the Straits of Juan de Fuca when we put up sails for the first time. There was not much wind, and we looked pretty silly with a baggy main and a tiny jib, but we were sailing. After a stop in beautiful Victoria, British Columbia, *Fram* was headed north again.

The day started out like most days that summer, except before it was over, we nearly lost *Fram*. We were on our way to the rapids at Hole in the Wall, one of three entrances to the Octopus Islands. We checked the current tables and began motoring toward the rapids. They lie between a rocky reef and a steep rock wall. As we approached the narrows, it became apparent something was wrong. We were bucking a swift current instead of going with it. We should have known we'd misread the current information and turned around before getting to the narrow rapids. But we didn't. Ahead of us were whirlpools and overfalls.

As we came into the slot between the rock on the left and the wall on the right, we could not go any farther. I sweat as I struggled with the wheel to keep us under some semblance of control. Huge whirlpools caught us and tried to spin us around. As I brought the rudder over to the stops to recover, the force of water on our keel heeled us over twenty to thirty degrees. I could not keep it up much longer. I decided to try and catch one of the whirlpools and, instead of fighting it, turn with it to make our escape. I waited for my opportunity, and when a nice big one rotating counterclockwise grabbed us, I turned with it, but our boat speed was too great, and we broke out before completing the turn, and now were headed for the rock. I was frantically trying to bring the bow around to the right, when another whirlpool caught us. This one was rotating clockwise. We barely escaped the rock, but when we broke free, we were heading straight for the rock wall not much more than a boat length away.

Desperate times call for desperate measures. I shoved the gearshift into reverse and rammed the throttle all the way forward. Water was boiling under the stern, and I thought the screaming engine was going to come off its mounts. The face of the rock wall was rushing toward our new bowsprit at eight knots, and then with a blur, the current swept us past sideways before spitting us out toward safety. Maximum reverse thrust slowed us just enough to keep us from crashing into the rock wall and bringing the new masts and rigging down around our ears!

Phyllis and I were both shaking when it was over. In retrospect, it was a stupid thing to do. We knew the violence of rapids. I should not have kept going when we discovered our mistake, and I certainly should never have tried to turn in the whirlpools. It would have been a fairly simple matter to just slow up and let the current wash us back until we could turn around. We had been extremely fortunate not to lose the boat or have major damage. We anchored in a quiet cove for the night to try and calm our nerves. At the height of the near disaster, Katisha, sensing our fear, dove into his hidey-hole and stayed hidden for hours.

In the morning, we carefully calculated the time for slack current and cruised through without even a ripple in the water. The Octopus Islands were a charming group of small rocky islands that could only be entered through one of three sets of rapids, Hole in the Wall being one of them.

In this quiet anchorage, we settled down to read. We woke up the next morning to a heavy downpour of rain and dark gray overcast skies. It looked like a good day to finish our books. The rain kept up until about noon, when suddenly the wind was screaming down from the hills, and we were slowly being dragged back toward the rocks. The anchor chain was stretched straight out from the bow, even with the engine idling in gear. I estimated the wind velocity to be at least fifty knots as it picked water up off the surface in great sheets of spray. With ominous teeth of rock closing in from behind, we had no choice but to raise the anchor and try to get into a more protected spot. We finally managed to tuck in behind a prominent point that shielded us from the worst of the wind. There was no place else to go other than where we were, because the only way out was through one of the three rapids. We felt trapped.

We were caught in a severe large scale storm with seventy-knot winds in our area. I was getting a little paranoid about the area around Hole in the Wall, so when the wind slacked off the next day, we were ready to move on.

August 18 was *Fram*'s second birthday. This was also the day that Thom and Karen left with *Aura* on their voyage to the South Pacific. We had hoped to see them off, but we were too far north in Canada.

A few days later, we tied up to a dock and invited friends Mike and Micky over for dinner. Katisha went exploring onshore as soon as we were within jumping distance of the dock. Later we heard a thud on deck, a wild scraping of claws, and then through the porthole over the dinette, a wild, wet, furry ball flew through the air, bounced off Mike's shoulder with a shower of water cascading across the table, and came to a stop on the settee across the cabin. Katisha's eyes were huge as he told us about his big adventure in loud, raucous meows. We went out to see where he had fallen in. Judging from the evidence on the dock, he must have taken a shortcut from shore to the boat by jumping in and swimming to our dock. He had done it before to get away from dogs and was a good swimmer. He did not leave the boat again that night. Raccoon eyes glinted at us from the shore.

We went with the tide and had a fast run up Johnstone Straits on the inside of Vancouver Island. This narrow passage was notorious for fast currents and rough water, and not many small boats attempted it. We now found ourselves among fishing boats and not many cruisers.

We followed the range markers through Chatham Channel, a narrow, shallow rocky pass that looks terrible with long ropes of kelp across the channel. We turned at Minstrel Island and went through the Blow Hole, another shallow, narrow, kelp-covered channel into Lagoon Cove. There we found a small marina on floats, a couple fishermen's shacks on log floats, and one house ashore, where the proprietors of the marina lived. Everything that came in was by boat or floatplane.

We anchored deep in the cove, where we watched an old fishing boat come and tie to one of the floating shacks. An old rusty fisherman dropped over an old rusty crab pot and puttered around for a few minutes, putting an old rusty pan on a propane burner in the cockpit. When he pulled up the crab pot, it had at least three crabs. He picked out the biggest one, dropped it in the pan, and threw the rest back. I knew we were in heaven if crabs were that plentiful.

We stayed in Lagoon Cove for three days and ate our fill of crabs and watched a black bear onshore fishing near the boat. We welcomed a couple of kayakers, who fought their way through an overgrown, mosquito-infested channel before reaching the cove. Their chart showed a passable shortcut, but it was no longer open. It had been a difficult passage, and we invited them aboard for a rest and then shared some of our provisions with them. They were on their way to Alaska via the inside passage, and they still had a long ways to go. Hardier souls than we.

We worked our way north, exploring hidden coves, rock-strewn passages, and more good crabbing spots. We fished for salmon along the way and usually could catch our limit in an hour or two. North of Vancouver Island and Northeast of Queen Charlotte Straits, we found a huge beautiful, secluded, and well-protected bay. We anchored in Claydon Bay and settled down to stay for a while.

Fram floated on water so still the trees onshore were reflected as if in a mirror. We were surrounded by this serenity for eight days while a gale pounded Queen Charlotte Straits only fifteen miles away. We did not see another boat or person. The forest completely surrounded the bay, except at the entrance, which was guarded by a small island. Onshore, a primeval forest so dense we could not penetrate on foot. After a few days, we had the spooky feeling we were the last people left on Earth and went fishing for a change.

When we came back from fishing, I called to Phyllis, "Look at that big seal sitting on the rock."

She stuck her head out of the hatch and said, "Your big seal just spread its wings and took off!" The biggest eagle I have ever seen stood about five feet tall with a wing span to match. Katisha didn't come out for the rest of the day.

In September, we started to slowly retrace our route south, fishing and crabbing our way along. We sailed back to Melanie Cove and lingered for a couple days with no other boats around. The apples were ripe onshore, and after carefully avoiding steaming bear plops, we gathered enough for apple butter and a pie.

As we made our way south, it was a time of reflection on the past two months and the future. We enjoyed the solitude and carefree days. We liked the feeling of relying on ourselves for our daily needs and the simplicity of a lifestyle that made baking bread or catching fish and crabs one of the major events of the day.

We generated our own power, and boat maintenance was an ongoing activity. Doing laundry by hand didn't seem like such a chore, with a washtub on the foredeck surrounded by the beauty of our anchorage and the shore beyond. We relished the joy of reading a good book from cover to cover, no matter how long it took, and sitting in the cockpit, watching a beautiful sunset. We liked going to new places, taking our home with us, as well as going back to places we enjoyed again and again. We confirmed that the cruising lifestyle was right for us.

I wanted to try and develop a business of working on boats instead of going back to Boeing. So I decided to spend the rest of my leave to see if it would work. I bought *Highlander*, a forty-five-foot power yacht, which burned in our marina and needed to be rebuilt. Later I bought a thirty-six-foot classic powerboat, *Sea Queen*, which also needed major work. We decided to make this a family effort. I would oversee the project and rebuild all the wood work. David, who was working for a boat dealer, knew engines and electrical systems, so that was his responsibility. Lisa was an expert wood finisher, and she took a semester off from the university to work with us.

I bought an old twenty-foot Sears delivery truck to use as a mobile shop. Parked beside *Sea Queen*, it would be much handier than my shop in our commercial building. It also turned out to be a perfect workshop for finishing *Fram*. They made a dismal pair. *Sea Queen*, painted a sickly light-mustard color with rust spots from bleeding iron fasteners and her topsides covered with a huge olive-drab tarp and the old truck in faded Sears aqua with assorted dents and a lot of rust on the corner posts.

When we finished *Highlander*, she was a beauty. It was ready in time for Dave and Sheri to take on their honeymoon in December. It had been a rewarding experience working on boats with two of our adult children, but unfortunately, as much fun as it was, I could not make enough money to accomplish our goal. We agonized over what to do. I returned to my job at Boeing, because I had to work until I could retire with a pension before we could cut the ties and go cruising.

When we sold *Highlander*, I got a slum apartment building. Dave got some cash and a promissory note that allowed him to go back to the university, and Lisa got the *Sea Queen*. Our family partnership did not make a lot of money, but everyone received something of value, and we had the joy of working together as a family. In the end, both boat-restoration projects turned out beautifully. It was now time to get back to work finishing *Fram*.

When we entered the Christmas season of 1980, we owned three boats and a big old truck and were broke.

Summer of 1981 brought shocking and sad news. Our sister ship, *Aura*, was lost! She struck a reef in French Polynesia and sank. We were relieved to learn that Thom and Karen were safe. This disaster happened on *Fram*'s third birthday, August 18, one year to the day after they sailed out the Straits of Juan de Fuca.

We were shattered and could think of nothing else. Was there any way we could help her? Could we divert to the South Pacific and go to the rescue? Of course, there was no way she could be saved. We needed to accept the fact as Thom and Karen must have. We still had *Fram*, and they had nothing and would need time to put themselves back together. It was a tragic and sobering loss. Their lives and ours would remain intertwined but be forever changed by this event.

We continued our preparations, adding more equipment and using the boat constantly as we learned as much as we could about her while we waited for the day when we could afford to buy sails. When Thom and Karen returned from the South Pacific in the fall, they had most of *Aura*'s sails that they managed to salvage. We bought them, and they were a perfect fit for *Fram*. Her sister ship's beautiful snow-white wings would live on and sail the oceans again. Thus, we will honor her memory.

In the summer of 1982, we invited Thom and Karen to join us on *Fram* for a cruise to Desolation Sound. We were waiting on the fuel dock at Campbell River to pick them up. They had not been on a boat since the loss of *Aura* a year ago, so we were anxious about how they would feel, being on *Fram*. I was fueling when this guy came waltzing down the dock, wondering if we needed crew.

"No," I said, "We are waiting for some friends of ours."

"Damn, I thought we were going to get to spend a week on *Fram*." Then I realized it was Thom.

Without a beard and with his hair cut short, he looked so different I failed to recognize him. I was embarrassed, but he was pleased to have fooled me. We were off for a wonderful week.

We headed north through Seymour Narrows, with the ebb tide, and found an anchorage for the night. We caught the early morning tide for the run up Johnstone Straits, averaging over nine knots. We had crabs from Lagoon Cove for Thom's birthday party by noon. That was after we had stopped to fish and he caught a huge red snapper.

We showed them our favorite anchorages and took them to Kingcome Inlet to fish for salmon. Everything was new since they had not cruised this far north into Canadian waters. They seemed to be having a good time, but it must have been hard for them to be on our boat, which was so much like *Aura*. Our hull had been built in the first passion of their dream. Now when they looked up, they saw the sails from their lost dream carrying *Fram* over the waves.

Salmon

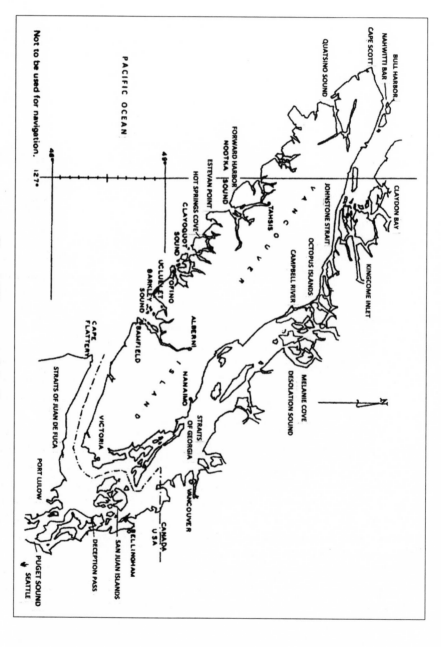

Chart of Vancouver Island

Chapter 17

Fate Intervenes

On January 15, 1986, our dreams and plans were jolted and our lives changed. Phyllis had exploratory surgery that became a mastectomy. She was diagnosed with stage III breast cancer, and our world was turned over. With that dreaded specter hanging over us, we tried to adjust our thoughts to what this meant for our future. The surgeon was confident that the chance of recovery was good, but there was some lingering doubt. Phyllis's attitude was positive, but we were both scared.

After she recovered from surgery, the recommended follow-up treatment was one year of chemotherapy. She adjusted to the reality of living with cancer quite well, but chemotherapy was a hard sentence, and it meant we would have to delay our departure for a year.

She was watching television on January 28, when the Space Shuttle Challenger's solid rocket booster blew up with the loss of seven astronaut lives. She called me at work to let me know about the disaster. This event shook me to the core. As the Boeing configuration manager of the Space Shuttle definition studies, I fought hard for a different configuration that would not use solid rocket boosters (which caused the explosion). NASA made a political decision and we lost the contract. This accident and the Columbia loss later should never have happened.

This tragedy broke open the dam of her pent-up tears, and for the first time, she wept. She cried the rest of the day about the cancer, the chemo, the delay of our plans, and most of all, for the lost lives. It was not a good start to the year.

Phyllis's surgeon gave her exercises for her arm to help restore its strength and flexibility. He was amazed at how quickly she improved and regained its full use. Weekend sailing and cranking winches were wonderful therapy, both physical and mental. Her doctor remarked that he would have to prescribe sailing to help his patients recover.

After she recuperated sufficiently from the surgery, it was time to start chemotherapy and the hardest year of her life. We continued our weekend excursions, and I think that helped keep her spirits up. Her strength and endurance were dramatically reduced, but she was able to maintain a reasonably normal lifestyle. We continued our preparation for going to sea. By having an extra year, we would have more resources and be able to add more equipment to *Fram*.

We proceeded in the belief that Phyllis would make a complete recovery. When she started chemotherapy treatments, we bought a piece of property in the San Juan Islands, where we would build a house someday. Planning for many years ahead helped her keep a strong, positive outlook for the future.

We decided since we were not going to be able to leave this year, we would circumnavigate Vancouver Island in Canada and get some ocean-sailing experience. I had three weeks' vacation available, and that was just enough time for a quick trip. Phyllis's oncologist prescribed oral drugs so she could continue her treatment while we were gone. It would be a good break in the routine.

The last week of June and the first two weeks of July were the best for favorable weather with the least amount of fog. Because the prevailing winds on the outside of the island were from the northwest, the recommended way around was counterclockwise, traveling north on the inside, around Cape Scott, into the Pacific Ocean and south to the Straits of Juan de Fuca and Puget Sound. The total distance was about six hundred miles with 250 miles on the North Pacific. It would be a good test for us, the first with *Fram* in the open ocean and on a coast that was one of the most rugged in the world and known for many shipwrecks. One of the buoys near Cape Scott off the northern point of the island had measured waves a hundred feet high, so it could be a real challenge. We had the best available charts, plus radar and loran—two electronic aids that made it much safer.

We left on Thursday—no Friday start for our big adventure. I'm not superstitious, but there is an old sailor's belief that leaving on Friday brought bad luck, so maybe it does not pay to take chances needlessly. We left our dock at noon and headed up Puget Sound. It was midnight with a full moon and radar guiding us, when we anchored for the night in the San Juan Islands.

By now, the long run to Desolation sound was a familiar routine, and we stopped at a couple favorite anchorages on our way to the end of the Vancouver Island. We had just entered Okisollo Channel, when we encountered our first real challenge for the radar as thick fog engulfed us. The chart showed a great jumble of islands, rocks, and reefs and only one clear passage through.

I was ready to turn back, but Phyllis said, "No, we have to learn to trust our radar."

I could only say, "You're right."

We kept going while Phyllis watched the radar screen in the wheelhouse and called out steering directions. We were doing just fine. Then the fog lifted a few feet off the surface, and I could just see under the overcast, but from down below, she could not. I decided to pull her leg a little. I steered a course toward a group of rocks, knowing that would certainly excite her, and it did. When she caught on to the joke, she made life a little difficult for me for a while.

We anchored in a small rocky bay in preparation for a long run north in the morning. It was 4:00 a.m. when we slipped out of the anchorage in the dark. We cranked up the engine and stretched *Fram's* legs under a leaden, overcast sky. We traversed Johnstone Straits, riding the favorable current all the way to the end. At eight thirty that evening, in a glorious sunset, we dropped the anchor in Bull Harbor, just inside Nahwitti Bar at the northern tip of Vancouver Island. We relaxed in the cockpit, absorbing the quiet, rugged beauty around us after a long and tiring day.

We tried to ignore the fact that six hours from now, we were going to cross dangerous Nahwitti Bar. This shallow bar is exposed to the full thrust of the northwest winds out of Alaska, which can create fearsome waves. The safest time to cross was at high slack tide.

After a few hours of restless sleep, the alarm rang. My sleepy brain knew I had to get up. This was the day. All the years of dreaming and planning had come down to this 2:00 a.m. departure, and I was nervous. Our anchor was up, and we were out of the bay when I had second thoughts about the challenges we would face, but it was too late to turn back. With a tightening in my gut, we approached the infamous bar. It was the only way around the north end of the island, so we had no choice.

We were across Nahwitti Bar and hardly knew it was there, except for the shallow readings on our depth sounder. We crossed at exactly the right time under a full moon in a glorious night with a small swell and no wind. We had timed it perfectly.

However, we had a real scare after crossing the bar. We saw a mass of strobe lights to the north. We couldn't tell how far away they were or what they were. Certain lights are used as aids for navigation at night, but strobe lights were not recognized as such. I turned on the radar, but it did not answer the question either. I still wasn't sure about all the strobe lights, but there didn't seem to be anything too close, so we just kept going. It remained a mystery until we later learned they were fishing boats. The fishermen just shut down their engines at night, turn on a strobe light, and go to sleep while they drift.

We motored in a gentle swell with no wind. The sky was ablaze with stars, and our introduction to the big ocean was one of majestic beauty. I saw the light on Cape Scott as dawn crept up behind us. The new day arrived along with the current, wind, and waves. In perfect wind conditions, we were exhilarated to finally be sailing on the ocean. It was a radiant morning as we sat in the cockpit, bundled against the cold with steaming cups of coffee, and watched the sunrise burst over the mountains of Vancouver Island. *Fram* slipped quietly along in the ocean swells, and our hearts swelled with joy at being there at last. It was seventeen and a half years since our first wild sail down Lake Pontchartrain in *Bravo*, and here we were in a magnificent ship of our own creation, living our dream.

By noon we were off Quatsino Sound, our first anchorage on the outside. Reluctantly, we left the sea as we turned and made our way into Forward Inlet and on to Winter Harbor. We were in another world. The day we were there, it was as if we traveled back in time when we found no other yachts and only a couple old fishing boats. Home to a large fishing fleet, onshore was a small store and several small shacks. It didn't appear like anyone was around, except for smoke from the chimneys, the only evidence of humans. We slipped into a shallow little cove, dropped our anchor and a couple of crab pots, and lay down to take a nap. It had been a long but wonderfully gratifying morning.

We moved on to Julian Cove in the afternoon and watched huge black-and-white eagles fishing as they swooped back and forth over the cove, ignoring our large black-and-white invader of their wilderness. We were breathless as we witnessed this amazing display close off our bow.

One large eagle sat on the top of a tree, being harassed by a raven that would not leave him alone. It flit around, pecking and cawing, and made a terrible fuss. Why the eagle, which was ten times as big, put up with it, I did not know. It could easily have crushed the smaller bird with its beak or one of its huge talons. Even when the eagle took off, that was not the end of it, because the raven attacked in the air, pulling feathers out as it flew. It looked like a fighter plane attacking a huge bomber.

Our days were idyllic as we sailed, wing and wing, down the desolate coast in steady twenty-knot winds, with waves rolling majestically under our stern. We explored a wonderland of rocky shores and dense forests. We feasted on the bounty of the sea and spent our solitude reading and reflecting on the crooked path that brought us to this place. We would sail many oceans and see many wonderful places, but we knew that in the end, we would once again return to the Pacific Northwest and one of the most spectacular cruising grounds in the world.

On the day we were to go around Estevan Point, we woke to a heavily overcast sky and a weather report predicting thirty-five-knot southeast winds in our area. We decided not to try and round that fearsome point of many shipwrecks in these conditions. We relaxed and read in our warm and cozy salon, redolent with the fragrance of fresh-baked bread. We were safely anchored in Friendly Cove, behind a hooked bite of land protecting the cove from the Pacific Ocean.

It has an interesting history. It was the location of a large Indian village until recently and was the site of the Europeans' first landing and base of operations on the Pacific Northwest coast. The Spanish and then the British, including Captain James Cook and later Captain George Vancouver, made their landfalls at Friendly Cove. All that remains today is a lighthouse, a few buildings, and a church.

When we anchored earlier, two fishing boats were already there. It was protected, but some swell came in and gently rocked the boat. By nightfall, the wind was howling and the cove was chockablock full of fishing boats sheltering from the storm. It rained most of the day, and the wind built up big seas. In our bouncy world, we ate and read and slept through a bumpy night.

When I woke up at 6:00 a.m. the next day, it was still raining and blowing and the fishing boats were still there, so I went back to sleep. By noon, it stopped raining and the wind had died. The weather report still showed a low-pressure system moving through, with another behind it but weakening. A couple of fishing boats were getting underway, so we thought we should too. We had the anchor up when we saw them turn inland instead of out to sea, but we decided to go anyway.

We prepared to round Estevan Point, the "Cape of Storms." We set a course straight out to sea to avoid a shallow area of reefs near the point. The first several miles went pretty well. Then the fog rolled in; we were hit with squalls, and the ghosts of fear crawled aboard. Dread crept up my spine as I thought of the many ships that came to grief when caught on this lee shore, unable to claw their way clear. With the aid of radar and loran, we approached the point carefully, staying far away from the rocky reefs awaiting the unwary sailor. When we reached the point, we were struck with the full impact of the wind and swells. *Fram* handled the rough conditions reasonably well, but I was worried about Phyllis.

I looked at her huddled in the corner of the cockpit and asked, "Are you okay?"

"How much longer until we're out of this?" she asked. "I can hang in there until we get to Hot Springs Cove," she assured me.

I saw she was exhausted. When we turned the corner and approached the entrance to the cove, at last we had some relief from the strong wind and big seas. We were welcomed by porpoises joyfully playing in our bow wave, and the sun broke through the fog. We relished this unexpected reward at the end of a nasty day.

One of my worries had been seasickness on the ocean, but so far it had not been a problem. Phyllis seemed to be particularly immune, and it was only when I was below for an extended period of time that I felt queasy. The question of how I would do on a passage would not be answered on this trip, because we were only sailing short distances and anchoring each night. Twenty-four-hour watches would be another story. I'll just have to wait and see.

In the morning, the bad weather was gone when we took the dinghy ashore and got an early start to the Hot Springs. The trail was a long rugged walk through a rank forest. The trees formed a dense dripping canopy over our heads, holding out the sun. Moss clung to the tree trunks and the ground. Our legs brushed rich green ferns as we walked on the soft, spongy earth. Much of the trail was a crude boardwalk, where it crossed marshy bogs or stairs in steeper spots. It was a one-and-a-half-mile hike but seemed much longer. Phyllis was pretty tired and was ready for a relaxing session in the warm water.

We slipped out of our clothes and lay in the luxurious embrace of the soothing hot pool. Steam drifted into the cool early morning air, sunshine danced on the ocean waves a short distance away, and birds sang in the trees. Time stopped for a while to let us enjoy this lovely natural oasis.

On the Fourth of July, we were on our way to Ucluelet, in Barkley Sound. The waves were the biggest we had seen yet. As we surged through the seas, I reflected back to the depressing day ten years ago, when I wondered if our ship would ever run before the wind and ride down the ocean swells. We waited a long time for this experience. When *Fram*'s bow rose and buried itself in the waves and her stern lifted to the following seas, it reaffirmed our commitment to go to sea. This has been an important and rewarding time while we learned how to handle our ship and ourselves on the ocean. *Fram* is a fine vessel that will carry us safely wherever we want to roam.

Riding the ocean swells

That day, we were sailing among the fishing fleet with a sea of masts and fishing gear around us. It was weird watching them in the huge ocean swells. The fishing boats looked like a swarm of grasshoppers, one moment sitting on top the waves and the next with only their bent legs showing as they dropped into the trough. We wondered what we looked like to them.

I was getting the nervous jitters as we approached Ucluelet. I worried about the narrow rock-strewn entrance to the inlet with such a large sea running. How and when could we take the sails down? We would be sailing into the unknown.

When we were off the entrance, I forgot my worries about finding the safe passage. All I had to do was fall in line with the fishing fleet going in. There was a string of boats coming from over the horizon into the entrance. One slowed and let us join their ranks. Fortunately, as we turned east, it put us on a beam reach, and with all our sails up, we were charging along at over eight knots and fit in nicely with their boats at that speed.

What was I going to do when everyone else stopped? In the meantime, with our large sails driving us fast, I had my hands full, just staying in the narrow slot between the crashing breakers on the fringing reefs. Phyllis was prepared to go forward and drop the sails as fast as possible, when we rounded the point into the inlet. Then it dawned on me that Ucluelet did not look very big on the chart, and there was an incredible number of fishing boats entering.

Where were they all going? I did not have long to wonder, as we came past the last little islet and turned into the inlet. There they were, stopped right in front of me, bringing in their outriggers and flopper stoppers. I was momentarily stunned by the solid wall of boats dead ahead, but I was just able to dodge the closest ones while *Fram* lost speed, and I chose a spot to round up into the wind to get the sails down. Phyllis was ready and brought the jib down immediately; the main followed quickly, and we were stopped. We would lower the mizzen and staysail as we motored through the protected inlet. It had been an exciting entrance that I would just as soon not repeat.

The excitement wasn't quite over for the day. The wind was still blowing as we entered the marina. It looked like there was room for us, so we motored past the end of several docks to get to the inside slips that were still empty. As I circled around to come in on the starboard side, I knew I was in trouble. The wind was too strong to make the turn, and my bow was blown off at a prodigious rate toward the dock and its supporting piling. The wind was in control, and I just hoped to minimize the damage. I put it in reverse and tried to back away, when a fellow sailor came running down the dock to give us a hand. *Fram* stopped just as the bow pulpit bumped against a piling. With that as a fulcrum and a stern line thrown to the guy on the dock, we worked ourselves into the pier. I was pretty embarrassed about the inept entrance but very appreciative of the fellow on the dock for saving us from any serious damage to ourselves or others.

(A year and a half later, we sat having a beer with a new arrival in Cabo San Lucas, Mexico, when the owner asked me, "Do you remember that day in Ucluelet when you lost it coming into the dock?" We were sitting on *Homer's Odyssey*, and Homer was the guy who helped us. What a small but wonderful world.)

We enjoyed our time in Ucluelet while we wandered the docks and stopped to talk to the fishermen. One told us yesterday was the roughest day of the fishing year so far, and they were running for shelter. I thought the seas were awfully big to be able to hide a forty-five-foot fishing boat with twenty-five-foot masts and outriggers in the trough of a wave. By nightfall, it seemed like every fishing boat in our part of the world was there. I took Phyllis out to dinner in appreciation for her courage on this great adventure. We were equal partners in every way and especially this, our dream and vision for a new life.

The next day was overcast, but there was no wind, so after doing laundry and buying groceries and beer, we headed out into the protected enclosed waters of Barkley Sound. It was warm and muggy, and the strong wind had abated. We found a lovely little bay with two other boats already there. Yesterday, *Lady Hartley* found the rocky reef at the entrance with her keel and warned us to keep a sharp lookout on the bow. I guess it was quite a bang when she hit, but she wasn't leaking, and the only thing damaged was their pride. We appreciated the warning and avoided the reef as we entered the bay. In these remote locations, most dangers aren't well charted, and we learned to be extra careful.

It was the sort of place that weaves a magic spell, and we just could not get enough of it. We stayed up late, sitting in the cockpit, listening to the gentle slap of waves on the hull, and drinking in the beauty of the place while watching Venus chase the sun into night.

The next day, I worked on a project that proved to be one of the most versatile and useful additions we ever made. I built a table of one-inch-thick solid teak on the back of one of the cockpit seats. It was a fish-filleting table, a workbench, a buffet table, a place to set the barbecue, and any number of other uses. We let the teak go natural and also used it as a cutting board. I could mount my heavy-duty vise on one corner, and over the years, I have made many replacement parts for our boat and other people's boats with the vise and that workbench. A large vise on a sailboat never failed to get attention, and *Fram* became well-known for that workbench. I installed a saltwater pressure water hose underneath it, so a quick rinse removed most of the fish mess in moments.

During our cruise, we caught a lot of fish. Katisha thought bottom fish were a whole lot better than salmon, and the only thing he liked better was crab. It became a daily ritual to catch his fish and fillet it for him on the table. Once I started the filleting and skinning process, he sat patiently and watched until I was finished and gave him his portion. He always made sure it was for him. He sat and meowed and looked at me until I told him it was all right, and then he pounced and it was gone.

We enjoyed exploring Barkley Sound, but time was marching on, and we had to start back to Seattle. We were up early and headed back out into the ocean swells with visibility less than a mile in heavy mist and rain. By the time we were three miles out, the wind was blowing hard, and we were beam on to the waves. *Fram* was slammed from side to side, with rain coming in torrents. When we turned southeast, we were motoring into the wind, which was worse.

It was hard on Phyllis as we slugged it out with the waves on our nose. It was the roughest ride we had experienced yet on *Fram*, and we were both uncomfortable, with nervous fear gnawing at us. Our best speed was three knots, and the noise of things breaking free and flying around inside the boat added to our anxiety. The coffee pot was clamped on the stove, but its lid, insides, and contents were decorating the galley floor, counter, and assorted crevasses.

In time, the motion eased once we were in the Straits of Juan de Fuca, and our speed increased to five knots. With limited visibility, we used radar and loran to keep us on course and away from shipping. I never dreamed the first time we would actually travel the straits would be coming in from the Pacific Ocean. After several hours, the wind died, and the rain stopped. With an incoming tide, we were swept along on a two- to three-knot current in addition to our boat speed, so we were making good time. We had our fishing lines out and were trolling for salmon near the shore when the engine went clickity-clack, *bang*, and I immediately shut it down.

The alternator-mounting bolt had broken again. This was the third time something had broken on the alternator support structure, and I knew I was going to have to do something more permanent than just replacing the bolt. Phyllis ran forward and raised a sail while I worked to jury-rig a fix for the alternator bolt. When we sailed past our destination for the night, Phyllis was near tears. By the time the alternator was fixed, we were close to Victoria. With the last moments of daylight, we came into the visitors' dock in front of the Empress Hotel and pulled into the last empty slip. It had been a long day, and Phyllis was completely exhausted.

Our circumnavigation of Vancouver Island convinced us our dream would become a living reality worth all the years of planning, working, and preparation. We passed our own final exam. Now we were ready for the real thing. By the time Phyllis finished fifty-two weeks of chemotherapy and her body recovered, we would be ready.

We spent about two and a half weeks on the outside of Vancouver Island, and it was not nearly enough time to see and enjoy all of its spectacular cruising areas. It was remote and primitive, with magnificent scenery, great cruising areas, and wonderful fishing. There were more rocks and rugged forbidding shorelines than one might like, but that was part of its majesty and beauty. It was not a place to take lightly. It could be very dangerous. There were few navigation aids, and dense fog could close in at any time. The seas could be huge, and the weather systems were influenced by storms and winds out of the North Pacific and the Gulf of Alaska. It was a fascinating place to explore and gave *Fram* and her crew important preparation for the years to come.

Salmon are big in the ocean

Chapter 18

The Final Preparation

Once again we set a date. We would sail away on August 10, 1987, my birthday. Our first goal was to be in Cabo San Lucas, Mexico, for Christmas. After that, our destination was not as clear. We planned for years to go down the coast to Mexico and then on through the Panama Canal to the Caribbean, up the east coast of the U.S., and cross the Atlantic to Europe. A few cruising acquaintances told us we ought to go west into the South Pacific. We would decide later, but for now, Cabo was our goal.

We moved *Fram* to Shilshole marina in Seattle, close to all the marine stores as we made final installations of equipment and preparations to go. We enjoyed the activity at Shilshole, and it was good for Phyllis to be in the heart of a sailing community. Also, it was easier to get out for the weekends. Our slip at the Duwamish Yacht Club was rented immediately, and we put it up for sale.

One item we did not have was a boom gallows. It was not safe trying to control a sail on a boom that is moving around in heavy seas. Topping lifts and sheets simply cannot hold a boom steady enough to work in safety. The noise and motion of the boom working back and forth when the main is lowered in a rolling sea is also disturbing as well as wearing on the gear. A boom gallows was an essential piece of gear on a cruising sailboat.

In December, we were once again on our trek north to the San Juans for the Christmas holidays. We left Shilshole in the morning on the twenty-first with a heavy overcast and light rain. We ran before southerly winds with the jib alone. The furnace made the boat warm and comfortable, and the autopilot steered as I watched for boat traffic from the wheelhouse. There was a football game on TV, so I started the generator and went down to the main salon to watch the game while Phyllis took over the watch. It was such a miserable day the only other boat traffic was ferries and an occasional freighter.

As we passed Foul Weather Bluff, it seemed like our course was a little erratic, so I opened the hatch and went out in the cockpit to see what was going on. The wind almost knocked me down. We were above hull speed as we charged down the waves with *Fram*, yawing and struggling when she reached the trough. We turned on the weather station and heard there were sixty-knot winds in the nearby Straits of Juan de Fuca, where we were headed.

Port Ludlow, the last good anchorage before the straits, was off to our port side; and suddenly it seemed like a nicer place to be in that wind, so I turned to the left. With wind nearly abeam, all of a sudden there was a loud crack like a cannon shot, and all hell broke loose forward. The jib sheet had parted, and the noise of its flapping and snapping was deafening as the jib tore itself to shreds. Phyllis started the engine and brought us into the wind while I went forward to work with the sail.

I had to get out on the bowsprit and manhandle the remains down. I crawled out across the pitching deck toward the bowsprit. As each wave drove under us, the bow raised about fifteen feet and then dropped into the trough, burying everything forward, including me, underwater. I was lifted clear on each downward plunge. That water was cold! When I was back in the warm wheelhouse, I felt like a frozen, half-drowned rat and was a little queasy from all the time spent in free fall.

When the anchor was down and I was warm and dry with a hot buttered rum in hand, life looked a lot better. However, we were sobered by how quickly a small problem became a big problem. It was before we wore safety harnesses while working on deck, and I felt pretty lucky that the sea had overlooked an opportunity to teach a fool a deadly lesson.

During the next several months, we focused on preparing for the big day. It was amazing how many things had to be taken care of in order to phase out a land-based life and, at the same time, prepare and stock a boat for an open-ended world cruise. Phyllis enrolled in a celestial navigation class and a weekend seminar on sail repairs and maintenance. I designed and fabricated a boom gallows for the main boom and had one built for the mizzen.

I revamped all of our running rigging and brought the lines to the cockpit, where we would be able to raise and lower the jib, main, and mizzen as well as reef the main without leaving the safety of the cockpit. This was important with only two people handling a large boat. The staysail would still be raised and lowered at the mast, but it was a small sail and easy to handle. We found that Phyllis needed self-tailing winches to handle many of the tasks, so we added several.

I finally told my boss I was going to retire so he could find my replacement. He didn't try to talk me out of it but asked me to stay until June 1. That made our schedule a little tighter, but it would work out all right, so I agreed. Phyllis finished her chemotherapy and was feeling good again, walking every day to get her strength back and was her normal cheerful self.

The first weekend in April, we sailed to Port Townsend for her seminar on sail repair at Hasse and Petrich, Port Townsend Sails. It was a productive weekend. She was thrilled with her class and impressed with the high quality of their cruising sails. We ended up ordering a new jib and mainsail and arranged to have the rest of our sails reworked to their standards.

Our three kids (no longer kids but young adults) were settled into careers and lives independent of their parents. David and Shari had finished school, and David was hired at Boeing, another Nansen engineer. Lynn enjoyed a career at Frank Russell Company in Tacoma and was single, living in the house she remodeled a few years ago, with a little help from her dad. Lisa and Doug were married in 1985, and she was working at Microsoft while Doug, the consummate host, was a flight attendant for Alaska Airlines. Following graduation from the university, they had been able to buy a house after selling *Sea Queen*.

We made one more excursion with all of them before I retired. We took *Fram* into Hood Canal for the first time, entering through the opened draw span of the Hood Canal floating bridge. It was a wonderful nostalgic time since this was the last time our family would all be together on *Fram* for many years.

We sold our commercial building and two of our four vehicles (including the Sears delivery van). Phyllis sang her last concert, and my retirement was effective on June 1, so we were committed. Even though I looked forward to that day for many years, it was a traumatic moment after thirty years with Boeing, many of them involved with the most exotic and advanced space projects created by man. They were exciting and gratifying years for the most part. I like to believe that through my professional life, I made some contribution that helped civilization advance a little. My anticipation of this day focused on allowing us the freedom to start a new lifestyle that would not have to end until we wanted it to.

We took *Fram* back to Port Townsend to haul out and paint the entire boat. We had to raise the waterline for the third time. *Fram* was getting fat. It couldn't have been all the scrap metal in the bilge (carried for repairs), and I was sure it was not the spare parts or boxes of screws and bolts or even extra pieces of wood. Phyllis claimed her supplies did not weigh anything, particularly not the sewing machine, microwave oven, food processor, or canning jars. It might have been the welder or little table saw I squeezed into the bilge underneath the dinette or those reels of copper wire from Boeing Surplus Store that were causing us to ride a little low in the water.

The Travelift operator told us his new transducers weighed us at thirty-three to thirty-five tons, and we were not quite at full cruising trim. We still did not have our full fuel load or freshwater tanks filled. It was a happy day when we went back in the water, with everything finished. *Fram* looked elegant in her bright new paint, ready for her grand adventure.

***Fram* is ready to go to sea**

Many of the items we added were to back up another item; the engineering term is *redundancy*. America sent men into space and to the moon and returned them all safely with redundant systems. That means, in the simplest terms, to have alternate ways of accomplishing a task.

I was part of that team and the concept worked. It worked as well on a sailboat sailing the high seas as it did for an astronaut in a space capsule. The most graphic example of redundancy occurred on Apollo 13, when a pressure vessel ruptured with Apollo near the moon and destroyed the capability of the service module to return the three astronauts to Earth. A near disaster was averted because they had redundancy (an alternate way) to come back. They used the Lunar Landing Module to return safely to Earth.

My goal was to have at least two ways of doing every task on *Fram*. Some people thought I was crazy, but it is not too difficult and was effective; besides, it let us spend a lot more time enjoying and a lot less time worrying.

We sent out invitations for a party on Sunday, August 9. If we thought we were busy before, it was nothing compared to those last frantic days. Phyllis bought provisions, and I worked to finish a complex electrical system. We also took care of last-minute personal business. Our wills were brought up-to-date, and papers were prepared to give Lynn power of attorney to act for us. We moved all our excess belongings off the boat and into a storage unit and prepared for a big party.

We moved through that last week in a daze of hard work and disbelief that the time was now. Many years passed since the critical decision was made one stormy night on the Straits of Juan de Fuca, with fog rolling in from the Pacific Ocean. The struggle that followed was long and hard, but the time finally arrived.

But now it was *party time*! Everything that was going to get done was done. The boat looked fabulous. We had a huge Mexican flag flying at the starboard spreader in honor of our first planned foreign port of call. We had a gigantic American flag on the fantail. All our burgees were up, and just for a little color, a couple hundred balloons were strung on the stays. Somehow everything was stowed away. New carpet was laid the night before by the captain, and new cushions and covers were in place. There was tons of food for the party. We had a keg of Redhook Ale, Ballard's finest, on its way. *Fram* was on the large net dock at Shilshole with plenty of room for food and beer and crowds of people. The weather was typical Seattle August weather—perfect.

People began to arrive, and we were delirious with joy. Friends and relatives appeared, many from far away. We were truly touched. They came to wish us well and to say their farewells. Some we had not seen for years and some were very close and had watched our dream unfold. Our guests shared our happiness this day as we started living our dream. Our beautiful ship was ready to carry us to the far corners of the earth. Our commitment had been total and the time of truth was *now*!

Bon Voyage party

Part III

Living the Dream

Fram anchored in Moorea

Chapter 19

The Dream Unfolds

August 10, 1987, was the first day of our new life! Today was my birthday, and I was fifty-six years old. The future will be different from anything we experienced before. We were doing what we envisioned and dreamed of for many years. The impact of that reality has not yet set in. It had been terribly hard saying good-bye to our kids. In a few minutes, we would untie the lines and leave. Leave: to go away, depart, to set out. For years, all our thoughts and lives hinged around that word, and now we were leaving.

Crew Bob Perego was aboard and would sail with us to San Francisco. Phyllis was still recovering from the year of chemo and recent reconstructive surgery, and we worried she might not be strong enough yet for this first ocean passage. Bob was a good friend, who had experience on the ocean, and we looked forward to his company.

The lines were cast free, and Seattle grew small and hazy behind *Fram*'s bubbling wake. The wind was at our backs as it should be on a cruising boat. We rigged the whisker pole for the first time, and I was glad to have Bob's help. It was big, heavy, and cumbersome to handle, but it worked fine once we got it set. We will have to find an easier way for Phyllis and me to handle it by ourselves. With the pole out and the new mainsail set, we ran wing and wing up the sound on an outgoing tide. We reached Port Townsend in record time and tied up to the dock by the sail loft, where we picked up our new sails and repaired jib, which was shredded in that wild gale last year.

While Bob and I made final adjustments to the pole, Phyllis went to town and managed to find a bookstore, a bakery for my birthday cake, and an ice-cream shop for treats later in the trip. I set up a new series of loran waypoints. We would not be using the old ones for a long, long time. It still did not seem real, except that I was nervous. Tomorrow we would be going out the Straits of Juan de Fuca to Neah Bay, our last anchorage. We went to bed early after a little birthday party.

One of the changes we made today as we embark on ocean sailing, was to keep time using the 24 hour clock, which is traditional for ships at sea. We were underway at 0355 to catch the outgoing tide. The dock lines were stowed since they wouldn't be needed for a while. We motor-sailed with the favorable tide into a gentle westerly breeze. Later the fog found us, and the visibility dropped to a few yards, but unlike our experience in *Koru*, this time we were ready. The radar watched for ships, the loran gave us position, and the autopilot steered. The compass had been swung and was accurate. The decks and hatches were watertight, the dodger kept the mist and spray off our faces, the new sat nav was checking up on the loran and beeped away whenever it received a fix, and we were much more experienced sailors. We had waited and prepared for sixteen years for this day. No turning back this time.

We stopped in Neah Bay and dropped anchor for the night. The straits were behind us, and the Pacific Ocean was ahead. Bob brought his halibut fishing gear and some tuna lines, and we planned to swing out to the Swiftsure Bank tomorrow and catch some halibut. We also set the crab pots for the last time, hoping for a final gift from the sea. We went to bed early but decided to sleep in and not try to rush our departure. There was no need. No anchorage tomorrow night. The weather fax, a new addition, showed the North Pacific high-pressure system in place and stable, with light to moderate winds on our route. The satellite photos showed light clouds over the entire area. Neah Bay stayed exceptionally calm throughout the night, so we had a good sleep.

The crabs cooperated and sacrificed themselves to our pots. We had four altogether, so somewhere along the line, we would have a feast. The wind was light as we made our way out of Neah Bay and steered northwest for the Swiftsure Bank. The bank is off of the coast of Vancouver Island, not far from Barkley Sound. The Pacific swells coming into the entrance of the straits created uncomfortable lumpy seas. The mainsail did little to help the motion, but we left it up as we motored on. It was not long until Bob was verifiably sick. He took some of his own seasick pills, but they didn't work. Phyllis and I put on transdermal patches as a precaution and felt fine. By the time we were at the Swiftsure Bank, Bob could hardly tell us how to rig the gear, let alone do any fishing. We found the bank with no problem, using the loran and our new depth sounder that painted out its contours like a photo.

Fishing was nearly impossible with *Fram* rolling from toerail to toerail in the swells; however, we did catch one small salmon. Bob was having a terrible time, and we were not having much fun either, so the lines came in and *Fram*'s bow turned southwest. We were on our way to California.

We went out sixty-five miles and turned straight south. The weather fax indicated we should have good following winds, and there was a spot near the Oregon border about sixty miles out, where the sea temperature reached sixty degrees Fahrenheit. That was supposed to be the right sea temperature for tuna. If we could not catch halibut, maybe we could catch tuna. Another of our new toys was a sea-temp gauge that measured the temperature of the water, and it was very accurate, so we would know when we arrived at the right spot.

When we turned southwest, the wind was on our quarter, and the motion became much easier. We continued motor-sailing in the light airs, as we were anxious to get away from the entrance to the Straits of Juan de Fuca and all the ship traffic before dark. It was not unusual to have five ships in sight at one time. Phyllis talked Bob into trying the patch, and they were both below, sleeping, while I was on watch.

One of the six ships in sight was straight ahead, and I expected it would soon pass by like the rest, but that did not happen. I had to detour around a giant trawler bristling with antennas, sitting thirty-five miles off the mouth of the Straits of Juan de Fuca. Then I saw the Russian flag.

I looked back a few times as we left land behind. This was the day that I waited for for so many years. When Cape Flattery and Tatoosh Island faded in the haze, it seemed strange to realize that we would not see them again until our return, many years in the future.

By evening, we left the ship traffic behind, and the engine was silent. Sitting in the cockpit alone, I had a chance to contemplate the scene around us and feel the loneliness of being on an ocean with no other boats or land in sight. It was a strange feeling. As I looked toward the horizon, it was much different than I expected. It was not a straight flat line but, rather, a mosaic of hills and mountains. A mound rose out of the sea, growing until it reached a peak before melting away to be replaced by others. It was a fascinating spectacle that I have never grown tired of watching, as the waves join and build and then flow on their separate ways. This, our first night sailing on an ocean in our own ship, thrilled my soul. It was even sweeter because of how much effort it took to be here in *Fram*, created by our own hands to fulfill our dream.

We split the watches into three hours on and six off, as Bob had recovered and was feeling chipper again. I worried for many years about this first night, but it was superb. I didn't think I would be able to sleep, but I did. I worried about being sick and all the motion keeping me awake, but I felt fine. Even the autopilot growling right under my ear didn't keep me from sleeping. I could set one of my biggest worries aside.

The morning of the second day, Phyllis woke me at 0530 to help take down the mizzen, as the speed gauge indicated 8.5 knots. That was driving *Fram* too hard. For safety, we established a rule that all sail changes at night would be done by two people, and nobody went forward without someone else in the cockpit. In addition, a safety harness was to be worn at all times, with it clipped on whenever we came out of the hatch.

Phyllis taking a sunsight

We were about sixty miles off of Grays Harbor and on a southerly course. After breakfast, the wind slacked some, and we replaced the staysail with the jib. The sun even came out for a moment. The sea-temp gauge read 59.5 degrees, so Bob and I rigged the two tuna hand lines. About a half hour later, we had two fish on simultaneously. Because of our speed, they were surfing behind us, and we saw them on the surface, with a rooster tail behind, while they beat the water with their tail at a fantastic rate. Their tail moved so fast we could hardly see it. We pulled them in, hand over hand, but lost one in the process, because we were using barbless hooks. We were thrilled that we landed a twenty-pound albacore tuna. We caught two more before we pulled in the lines. We froze one whole for Bob to take home to show his girlfriend and filleted the rest. We didn't have room in the freezer for any more.

What a magnificent fish they are. As an engineer, I marveled at their amazing design. Their streamlining is incredible. Their fins either retract into covered recesses or fit smoothly into perfectly fitting pockets. They have variable-angle vortex generators on the top and bottom of their bodies to prevent flow separation over their tails. Their eyes retract flat against their heads, and they are the only warm-blooded fish.

To achieve their high swimming speed, tuna need a higher body temperature in order to metabolize their food fast enough to sustain their high energy output. Since they do not have insulation on their bodies, like water-born mammals, they have two blood systems instead. One is warm, the other is cold, and they have heat exchangers between the two systems. They migrate from Asia to the Americas and are eating machines, so when you find them, they will attack any lure.

One of the pieces of equipment we added to *Fram* before we left was a wind-steering vane. Even though we had a reliable autopilot, the advantage of a steering vane was that it didn't use electric power. We chose a Sayes Rig that worked well on heavy boats. It had a small sail we could set that kept the boat in the same relative angle to the wind, by controlling an oar that was connected by an extension to the rudder. We called this vane Fred, after Fridtjof Nansen. We liked the idea of having Fridtjof sailing with us on our *Fram*.

That evening, we reduced sail, so we would not have to make a sail change at night. We also switched to Fred for the first time. It worked well as the seas built during the night. Before long, we were sailing at six knots with *Fram* rolling something fearful as we quartered down the big seas that were now about twelve feet. Sleeping was hard as we were being tossed around on our bouncy bed, and it was a relief not to also have the autopilot growling in our ear.

During the night, the moon and stars came out momentarily. It would have been nice to see them a little longer. We saw three ships but nothing close. By morning, the wind was down, so Bob started the engine to charge batteries and give us a little boost. It had not been running long, when the engine warning horn gave one short blast and was silent. I was up in an instant. Something was wrong. We shut down the engine and discovered the V-belt driving the alternator and water pump had broken, and it also broke the warning-system wire. It was lucky the horn beeped that one time, or we would not have known anything was wrong until the engine overheated and seized up.

It wasn't easy replacing the belt, but at least I discovered I could work in the engine room in a large sea and not get sick. Two belt failures later, under equally unpleasant circumstances, it dawned on me what the problem was. When we started the engine with the batteries low, the large alternator with the new regulator I recently installed put out about 150 amps, and the single belt I had used for years just could not carry the increased load for very long.

The wind became rather fluky, and with the large seas, *Fram* was rolling like crazy. Bob renamed her *Motion Machine*. We were finding it hard to adjust to the everlasting movement. The noise in the autopilot hydraulics was getting on my nerves, so I decided to try and find out what was wrong. Just before we left, I made an emergency tiller for the rudder, so it looked like a good time to try it out. I tried steering with it and was shocked. The forces were much higher than I had anticipated, and the tiller was not strong enough to be of any use.

One of the advantages of the Sayes Rig wind vane was its direct connection to the rudder, and we could easily use it to turn the rudder by hand. While Phyllis hand steered using Fred, Bob and I disconnected the hydraulic ram and bled the system. It made me nervous to have the hydraulic steering ram removed and the rudder hanging free. Everything seemed all right, so we put it back together, except I discovered that the steering arm on the rudderpost was too short for our system. We hooked it back up and tried not to hear the groaning. There was nothing I could do until I had the correct arm.

In the morning, we passed the Oregon/California border. The wind was up to twenty-five knots, and with a reefed main and jib, we enjoyed an exhilarating sail in bright sunshine. The wind continued to build, until *Fram* was going too fast, so we lowered the jib and replaced it with the staysail. Lowering the jib at the end of the eight-foot bowsprit was not much fun in that wind. We ran wing and wing before the wind with the smaller staysail as we raced over the waves.

Our spirits were exuberant. This was ocean sailing at its best. We were averaging 150 miles a day. Phyllis served delicious crab melts for lunch and tuna for dinner. We have had wonderful meals on the whole trip. It was our fourth day at sea, and we were now into the rhythm of it as our bodies adjusted to a new reality.

Late in the afternoon, there was an incident that made us all nervous. It began when we saw a freighter pass us a few miles away, going in the opposite direction. After it passed, it made a 180-degree turn, came back, and ran parallel to us for a while. All of a sudden, it turned and came straight toward us. It was less than a half mile away before it turned once again and resumed its position off our beam. We debated about calling it on the VHF radio but decided not to. We wondered if it was expecting a rendezvous and could not decide if we were the right boat. It had all the ingredients of a drug transfer, and we wanted nothing to do with it. We felt alone and vulnerable as it continued beside us, until after about an hour it turned away and disappeared over the horizon.

When I came on watch at midnight, it was a crystal clear night, and the stars glittered in magnificence. I had nearly forgotten there was a Milky Way. The broad white river of stars spread across the firmament, light-years away, and yet was an amazing presence above our swaying mast. Time passed quickly as I sat in the cockpit, gazing at the splendor of the heavens. The moon broke into my reverie and startled me when it peeked over the horizon just before midnight. I could have stayed and watched all night if I hadn't been so tired.

Phyllis relieved me while I went below to sleep. With *Fram* running before the wind, she rolled continuously from side to side, and with the waves about twelve to fourteen feet high, she also moved up and down and pitched at the same time. The autopilot groaned constantly with every wave but maintained our course in spite of being under great strain. It still amazed me I could go below and sleep without any problems in rough conditions. Phyllis and I still slept in our king-size bed in the aft stateroom, with pillows wedged all around to keep us from being thrown about. It felt weird, like sleeping on a bowl of Jell-O, but we managed to sleep anyway.

Bob woke me early for my watch at first light, because he thought it was time to reduce sail again. The wind roared as it continued to increase through the night, and the seas were becoming huge. We lowered the staysail, and with only a double-reefed main, we were riding a watery roller coaster at over eight knots. Our wind gauge was showing twenty-five to thirty-five relative (to our boat speed), so the actual wind was closer to forty-plus knots and stayed that way as the morning progressed. These were far and away the biggest seas we had ever seen. All around us were eighteen-foot mountains of water with white frothy wave tops blowing off into great white sheets of foam. We were humbled and thrilled at the same time with the grandeur of those waves.

The bright sunshine created a spectacular sight as it shone through the waves when we surged down into their shadow. The water was iridescent blue, topped with a creamy white cap as the crests curled into an effervescence of foam, towering over our stern. With nagging fear, we watched the cliffs growing out of the chaos behind us . . . surely this one will explode on top of us. Then like a dancer raising her skirts, the stern rose, and, we surfed down the face with spray flying. When we reached the trough, the bow dove into the next wave, the autopilot struggled to keep us from rounding up, and then we were climbing again. We shouted our joy. This was what we had built *Fram* to do, and we were having a blast. All those questioning cold, dreary nights looking up at her landlocked bow were washed away by the surging waves.

After a few hours at this mad pace, we eased the motion by dropping the main and raising the staysail. This slowed our speed to about six knots and relieved some of the strain on the steering system. We were still enjoying the spectacle of the huge waves, howling wind, and restless wake.

Big seas off West Coast

By midafternoon, we entered the shadow of Cape Mendocino, and the wind and waves moderated. After our wild day, we took turns sleeping through this last night before landfall. Midway into my night watch, the wind died completely, so we lowered the sails and motored through the night toward San Francisco. Haze and then fog enveloped us, so the radar became our eyes as we approached the coast with its concentrated ship traffic. When Bob woke me before daylight for my watch, his eyes were red and glassy from constantly staring at the radar as he changed course to avoid all the traffic.

In the morning, the fog became low-lying overcast, and we were overwhelmed with a sense of satisfaction at making our first landfall after five days at sea. We were feeling like old hands by now. The Golden Gate Bridge came into sight just before noon, and we entered with dolphins bounding out to greet us as they had many times along the way. Phyllis served a great lunch of salmon quiche with ice cream for dessert as we came under the bridge in the brilliant sunshine and toasted a successful first passage.

San Francisco Bay lay before us, and the city glittered like a pile of jewels on its bordering hills. The dream of sailing under the Golden Gate Bridge finally came true. Our first and biggest hurdle of cruising was over. We untied our lines and left. Then we spent five days at sea on one of the roughest coasts in the world, arriving safely in San Francisco still exuberant and happy. Our dream was now a reality.

Sailing into the bay was lovely, but as we approached the entrance to Pier 39, I began to realize why San Francisco Bay was so famous for its difficult conditions. It took me two attempts to make the entrance to the marina, and then I was not so sure I wanted to go in. The wind was blowing thirty knots, and the current was running three knots, and I could just imagine the problems I was going to have trying to maneuver in a confined marina. Besides, the harbor tour boats were going in and out at regular intervals, filling the narrow channel near the breakwater. We had not come so far to turn back now, so in we went, with our bumpers and dock lines ready. As we rounded the end of the piers and headed in, we did not see many options, so with the wind and current on our beam, it seemed like the logical thing to do was to land on the end slip of one of the first two piers.

The first one had big signs saying, NO LANDING.

The second one said Members Only.

That did not sound quite so intimidating, and since we were drifting toward it anyway, it looked like a good place to stop temporarily. We made a reasonably good landing by just letting the current and wind crunch us against the dock. With the lines secured, I headed toward shore to find the marina office, leaving Bob and Phyllis to watch over the boat.

As I came up the ramp, a young Hispanic man was running down the dock, trying to get my attention. I could not understand what he said, but I gathered he was trying to tell me I could not moor at the end of the dock. I told him I knew that, but I had to find the marina office so they could tell me where to go. He finally gave up and pointed toward a door at the end of the pier and followed me as I opened it.

What a shock! I was still in heavy-weather clothes, and after five days at sea, I must have looked pretty grubby. I felt like Alice stepping through the looking glass. I was in the middle of a carnival, with crowds of people dressed in shorts and T-shirts and halter tops. Off to one side, carousel music was playing as its herd of horses went round and round, with their small riders squealing in delight. On a stage in front of me, a band played to a small knot of people. I stood still with my mouth open as I stared in amazement, then I realized the guy was tugging at my sleeve and pointing across the pier to a large gateway.

Through the gateway and around the corner was the marina office. As I walked up to the door, a young lady was locking up. She stopped and asked what I needed. I told her we had just arrived from Seattle and needed a slip. She asked me where I was moored now.

When I told her where we were, she said, "Oh dear, what the hell are you doing there? How big is your boat?" She wanted to know.

"A little over fifty feet with bowsprit," I responded.

"You can dock in K-10. Here's a key. You can come in tomorrow and register." She said as she handed me a key.

"Move right away. The tour company gets real upset if anyone docks at the outboard slips," was her parting remark.

At that, the young man took off like a shot to tell his boss I would be moving. In the meantime, Phyllis and Bob had been regaled by demands and insults and threats but stood firm that they were not going to move the boat without the captain. As I made my way back across the midway to the dock, I saw the tour boat heading out the channel past *Fram* with plenty of room, but the skipper was shaking his fist from the wheelhouse. Oh well, welcome to San Francisco.

We stayed four weeks. Most of the time at Pier 39, but several times, we went to the state park at Angel Island. After our first entertaining visit there, we had to go back again to see if the first visit had been an anomaly or whether people always moored that way. We had never seen anything like it, with boats tied to two or three or even four mooring buoys. By late Saturday afternoon, our sides ached from laughing, and the moorage area was a spiderweb of interlacing lines.

The standard technique seemed to be for some hunk of a guy to come toward a mooring buoy at full throttle, with a lovely bikini-clad woman on the bow with a special hook (the Happy Hooker) ready to snag a buoy. Sometimes this was done successfully, except that the boat was going too fast to stop, and she either ran out of line or could not hold on. This would elicit the following comment from the cockpit, "You stupid —!" The next approach was a little slower and the hookup successful. Now came the attempt to back up to another buoy. The strong current insured it would take at least three attempts, accompanied by more juicy language. When the captain finally realized the line was not long enough to reach the second buoy, his head disappeared as he dug through the lockers, looking for more line. By this time, some kind soul in a dinghy would row over and offer his help, rowing a line over to a buoy. Often this line was not quite long enough, and he would be holding the buoy with one hand and the end of the (too short) line with the other while the current tried to pull him apart.

"I need more line, you stupid —," he shouted.

With the second line secured, the boat was often too close to the next boat, so a third line would be required. The process did not end then, because it took another hour or two to get the tension adjusted just right. It was like watching a nervous violin player trying to tune his fiddle before his first concert. Just as everything seemed to be satisfactory, along came another boat to tie to the same buoys, and the whole process would start all over again. By the time the place was a tangled snarl of crossed lines, somebody would decide to leave, and the unraveling process began. We concluded that the key sport at Angel Island was mooring.

I went ashore one day and asked one of the park rangers why they moored that way. He said he didn't know for sure, but he thought it was because they had so many collisions due to winds and currents, and the multiple ties seemed to help.

"Anyway, it's the tradition here," he said as he shrugged his shoulders.

When we were not observing the show at Angel Island, we divided our time between sightseeing in the San Francisco area and installing a few more items on the boat. We painted the decks white. Phyllis hated the way they looked, but later in the heat of Mexico, we found that the white decks kept the interior much cooler.

Lisa and her husband, Doug, came for a visit; and we rode the trolley and walked all over San Francisco. We explored the many fine restaurants and generally enjoyed being tourists instead of ocean sailors for a while. They brought the stern ladder I ordered before we left and a cruise generator (that made DC electricity when we ran the engine) that was a gift from one of our friends at the Duwamish Yacht Club. I also had a new rudder arm sent down from Seattle.

Another alternator belt broke on the engine one day as we pulled out of the channel by Angel Island on our way to Sausalito to fuel. We had an exciting few minutes raising sail and maneuvering out of the channel, as we still were not used to the wind and current in San Francisco bay. It was my last belt, so we set a course toward an anchorage near Sausalito to make repairs. As we sailed into the shadow of the hills, the wind died.

We drifted slowly to a stop, and while I debated what to do, a gust came screaming down off the hills and hit us broadside. It laid *Fram* over forty-five degrees, and from below, there was a loud crash of breaking glass, and then the wind was gone. Our two cases of California wine had not yet been properly stowed, and we did not want to look. Fewer bottles were broken than we expected, but it was still a sorrowful sight. We cried over our forward bilge full of expensive wine. We finally used the Callegari as a tug and pushed *Fram* into Sausalito. That big gust was the last gasp of wind for that day.

By the end of four weeks, we were ready to leave. San Francisco in August was a cold, foggy place, and we were ready for some sunshine and warmth. Once again, we passed under the Golden Gate on our way south. It was a gorgeous sunny day with light winds, so we were motor-sailing. The swells were hardly noticeable, and we felt like we were on a lake as we slipped along with the sails just filled and the engine throbbing gently. The day passed quickly, and early in the afternoon, we slipped around Pillar Point into Half Moon Bay. It was a nice anchorage behind a breakwater. *Genesis* from Seattle was there, and while we were putting the anchor down, another Seattle boat, *Nua Nua*, joined us. As we sat in the cockpit viewing our surroundings, we watched a wind surfer skimming around the bay. As he came by, we both thought we recognized him but decided no, that was not possible.

The next time by, he dropped off his board and said, "Hi, aren't you the Nansens?"

We were amazed to see Arnie, who was one of the owners of the Duwamish Marina and Boatyard, where we hauled *Fram* for many years. He also launched *Nua Nua* when she was new. What a strange place to meet old acquaintances.

Our weather fax showed nice stable conditions, so it was time to move on to Monterey. We left early on September 17 for an easy run with light winds and some fog. Along the way, we saw some of the strangest-looking fish we had ever seen. At first I thought they were some large dying fish that floated to the surface as they lay on their sides with a fin slowly flopping in the air. On closer inspection, it looked like they were just the head of a fish with no body. It was not until we went through the aquarium in Monterey that we discovered they were California sunfish, coming to the surface to sleep. Just one of the strange sea creatures we would see.

We first experienced ocean surge as we docked at one of the marinas. We nearly slammed into the dock when *Fram* made a rapid side step in the surge, which I hadn't expected. The inland waters of the Pacific Northwest had not prepared me for handling surge conditions. We were excited to be in Monterey and walked its historic streets while we imagined the time when Steinbeck wrote *Cannery Row*. We were also enthralled with the fine aquarium.

After a couple days, with the wind still light, we decided to use the opportunity to head for Point Conception, even if it meant we would have to motor-sail. It was foggy but calm as we left picturesque Monterey, past some of the old cannery buildings and the kelp beds near the shore. With the seals and sea lions barking at us from the breakwater, we were engulfed in light fog. Most of the day was overcast and foggy, with only a brief sun break. By nighttime, the fog wrapped us in an impenetrable blanket. The only light was the soft radiance of the radar screen in the wheelhouse, our running lights, and the little halo of light surrounding the compass in the cockpit. The rest of the boat might not have even existed, for it could not be seen in the intense blackness of the night and the dense fog. Our eyes were glued to the radar, watching the track of ships as they crawled across the screen. Their numbers increased steadily as we approached Point Conception. This was our first all-night passage without extra crew, so the worry of all the ships charging unseen through the thick fog around us kept us on our toes.

Phyllis was on watch, when all of a sudden I was awakened by shouting voices coming from the VHF radio, apparently from two freighters on a collision course. They were shouting at each other to turn, not to turn, hold course, change course, or something else. Somehow they missed each other, but it sure woke me up. Platform Harvest, an oil rig nearby, with radar and plotting equipment, acted as a traffic director to help keep ships from hitting each other or the oil rigs. We checked in with him earlier to let him know that our little boat was also out here.

Later I was again awakened by the loud, firm voice of Platform Harvest warning a freighter, "Sir, you are on a collision course with an oil rig, please turn, *now!*"

In the morning after the fog thinned, we caught two nice tuna. At the time, we were close to Point Conception, dodging freighters and oil rigs while we hauled in our fish. At noon, we passed within six miles of the fearsome point, but on that day, it was behaving like a lady, and we motored past on our way into Cojo anchorage just around the corner. We were fortunate to have avoided the winds that often blow there. I had been reading Richard Dana's *Two Years Before the Mast*, and Point Conception sounded like a nasty place to be. It has another distinction. It is the imaginary dividing line between Northern California and Southern California. We believed it; as we came to anchor inside the kelp at Cojo, our heavy sea clothes were suddenly stifling hot. Layer after layer came off, until even a T-shirt was too much. We finally arrived in the warm part of the world.

Cojo was our first experience in an open roadstead anchorage, and it was a little disconcerting later in the evening when the wind shifted around to the east and was blowing twenty to twenty-five knots, putting us on a lee shore. Our anchor chain stretched out like a steel bar, and the waves began to build. I started the engine and put it in gear to take some strain off the anchor while we tried to decide if we should leave. Then the wind died. Our decision had been made for us. The remainder of the night was pleasant with only a slight swell to gently rock us asleep.

In the morning, I was up early to greet the new day and check the local weather report on the VHF radio. When I switched it on to channel 16, we were greeted with a series of high-pitched shouts, some of them approaching a scream. Obviously there was some sort of crisis happening, and there was total chaos on the radio. Two heavily accented male voices were so excited the pitch was about two octaves above normal. The third was a female voice so high-pitched she was practically screaming. It took several minutes to realize that she was the coast guard in Long Beach, and the other two voices belonged to the captains of two ships that had collided off of Point Conception in the fog, just a short distance from where we were anchored.

We listened in fascination as the story unfolded. One was the ore carrier *Pac Baroness* with a load of copper ore, and the other was the Honda car carrier, *Atlantic Wing*. The accident had just happened. After a few minutes, the panicky coast guard voice was replaced by a calm male operator, and the story became clearer as he drew out the pertinent facts and started to get help on the scene. It was too foggy to bring in helicopters, so they called on crew boats from one of the oil rigs and other ships in the area. The *Atlantic Wing* was stuck bow first into the side of the *Pac Baroness*, whose captain thought it was sinking. The crew was evacuated to the *Atlantic Wing*, but the captain refused to leave his ship.

The discussions went on and on as the *Pac Baroness* settled lower and lower in the water. The captain of the *Atlantic Wing* kept pleading for permission to back away as he feared the *Pac Baroness* would pull him down. The coast guard advised him to do what he had to do to save his ship, so he backed the *Atlantic Wing* free, exposing a great torn hole that had been the bow of his ship. The captain of the *Pac Baroness* finally left his ship, which sank shortly after she was taken in tow. The *Atlantic Wing* limped back to Long Beach under her own power. It was a captivating few hours, listening to the drama unfolding so close to us.

It seems nearly impossible that such a collision could occur with modern radar and the oil rig Platform Harvest monitoring and advising passing traffic, but we heard the conversations on the VHF radio the night before and listened to two narrowly avoided collisions. The quality of seamanship on many of the freighters must be marginal, and when a large number are in close proximity, as occurs at Point Conception, it can be treacherous.

We later met a couple, who, in their small boat, had been run down off of Point Conception by a freighter that did not stop, even though later investigation revealed the bow lookout had seen the collision. One of the problems with these ships was a language problem. That lookout could not speak English and was unable to communicate with the bridge. Fortunately, their badly damaged sailboat stayed afloat, and they survived. After a lengthy investigation, they were able to find the guilty ship and received some payment for damages.

When the excitement calmed down and the fog was replaced by sunshine, we left Cojo for Santa Cruz Island. As we motored across the Santa Barbara Channel, we were reminded we were in Southern California. The sea was glassy calm, and the weather was nice and warm. We passed within fifty feet of two large whales as they came up alongside of us. It was a shock to see these huge monsters rising above the surface; their bodies seemed to go on forever. We turned away to give them plenty of room. It was another first for us to see whales other than orcas so near. Our anchorage for the night was another open roadstead. The island was dry and sandy with scrubby brush. We weren't in the Pacific Northwest any longer. By daybreak, the wind shifted, and we were dangerously close to the rocky shore, so we raised anchor and were gone.

The wind died by the time the sun was up, so it was another day of motoring as we proceeded through the thick Los Angeles smog to King Harbor at Redondo Beach. We anchored inside the breakwater for the night and made inquires about dock space, because we planned to spend several weeks in the Los Angeles area. When we told him our length, the harbor master laughed but said he would see what they could do.

Later, a dinghy stopped by with Bob Bichin and Gina from *Predator*, welcoming us to Redondo Beach. I was on deck at the time, and Phyllis was below. Gina was a cute little blonde, but Bob did not look like your typical yachtsman. He was a great bear of a man with a big bushy beard and long wild hair, wearing black leather pants and a vest. He was covered with tattoos and enough gold chains hanging down his bare chest to anchor our boat. Phyllis stuck her head out the hatch about then to see who I was talking to, and I heard an involuntary gasp when she saw Bob. Biker Bob and Gina were friendly and helpful during the next few weeks while we were at Redondo and at the many anchorages we shared along the way and in Mexico. The harbor patrol stopped by a little later to say that they had a slip for us. A nice start to a pleasant three-and-a-half weeks we spent in King Harbor. We also met many other sailors with experience cruising to Mexico.

We were here for our nephew's wedding and entertained many members of my family onboard. It was a special time to say good-bye before we left for Mexico. But we had more work to do, so we were also busy with the boat. We bought and stowed enough food provisions for a year. I rebuilt the alternator mounting system that had failed so often, converting it to a double belt drive. I mounted a high-capacity (sixty gallons a minute) engine-driven bilge pump and installed the 2.5-kilowatt, 110-volt cruise generator that was sent to us from Seattle.

When the time came for us to give up the slip at Redondo, we moved to Long Beach and found a visitor's slip for a week. Long Beach Marina was expensive, so it was not a place to camp for a long time. While here, we contracted to have a Bimini cover made for the cockpit. We also bought a sixty-five-pound Danforth anchor as a spare and three hundred feet of three-fourths-inch line for our second bow anchor. I had one of our twin backstays modified with insulators for use as a ham radio antenna. The radio and tuner were onboard but not installed. I only had my novice license, which would be sufficient to get a Mexican license, but knew that somewhere along the line, I had to bite the bullet and get my code speed up to thirteen words a minute so I could get my general license.

Soon we were ready to leave the civilized world of supermarkets and marine supply stores. David and his wife, Sheri, arrived for a visit. Since Sheri spoke fluent Spanish, we arranged to spirit her away for a couple of weeks to make the trip with us to Mexico as our interpreter. David had to return to his job in Seattle, so he would miss this trip.

Before leaving Long Beach, we went to the Mexican consulate to get our boat papers. The consulate visit was a small taste of what we would experience in the future as we dealt with Mexican officials. We had been in line for more than an hour, waiting to get into the building, when one of the clerks walked down the line, asking what we were there for.

When we said we were there to obtain boat papers, he said, "In there, second floor, and only one of you."

Since Sheri spoke Spanish, we handed her our papers and passports and pointed her toward the door. She had been gone about five minutes, when I remembered she did not have any money with her, and it was going cost something for the papers. So I went rushing off to find the clerk to let me in. When I reached Sheri, she was just explaining why she was going to have to go and find us since money was the first thing she needed. After being shuffled around through several offices to have the various papers stamped, we were happily reporting our success to Phyllis, when she asked about Katisha's entry papers.

"Ohhhh . . ." In all the hassle, I had forgotten all about the cat, and Phyllis was pretty upset since she had gone to a lot of trouble to make sure he had all the documents required by Mexico. Well, I was not about to go back through the line again and try to explain about the cat. I didn't think they really cared anyway. Katisha had all of his shots and a certificate of good health, so we decided to go on to San Diego for our fishing licenses. He would just have to be an illegal alien.

We left Long Beach in the afternoon, and it was well into a lovely moonlit night when we arrived at Dana Point, where we made our way to the inner anchorage for the night. In the morning, we motored to the fuel dock to fill all our diesel, gasoline, and propane tanks.

The fuel dock looked innocent enough; there was adequate room, and the current didn't seem very strong, but I again missed observing the effect of the surge until we were alongside the dock. The first lines were thrown across to the dock attendant and made secure to the cleats, and then I thought the side of the boat was being ripped off as the boat lurched away in the nearly invisible surge, causing the mooring lines to squeal in protest. I doubled up all my lines, but we were still moving back and forth with a great deal of groaning—first the lines as they stretched tight and then the bumpers being squashed flat against the dock. We loaded 350 gallons of diesel, 12 gallons of outboard gas, and filled one propane tank. With everything full, I was anxious to escape the surge at the dock; so when the hoses were ashore, the bill paid, and the engine started, I was ready to cast off. We cleared the dock smartly and were on our way—I thought!

As we passed through the breakwater, Sheri asked, "Where's Katisha?"

At the same time, the VHF was calling, "*Fram, Fram.*" The voice asked if we were missing a cat since there was a strange one at the fuel dock.

Well, back to the fuel dock we headed as I shook my head in disbelief at having to brave that dock again for a cat. I thought I could swing by with the stern, and then someone could hand him across so we would not have to dock. We should be so lucky. When we got there, it was apparent from the shouts and arm waving that he had gone ashore somewhere. Besides, there were now two boats at the dock, and there was just barely room for us to squeeze in between. We made it without hitting anyone, and with the help of the people on the dock, *Fram* was secured.

Phyllis went cat hunting ashore. She found him hiding under a car in the parking lot, reeking of diesel, in which he had rolled. He was a mess and scared. We paid our dues for leaving him behind since this time the departure was much more difficult because of the proximity of the other two boats. By using a spring line, I swung the bow out far enough to clear the forward boat, and we were once again on our way. Katisha smelled of diesel for days, but he wasn't anxious to go ashore any time soon. In fact, it would be more than a year before he was off the boat again.

We arrived in San Diego that evening in a driving rainstorm and were fortunate enough to get the last available slip at the police dock. In the morning, we bought our Mexican fishing licenses. After topping up our water tanks, we were ready to leave the next day. Back at the dock, we visited with several Seattle boats also getting ready to leave for Mexico.

It seemed strange to be leaving the United States, this time for many years. Our dream was unfolding, and now we were ready to step into its first living moments in a foreign land.

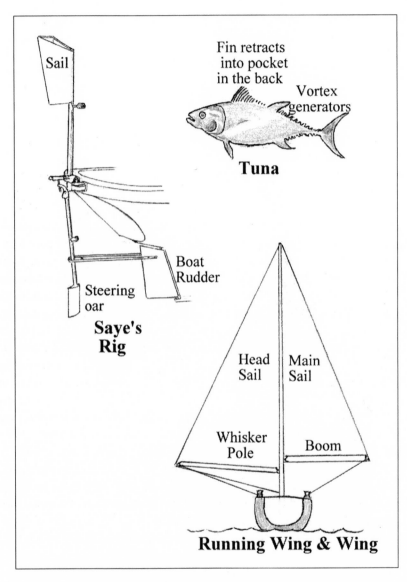

Sayes Rig, tuna, and running wing and wing

Chapter 20

Mexico

We left for Ensenada, Mexico, a little over sixty nautical miles south of San Diego at two thirty in the morning on November 6, 1987. This was our last United States port, and we were outward-bound for the world. Nobody else was around as *Fram* slipped away into the dark. We motored down the bay past Point Loma, and it was still dark by the time we were at the Mexican border. Phyllis and Sheri were both asleep. The weather was clear with just a whisper of a breeze from the south.

In the light conditions, I was afraid we would arrive in Ensenada too late to check in. When we entered the harbor at two forty in the afternoon, it looked like we would not have enough time to drop anchor and be in town before the clearance offices closed at three. About then, a young man in an outboard-powered *ponga* roared up to us with the offer of moorings for rent.

When I asked him how much, he replied, "Five dollars a day."

"If you can get us to the port captain by three, we'll take it."

"No problemo, follow me," he shouted as he turned toward shore.

He led us to a mooring float just off a small rickety dock. As I secured the mooring line to my cleat, he brought the *ponga* alongside and said, "Come with me, hurry."

We grabbed our boat papers, jumped in his boat, and took off for the dock.

"One momento. I get the driver."

After a few shouted sentences in Spanish, another young man ambled out of the shed that apparently was the office. He waved us toward an old battered Ford Falcon that was hardly distinguishable as an automobile. Phyllis and Sheri climbed in the back, and I sat in front with the driver. I had to be careful, as there was no floor, except near the door. It had been cut away to accommodate a transmission that Ford never intended to be installed in a Falcon. I don't know what kind of vehicle it came from, but the gear shift stuck out at a peculiar angle, and I never did figure out how the driver got it into the gears he wanted, but he managed to get us around. He didn't speak English, but we had Sheri, so no problemo—he knew where to go.

We entered the port captain's office as everybody was getting ready to leave. They ignored us and we stood there, uncertain about what to do. Finally one of the ladies reached out for our papers as Sheri hastily told her we wanted to check in and out. She looked at us with a blank stare, rolled her eyes to the ceiling, and silently took our papers. She shuffled through them, kept a copy of our crew list, stamped some others, and sent us off to immigration with instructions of what to do and what to bring back. We piled back into the perambulating wreck, and off we went. It was after three, but the port captain's office had called ahead, so the immigration officer was waiting for us.

After checking our passports and stamping our tourist cards and crew list, he sent us back to the port captain's office with further instructions. Our driver was able to get the car started again and took us back to the port captain's office, where he signed our clearance papers. Once more, we made the rattling excursion to deliver a copy back to immigration. We were finished by three thirty. All our papers were signed and stamped, and we were only four dollars poorer for the transportation cost. We did not say anything about Katisha, and they had not asked, so he was now smuggled into a foreign country.

Our first contact with Mexican officials had been surprisingly pleasant, and in the future, they were nearly always polite and easy to deal with. Their system did not always make sense, but we never had any problems.

We left before noon the next day and sailed through the afternoon into a lovely moonlit night. Sheri was nervous about standing her first night watch, but with good sea conditions, her biggest problem turned out to be ship traffic. We were about fifteen miles offshore, and there was often a ship in sight. We changed course several times to avoid close encounters. Cruise ships were impressive with all their lights blazing, making it difficult to see their navigation lights. We were always a little uncertain of their course.

Sheri woke me up at 0230 when three ships appeared to be converging on us. I changed course to give them more room, but one changed course toward us, traveling slow. He changed course whenever I did, and I was worried about his intentions. He passed about a hundred yards off our starboard and flashed a signal light with a dash and five dots as he came by. I did not respond and we kept going. It was a small ancient freighter with an old engine turning over so slow I could count the revolutions. I wondered if it was a drug runner, who thought we were his contact. Perhaps it was our black hull that attracted them. I was relieved when it turned away and was finally out of sight. This was the second time an old freighter pursued us. I didn't like the feeling at all.

The next morning, we found half-dozen squid on deck and one on the cabin top. How it got there was a mystery to me. There were also two flying fish, and Katisha had his first taste of that delicacy. After that, he knew the instant one came onboard, and it was the only thing that tempted him to go outside of the cockpit at sea.

It was a brilliant clear sunny day when Cedros Island was just visible at about twenty miles. I dropped the tuna gear in, and the line was not even tight when I had a fish on the hook, so the morning was prolific. We celebrated with champagne and orange juice for breakfast as we motored down the east side of the island. With seabirds our only companions, we anchored off of a spring surrounded by palm trees. We spent the afternoon basking in the sun as we relaxed and read. With all the years of hard work and preparation behind us, this was why we came to Mexico.

Day dawned brilliant and clear as we set sail in a perfect fifteen-knot north wind. The Baja Peninsula was visible in all its stark majesty. The ruggedness of the mountains complemented the blueness of the water as it slid beneath *Fram*'s wake. We let the vision soak into our beings. As we approached Turtle Bay, the wind decreased and long gentle swells made spectacular breakers on the reefs on both sides of the entrance into the bay. We joined eleven other yachts anchored there to watch the sunset. It was magnificent, with the mountains looking like dark paper cutouts against the crystal clear sky. One of the nicest days we ever spent.

The next day was not as nice. Turtle Bay was large with room for many boats. We were anchored in about twenty-five feet of water off an old rickety pier. The next afternoon, we went ashore and climbed up to the pier on a dilapidated ladder hanging precariously over the water. We were instantly surrounded by a mob of kids of all ages. They wanted to watch the dinghy or be our guide into town. We finally asked one of the boys to watch the dinghy and told the others that we did not want a guide, but one teenager tagged along anyway.

Our mission was to see the town and buy some beer and vegetables. The town wasn't much to see with its narrow dirt streets, small humble houses, a few battered vehicles, and many children playing in the dust. Our unwanted guide led us to the beer store and then on to a primitive grocery store, where we bought a few onions. There was not much else to choose from. By then, we had seen enough, so we made our way back to the pier. We gave the unwanted guide a U.S. dollar and the dinghy watcher five hundred pesos, but they were hostile and demanded more money. I was not happy with them as the dinghy watcher had watched the dinghy by taking it on a tour of the bay at full throttle. We gave them a little more money, just to be rid of them, but it just encouraged the other kids to also demand money. We were happy to be back on *Fram* and away from all the hassling.

We were not quite finished with the irritations of Turtle Bay, however. In the evening, a couple of large rusty Mexican fishing boats came in, and one of them anchored close behind us, with the second one tied to his stern, swinging free. The crew in the second boat jumped in and swam to the first, and they immediately started a party. By the time we finished dinner, the party was loud and boisterous. The crew spotted Phyllis and Sheri and were yelling, trying to entice them to join the party. Since they were anchored close to our stern, we worried about being bumped in the night. We decided it would be much nicer at sea than sitting in Turtle Bay, trying to contend with a bunch of drunken fishermen. We prepared to leave, and while we were pulling up the anchor, the fishing boats also pulled up their anchor and headed out. Oh well, it was a nice night, and we had seen all of Turtle Bay we wanted.

Another night slipped by, and when morning dawned, we were entertained by marlin jumping high out of the water all around us. Soon we saw dolphins in the distance, and then we were amongst them. Thousands and thousands, everywhere we looked were dolphins as far as we could see in every direction—swimming in rhythm, diving and leaping in formation, and tail dancing. They raced beside the bow and slapped the bobstay chain with their tails, rattling all the rigging with their exuberance.

In her excitement, Sheri forgot her fear of going out on the bowsprit and watched the graceful water ballet from that vantage point. We were enchanted. Phyllis spotted one odd-looking dolphin, and upon closer observation, we saw that it was a seal awkwardly swimming, leaping, and diving with the dolphins in their rhythm and right beside them—a clumsy ballerina in a graceful ballet. We traveled in their midst well over an hour before leaving them astern.

Magdelena Bay on the Baja Peninsula is a whale sanctuary, where the gray whales come to calve from January to April each year. During those months, there are many boats visiting the bay, but today, we found fishing *pongas* and fisherman shacks on the beach. We were the only sailboat in the anchorage. In the morning, a fisherman came by with lobsters to trade. He wanted cigarettes and beer, but since we did not have any cigarettes and only a few beers, we traded him a bottle of wine, a shirt, and a can of Spam for nine lobsters. Now that was Mexican cruising at its best.

Lobster and champagne at sea

The wind woke us during the night as *Fram* surged against her anchor chain, but by morning, the wind moderated a little, and it looked like we would have a nice sail for our last leg to Cabo San Lucas. We were on a broad reach with Sheri on watch, when strong winds and waves hit us at 0100. I awoke immediately with the sudden violent motion and noise. It was as if we passed through a doorway from moderate weather to near gale conditions.

Sheri was on her way down to wake me just as I bounded out of bed. We double reefed the main and slowed the boat. The wind was blowing twenty-five to thirty, with steep confused seas. We took several breaking waves over the side, but at least the water was warm on our bare feet as it sloshed through the cockpit. At daybreak, as suddenly as it came, the wind was gone, and the seas were calm. It was hard to believe.

With the dawn of a lovely morning, Sheri caught our first dorado (mahi mahi). The water temperature was eighty degrees, and we were in a different world as we motored along with a white sandy beach on our port side and sport-fishing boats chasing marlin, dorado, and wahoo churning up the water on our starboard. As we passed by the famous Arch of Cabo San Lucas and Lover's Beach, we were bursting with joy as we arrived at this, our first cruising goal.

Bob, on *Predator*, called on the radio with a place for us near them. We anchored with a bow and stern anchor over a clear sandy bottom near the beach in about twenty-five feet of water. We launched the dinghy and went to check in. It turned out to be an interesting experience.

The offices we needed to process our entry papers were located at opposite ends of town. When we had to return to the Capitán del Puerto's office a second time, we found we were still short one copy of the crew list. No problemo, we could get a copy at the copy store owned by his cousin. But now they were closed for siesta, and by the time they opened, the Capitán del Puerto's office was closed, so mañana would be "okay."

We soon learned to have an extra copy handy, just in case. We were getting used to time, Mexico style. At least we got plenty of exercise walking all over the charming town with its attractive shops. That evening, we took the dinghy to a restaurant on the beach and had a delicious dinner with drinks; for the three of us, it cost less than $25. We were going to like Mexico. Sheri had become a good crewman, and we were happy to share this special experience with our daughter-in-law. We were sorry when she left us.

Anchored in Cabo with Katisha

Now we were on our own with a strange language. Phyllis worked at learning Spanish, particularly the names of the different fruits and vegetables. She found her favorite vendors in the market, and they soon recognized us and were friendly and helpful with our awkward Spanish.

We settled into an easy routine. With Phyllis's natural outgoing personality, we soon became informal greeters of the newly arrived yachts. We found that people who set out in small boats to cross an ocean were always interesting, no matter what their background, education, profession, or nationality. Wherever we went, this was nearly always the case.

We ate out a lot and had some fabulous meals. It did not take long to find that Mexican food in Mexico is much different than we were used to in the U.S. We also ate at the little taco stands on the street corners and soon became addicted to fish tacos. I discovered that the local bars had American TV, which meant I could watch football and could follow my favorite Seahawks.

Each day at cocktail time, we watched the sunset over the hills behind Cabo San Lucas—each day a new work of art. The colors were the mauves and purples of the desert splashed with brilliant reds and gold. But what made them so special was the crystal clear silhouette of the hills, with the tops so distinct you could count the branches on a bush at the crown. Sunsets are beautiful all over the world, but I will never forget the stunning glory of those at Cabo from our anchorage.

Our social life was full, with people invited to our boat or we to theirs. As Christmas approached, we decorated the boat in our traditional fashion but found it difficult adjusting to the brilliant warm sunshine all around us, when it should have been cold and snowing. Phyllis and Connie from *Beliza* gave a brunch onboard *Fram*, and in a warm tropical breeze, we were joined in the cockpit by newfound friends, singing Christmas carols.

Lynn arrived to spend a week with us during the holidays, and even though she felt queasy on our bouncy boat, she enjoyed Cabo and our relaxing lifestyle. Her visit was bittersweet as it reminded us of how far we were from home and our family. With our endless focus on living our dream, our kids grew up and were now living their own lives, and we were no longer part of them. This Christmas was especially hard, our first away.

Getting water at Cabo was an interesting experience. I took our water jugs to the fuel dock, where they would pass down a water hose if they happened to notice me standing there in my dinghy. Sometimes they ignored me. Then another boat passed the hose over after filling their own tanks. I was never sure what to expect.

Ralph getting water in Cabo

Fueling was more of a challenge. This dock was eight to ten feet above water level and rested on disintegrating steel pilings. Over the years, the constant ocean swells had torn away a couple feet of dock. We anchored away from the broken pilings so we wouldn't drop onto the fangs of broken steel pilings waiting dangerously and expectantly in the surge. Then we backed close enough to throw a line to the dock attendant, and the boat was stern-tied to the dock. The diesel hose was passed across and also a water hose. Payment was made by throwing a weighted coffee can back and forth between the dock and the boat. This whole fueling operation can only happen after you have gotten a fuel permit from customs and had the port captain sign it, which is at least a whole day's effort.

We stayed in Cabo longer than we originally planned. We thought we would go north into the Sea of Cortez, but experienced Mexico hands told us it was cold and windy in the winter, and we should go south to the mainland and come back in the spring when it was nice. So we decided to follow their advice and made plans to sail south to Acapulco.

Our friend Jay from Denver arrived to sail with us to Acapulco. He brought us a packet of mail and a new three-hundred-foot stern anchor line. The day before we left, we took him to dinner at a little out-of-the-way restaurant that the yachties called the Sand Box. It was an open-air affair, with a roof and a little kitchen stuck off in the corner. The floor was about six inches of sand. Tables and chairs were placed haphazardly about, and it took some juggling with your rear end to get the chairs to set solidly enough to keep from falling over.

When we arrived, there were two other tables occupied, one with a couple of gringos and one with three locals—a man and two women. It was apparent they were celebrating some special occasion for one of the women. We had drinks and our dinner was just being served when a mariachi band arrived—not just any mariachi band but the best one in Cabo. There were twelve musicians and a very good female singer. They started in and just kept playing all through our meal. It was terrific.

When the meal was over, we were all dancing barefoot in sand up to our ankles. Jay tried to give the band a tip for playing so long, but they kept saying it was okay. We were worn out by the time we left, and I think Jay may have gotten a slightly distorted picture of our life in Cabo, but sometimes it was like that.

Saturday, January 23, 1988, we were checked out and had our import permit to take the boat to the mainland. The weather reports were mixed. Our local weatherman indicated some strong winds and rough seas coming out of the Sea of Cortez, but the weather fax looked good to us. The weather and sea conditions were nearly perfect, with the boat sailing virtually upright. We did not have to touch a line or a sail. As the sun fell into the ocean, it was replaced by a half-moon that lit up the clear sky. It was hard to imagine cruising being much better than this.

The next day tried very hard to be better—the sun did its part, the sky participated by giving us a beautiful sunrise and cloud-free heavens, and the wind kept blowing gently aft of the beam. The seas were pleasantly small, but Murphy of Murphy's Law apparently sneaked aboard. We discovered that the roll-pin in the propeller shaft coupling had broken.

Fortunately, before we left Seattle, I had mounted a pulley on the propeller shaft to use as part of a shaft brake. When the coupling pin broke, the only thing that kept the shaft and propeller from backing out and jamming the rudder was this pulley, which was now backed against the stuffing box. It could have been disastrous.

If the shaft had backed into the rudder, the autopilot had enough power to bend or break it, which then could have torn out part of the stern, not to mention having the shaft and propeller drop out into the sea. I did not have a replacement roll-pin and had to use a five-sixteenths-inch stainless-steel bolt that I knew would not last very long. I then set the shaft brake that relieved the load on the tenuous bolt. I put off a more permanent fix until we reached Acapulco. As it turned out, it took about five permanent fixes and a year to discover all the complicating factors that led to the failure, but that is another story.

Even the coupling problem couldn't put much of a dent in the joy of this trip. The water temperature was rising as we journeyed further south. It was up to seventy-seven degrees, and the air was correspondingly warmer.

Normally, if there are no unusual conditions, the air temperature at sea was within a degree or two of the water temperature. As evening turned into night, the wind moderated until we were running at about three to three and a half knots. It was so quiet and lovely we ate below in style with normal dinnerware and wine goblets.

The next day was our fourth day at sea. We only made 118 nautical miles noon to noon, but as far as I was concerned, we had arrived at our destination—not a physical place but, rather, what our dream had been for so many years: sailing the ocean with a gentle breeze on our quarter, with a clear blue sky, water that was the bluest of blue, warm balmy air, and nothing in sight for days on end, except ocean and sky. The dream was now reality!

The light from a half-moon was magnificent, and yet the stars were clearly visible. Throughout the night, we watched the stars of the Big Dipper emerge from the sea and rotate through the sky around Polaris and, in the early morning, dissolve in the light of dawn as they slipped toward the horizon. As we sailed south toward the equator, Polaris dropped lower and lower on the horizon. Now for the first time, we could identify the Southern Cross. We were in the tropics, and I sat in the cockpit in shorts and a T-shirt on night watch, listening to the rush of the bow wave, the gurgling of the stern wake, and groan of the lines. We were running wing and wing before the wind with the boat gently rocking back and forth. We did not miss seeing land, and it was more relaxing out here than at anchor. We were now true passage makers at home on the ocean.

The water temperature was eighty-four degrees, and it was hot. We were on a course toward the mainland, and we expected to be in Acapulco in the morning. Jay was on watch when the first lights of the resort city became visible just after midnight. By the time I came on watch just before dawn, the lights were brilliant and beckoning the sailors back from the sea.

At daybreak of our seventh day, we entered the famous harbor of Acapulco and circled around to the Yacht Club, where we anchored next to some old friends. We had come 730 nautical miles from Cabo, and the nicest passage we had ever made was now part of the treasure of our memory.

We enjoyed our stay in Acapulco. The Yacht Club was lovely, and we only paid a few dollars a day to use its facilities, including a cooled swimming pool, big showers, secure landing for the dinghy, and their bar and food service. We ate most of our meals at a little *palapa* restaurant across the street that was excellent and cheap. We could not afford to eat on the boat for the same price, and unfortunately, the Yacht Club prices exceeded our meager budget.

There were large supermarkets in the city, where we could buy anything we needed. The bus service was cheap and frequent. The harbor was calm and protected from the ocean swells that we had lived with at Cabo, so it was a treat to have the boat lying still at night, although during the day, it kept up a rocky dance because of the water-skiers.

All was not so nice. Pickpockets abound as I found out by having my pocket expertly picked while on a bus. My wallet had four hundred dollars in cash that were our funds for the next month's living expenses. I thought I was being careful, but a few seconds of distraction and my stolen wallet and the two culprits were lost in the crowd.

Acapulco was hot as we trudged the dusty backstreets trying to find a roll-pin to replace the one that broke at sea. While Jay (who spoke a little Spanish) was with us, we searched for a shop that might have such a thing. It was hilarious as Jay tried to describe with words what I drew on a scrap of paper. They understood boat and propeller and even shaft. But the idea of a roll-pin just escaped all our efforts at communication. Each shop in turn tried to come up with a solution for our problem, but in the end, after much head scratching, it was not a roll-pin. I bought a handful of bolts and just kept an eye on things, replacing them as needed.

Early on February 10, we left heading north for the Sea of Cortez. Jay was on his way home as we cleared the harbor at 0430. I put out our one remaining hand line and also the rod and reel. Dawn brought clear skies and no wind, so we were motoring as Phyllis fixed breakfast. Suddenly, a marlin hit on the rod and reel, gave a mighty leap, and was gone.

After breakfast we had another strike. This time the pole bent double, and the line sang as a big marlin came out of the water and stood on its tail, thrashing to shake itself free. There was wild chaos for a few moments as we pulled in the hand line, slowed the engine, and turned the boat around. Thank goodness we had no sails up. The fish was running fast, and the reel was smoking as the line ran out. I could almost see the spool by the time Phyllis turned around and ran back toward the fish. I began to reel it in and the fight was on. It took us an hour and a half to wear him down. He had also worn me down but not quite enough.

Phyllis drove the boat toward him as I reeled in as fast as I could before he took off and ran the line out again. He ran and we chased. We saw him far behind us as he leapt out of the water and danced, trying to get free. After a valiant fight, we finally brought him alongside, and I hit him on the head with the end of the gaff. At that moment, not a marlin but a magnificent sailfish unfurled his sail to its full extent as it turned vivid, iridescent neon blue. It was the most beautiful fish I had ever seen, and we wept at having killed such a glorious creature.

How can two people lift such a huge fish onto the deck of a sailboat? Fortunately, we had halyards and winches. I lassoed his tail with the main halyard and winched him aboard while Phyllis pulled him forward over the foredeck with the jib halyard. Laid out on deck, he was over eight feet long, and I estimated him to be a little over one hundred pounds. It took another hour to fillet it and get the meat into the freezer. Katisha didn't want anything to do with a fish that big and sat safely in the cockpit, peeking around the corner at all the action.

The sailfish

We stopped in Zehuatanejo, a lovely little place, to do some boat chores. Phyllis varnished the teak rails while we were there, but because of the heat, it dried as she put it on and, after a week, began to break down and peel off. She was disappointed, because it was time-consuming and a lot of work. As usual, I had several maintenance chores to do, which included replacing the bolt that replaced the roll-pin.

After a week, we left for Manzanillo, two hundred miles north. We had a miserable sail into strong winds and boxy waves. It was like running into a solid wall as we clawed our way north. We slept in the cockpit, because it was so rough below. Somehow the miserable conditions didn't seem so bad with each other's companionship. At least, it was warm. The boat and we were taking a beating, and it was a long slow grind before we turned into the harbor at midnight three days later. We don't like to enter a strange port at night, but the radar did its job, and two exhausted people crawled into bed after setting the anchor that night.

Las Hadas was a gigantic fairyland with fabulous facilities, fascinating architecture all painted white, all kinds of shops, several hotels, many restaurants, and condominiums—all beautifully maintained. A pretty fancy place for poor yachties like ourselves. On the bay, there was a nice sandy beach and a small marina. Outside the marina was a large anchorage, where we anchored, along with other yachties. Las Hadas encouraged the cruisers to anchor there by charging a minimal fee for use of the facilities. I think we added atmosphere, or maybe they just wanted to keep our ragtag bunch away from their more free-spending guests. In addition to the yachts at anchor, the little marina was filled with maxi-racers, who arrived after a race from California. The place was jumping.

Our high school friends Alan and Charlotte were waiting to spend two weeks with us. This adventuresome couple traveled extensively but had never spent any time on a sailboat. We wanted to give them the experience of our new lifestyle.

Saturday, we visited the open market in nearby Santiago to buy fresh food. They were amazed by all the little stalls selling fruits, vegetables, fish, chickens (alive and dead), eggs in flats, meat laying in the sun, small stacks of canned goods, honey in old wine bottles, mountains of melons, odd assortments of cheap tools, and many other peculiar items. We spent less than $30 and left burdened down with supplies for the next two weeks. They could hardly believe it.

On Sunday, we played jet-setters and did all the things you do at Las Hadas. We lay around on deck chairs, with beautiful monogrammed beach towels draped over as if we belonged there. We had drinks at the bar in the swimming pool, made famous by the movie *10*. Now we felt positively decadent, easily forgetting our humble floating home anchored nearby and the miserable passage that brought us here.

It was quite a contrast to the market the day before. We were brought back to reality on Monday, when we loaded purified water by jerry jugs from the dock and checked out of the port. Our first anchorage was at a small bay just a short distance away but a nice spot with no visible habitation. We snorkeled with spear guns, but Alan had the only success when he came walking up the beach with a puffer fish on the end of his spear. It had blown itself up into a round ball, with spines sticking out all over.

"Hey Ralph, what do I do now?"

Wednesday, we moved on north to Bahia Navidad, where we met Philomena (Phil), owner of the *palapa* restaurant where all the yachties hung out. We immediately became part of the social whirl of Bahia Navidad. We ate out at Phil's, we visited the small village across the bay, we had friends over for drinks, we met new people, and we visited the other yachts and said good-bye to friends who were leaving. It was one continuous party with a constantly changing cast of characters.

On Saturday, there was a big farewell party for the boats leaving for the South Pacific and the Panama Canal. With Phil's wonderful food and many drinks, everyone had a good time. When we got back to *Fram* after all the celebration, it was late, and we were tired. It had been our practice while we were on the mainland to lift our dinghy out of the water at night to discourage theft.

When we finally went to bed, Phyllis asked me, "Aren't you going the lift the dinghy?"

I was tired, so I answered, "It'll be all right. There are lots of boats around." I rolled over and went to sleep.

I woke up in the night, knowing something was wrong and immediately thought about the dinghy. I got up to check and it was gone! What a sickening feeling. The painter (rope) had been cut. We lay in bed waiting for dawn with a terrible sense of loss. Besides being our transportation, it was also our life raft. We told the fleet about the theft on the radio net at 0830. At the same time, two other boats reported their dinghies also gone. A little later, *Lady MacLin* came on the radio, saying that a Mexican fishing *ponga* was alongside with the remains of two dinghies. I went over immediately and saw that they were from the other two boats. They did have the seat, gas tank, and three floorboards from our Callegari. The inflatables had been slashed in many places, and their outboard engines were gone. After many questions, we learned that the fishermen knew the location of the *rojo* dinghy that was still out at sea because it had been too heavy to bring back.

They needed more gas to go get it, but if I had gas, they would take me. The tank from the Callegari they brought back was nearly full, and the cap was sealed, so even though it had been floating in the ocean, it looked all right. Off I went with three Mexican fishermen, headed out to sea. They could not speak English, and I could not speak Spanish. One fisherman stood in the bow, holding a bowline to steady himself, and directed the driver. How they managed to find the dinghy was amazing, as it was over two miles offshore, completely deflated and awash. I did not see it until we were within a hundred feet. There were four long slashes in the main compartments, and the engine was gone. It was obvious that the thieves were only interested in the engines and had no use for the dinghies.

It was nearly impossible for the three of us to wrestle the swamped Callegari aboard the *ponga*. My next pang of worry came when the Mexicans could not get their outboard engine started. What a predicament! We were two miles offshore and drifting. All three of them worked themselves into a heavy sweat before it finally fired. Maybe a little water leaked into my tank after all. I offered them the rest of the gas when we were back, but they said no. They did accept a reward of $20 for each of the returned dinghies. It was possible they were part of the theft scheme, but I liked to think not. I was glad to have the dinghy back, but it was a pathetic sight as we hauled it aboard *Fram* and hung it from the main halyard, looking like a dead carcass with long slashes exposing its insides.

Alan and I tried to repair it with borrowed patches and contact cement, but the patches didn't hold, and all the air leaked out after a few minutes. We needed a special two-part glue to do the job, and that was not available in Bahia Navidad. Meantime, we bought a damaged but repaired (and still leaking) Achilles from a fellow yachtie. Not perfect, but we had dinghy!

With heavy hearts, we sailed north to Tenacatita. It was a perfect sail for Alan and Charlotte, with gentle winds and fair skies and the finest array of sea life we had seen. Whales, dolphins, marlins, dorados, giant rays flipping in the air, and even a poisonous sea snake we had not seen before. In spite of our loss, we had fun. Wednesday, we were having breakfast when we received a call. Some outboard engines had been found. Dare we hope that one was ours?

We were underway immediately. When we arrived at Phil's, our engine was there in a big plastic bag with a lot of sand and a Mexican filleting knife in the bottom. It had been hidden under an upside-down *ponga* on the beach near town. The bar lock that secured the engine to the dinghy that I thought was foolproof proved me the fool. It had been sprung open and slipped off without even bending it or undoing the padlock.

I cleaned the sand off the engine, looked it over for damage, and clamped it on the Achilles. It started on the first pull. It was a wonderful feeling to have lost something vitally important to our way of life and have it returned. It doesn't often happen like that, but when it does, it's a time of rejoicing and thanksgiving. We had a big party at Phil's that day!

Alan and Charlotte left the next day after spending an eventful time with way too much adventure with us, but now we had to be on the move again. We were on our way to Puerto Villarta, many nautical miles away.

We had another miserable windward sail to Ipala and arrived before dark, totally wrung out from another terrible beating. We shared a glass of Chivas Regal with our friends on *Malaika Moja*, who were a few miles behind us the whole way. It was that kind of day. It warranted a good stiff scotch.

The next leg would take us around Cabo Corrientes into Bahia Banderas and Puerto Vallarta. The cape was known for its rough conditions similar to Point Conception. We planned to minimize that possibility by leaving early since the wind seemed to build up during the day and reached its maximum in the afternoon. We motored around Corrientes early in the morning in a dead calm. Our luck seemed to have changed; it must have been the scotch!

We wanted to go into the new marina at Nuevo Vallarta, but the tides were too low for our draft, and we ended up anchored in "the pond" in Puerto Vallarta instead. In 1988, the totally protected pond was a large dredged body of water that was part of a huge condominium development. Later it would be filled with docks and condos, but when we were there, we anchored in the middle, along with a few other yachts at no cost and with easy access to town by bus.

The tides were finally high enough for us to enter the marina at Nuevo Vallarta, where we put on water from the purification plant and diesel. Nuevo Vallarta was an example of development in Mexico at the time we were there. A huge sum of development money was spent to build a large marina for visiting yachts, but the entrance was too shallow to allow entrance most of the time, even for the average-sized sailboat. At the same time, the fuel dock was built to accommodate cruise ships. It was a real conundrum.

One of our most delightful stops was at the tiny enchanting village of Chacala, about fifty miles north of Nuevo Vallarta. We entered a small protected anchorage, encircled by a white sandy beach and fringing palm trees. We could have been visiting a South Seas island from its appearance. Nestled in amongst the palms were several thatched-roof *palapa* restaurants, and behind them we saw the small primitive homes of a village. We had just set the anchor on the sandy bottom, when a couple in a dinghy came rowing out from shore. They stopped by on the way to their yacht, anchored a short distance away, to tell us the Capitán del Puerto wanted to see our papers.

When I arrived at the small white-and-blue concrete building, located on a low hill overlooking the bay, I found a little old man in an ill-fitting uniform, who was apparently the Capitán del Puerto. He greeted me in broken English, inquiring where we had come from and where we were going. He also wanted to see our papers. I don't think he could read, but his assistant looked them over and told him they were all right. He did not check us in, just wanted to talk.

Later, we wandered down the single street of the little village with pigs rooting under the trees and chickens pecking in the dirt around the sleeping dogs. It was a lazy, warm sunny afternoon with hardly any life stirring as we walked back along the beach and stopped to visit with a couple from one of the anchored yachts. The restaurants did not have any business, so a lady came out and talked us into coming in for a lobster dinner. It was our farewell dinner on the mainland of Mexico, and when a couple of the other yachts joined us, we made it a party.

March 16, we left on the first leg of our crossing back to the Baja. We looked forward to stopping at Isla Isabella, a nature preserve sixty miles offshore. As we approached its rugged rocky outline, the island appeared as if flung out of the sea. Whales surrounded us as we entered the small rockbound bay, with cliffs jutting into the sky on two sides and onshore a small rocky beach with fishermen shacks above the high tide line. We anchored close inside the rocky reef. A hundred feet off our stern, swells entered and broke on the rocks beside us in sudsy cascades. Hundreds of frigate birds wheeled about the cliffs, and we watched them swoop in and land on their nests.

The next day, we went ashore and were greeted by several curious children. Since we were looking for the port official to check our papers, we made our way to a large building we saw from the boat. What we found was a partially completed massive concrete structure that was supposed to be a visitor's center and museum. When we entered through an open doorway, we discovered the building's present use. Women were gathered around several large cement benches, scrubbing laundry by hand, using rainwater collected from the roof of the giant building and stored in a cistern near the rear entrance. It was probably one of the world's most expensive laundry facilities in one of its poorest places.

The ladies told us the official had gone to the mainland. While we were anchoring the day before, we noticed someone in uniform leave in a small open fishing *ponga*. That apparently was the regular ferry to the mainland, sixty miles away. Its concession to safety was twin outboards, the only one we ever saw with two engines.

We wandered around the island, and every inch seemed to be covered with nesting frigate birds and terns, mating and raising their young. They showed no fear as we walked close to their nests. Outside the little bay, numerous whales sounded with great leaps and splashes. Since we limited our hiking to the lower slopes, we did not see the iguanas, but we knew they were there. Jacques Cousteau once called this The Galapagos of Mexico, and we felt like we were part of a film.

Anchored at Isla Isabella

In the morning, with time running out, we headed for La Paz, where we were to meet Doug and Lisa. The last day of winter turned into a comfortable sail into Los Muertos, a day's run south of La Paz. After anchoring for the night, the first day of spring found us becalmed in the channel just north of Los Muertos. I discovered a major fuel leak in the engine fuel pump and had it disassembled for several hours while Phyllis tried unsuccessfully to maintain steerageway with no wind.

It was ironic that this was the first windless day we experienced for several weeks. I finally finished installing the pump with only one nut holding it in place since I dropped the other one in the bilge and couldn't find it. I decided it was worth the risk of starting the engine to avoid the inevitable caustic comments from the first mate, if we failed to arrive in La Paz in time to meet the kids. I was lucky the single nut held. We made it to La Paz on March 22, one day before they were due to arrive.

Doug and Lisa brought mail and two-part glue for our dinghies. It wasn't long before we successfully patched both inflatables. I bought another nut for the engine fuel pump since I never found the one I dropped.

We explored the many charms of La Paz and its delightful, old-Mexico feel. It was one of the most prosperous cities we had seen, with a nice downtown shopping area and an attractive main street along the waterfront. Every place in Mexico had wonderful ice cream, and we walked along the street eating ice cream cones just like tourists. Many Americans lived there, and the well-stocked supermarkets had many U.S. products.

There were many beautiful islands outside of La Paz, and we explored several. The aerial photos we saw were enticing. Doug and Lisa had flown over them and described how they lay in stark grandeur, with spectacular azure-blue bays surrounded by white sandy beaches.

We enjoyed a brisk, exhilarating sail to Isla Partida, which was by far the biggest and best of the anchorages and beaches. We anchored there along with four other boats. We took the dinghy ashore and walked the white sandy beach that stretched all around the bay, shoaling for hundreds of yards from the shore. The water was bathtub warm and great for swimming.

We climbed the surrounding hills to get a good view of the island and the impossibly blue bay. The land was beautiful in a stark rugged majesty. The dry rocky hills appeared barren, but there was a vast array of plant life with many different kinds of cacti and low-growing bushes. Also, short, stubby trees with trunks with peeling bark that looked like potato skins. With occasional rain, this would all turn green overnight. The only sign of habitation were the fishermen tents. An amazing contrast on one side of the bay were mangroves that grow near saltwater and added a touch of lush green to the drab reddish-gray landscape.

Just north of Isla Partida was Ensenada Grande, where the rocks around the bay look like a cake covered with a dull red frosting that melted and sagged over the edges. It hung out over the water, where the waves eroded the rock beneath, making shallow caves along the rocky entrance to the bay. It was a strange and fascinating place.

While we were in La Paz, Phyllis took the test for her U.S. novice amateur radio license (ham). This was the first step working toward her general license before we leave for the South Pacific. With this license, she also received a Mexican license. She couldn't wait to join the local Mañana and Sonrisa nets. It fit her outgoing personality to be able to chat with fellow hams about what was going on where we were. She soon became one of the Sonrisa net controllers and was good at it.

Race week was an annual affair, and boats gathered in La Paz from all over the world. *Fram* was not a race boat, but we sailed to Isla Partita with the fleet and participated in many beach activities. It was a big party. The governor of Baja California Sur and the director of tourism arrived for the closing ceremony, lending a touch of importance to all the previous week's frivolity.

The morning after race week was over, most of the boats were gone, and I started the engine to charge batteries, when suddenly it was whistling, wheezing, and clattering. I shut it down immediately because it sounded so terrible. I suspected a broken valve and didn't dare run it, so we set sail for La Paz. It was an interesting challenge to sail into La Paz—down the narrow kinked channel, through the shoals while the typical tidal current was running—and anchor amongst the crowded fleet in the harbor, which was doing the La Paz Waltz.

I need to describe the La Paz Waltz. Due to shifting sand shoals in the shallow bay, tidal currents flow through in different patterns. Anchored boats find themselves moving around on their anchor every which way and in no relationship to each other. So you could anchor in a perfect location, only to find yourself bumping another boat doing the waltz in a different direction. It was an awkward dance. One day, we all stared in amazement when several huge gray whales swam through the shoals and anchored boats without touching a single anchor chain.

The engine problem went away on its own. As far as I could tell, it was only a valve that stuck open and then unstuck itself.

We continued to explore the haunting beauty of the Sea of Cortez and its treasure of amazing islands. One of the most beautiful was Isla San Francisco. The lovely circular bay of intense turquoise water was surrounded by a sweeping white-sand beach, guarded by a grand hill standing like a sentinel on the south side.

In the evening, sitting in the cockpit after dinner, we absorbed the beauty as we have so often in lovely places. The moon was brilliant, and the stars swept across the sky as if flung from the creator's hand. Across the sea, the mountains of the Baja thrust heavenward on the horizon in a great dark mass, with their crests a dull silver against the night sky. The water was glassy smooth, reflecting the moon and the stars. It was then we dared put the rest of the dream into words.

Mountains of the Baja

We said to each other for the first time, "We should sail around the world." Always before, it was a fleeting thought but never spoken out loud.

Our vision had been to sail the oceans of the world, wherever we chose to go. Here in this place of beautiful serenity, it took on a more definite form. We would sail to the South Pacific in the spring of 1989 and then explore as much of the Pacific as we can and stay as long as we were having fun before heading on west. I would like to go via South Africa, and Phyllis wants to go up the Red Sea and the Suez Canal into the Mediterranean. That decision can wait for the proper time; what mattered now was we had a new goal. The dream was alive and growing as we lived it.

The next day, we sailed across to the Baja to the anchorage at Agua Verde, guarded by a huge rock at the entrance. We wandered through the village with a few small shy children tagging along. When Phyllis gave them candy, they shrieked with joy and ran off to tell their friends. The road where we walked was filled with ruts, where it had washed out when heavy rain from thunderstorms in the mountains swept down through the valley. The villagers showed us their hand-dug well, where the floodwaters filled it with mud and debris, and the only water it contained now was brackish and mostly saltwater. Their only drinking water came from the visiting yachts or was brought by truck over the only road to civilization, the narrow dirt track climbing into the mountains. We gave them water from our tanks and promised to return. Later, a good, properly lined well was dug for these families by yachties and others who saw their plight and vowed to make a difference.

From Agua Verde, we made the last leg of our northern trek to Puerto Escondido, where friends were located. A strong wind made the trip more exciting than we expected. When we arrived near a series of rocky islands that lie to the east and south of Puerto Escondido, we were not sure which passage between the islands was safe, because our charts were so confusing. We watched a boat ahead of us go between the southernmost island and the land, so I decided to follow, even though our chart said No Ship Passage. Our hearts were in our mouths as we sailed at seven knots past the rocky headland, wondering if there was a hidden reef waiting for us or if we would be on the rocky lee shore in seconds. We heaved a sigh of relief when we were safely past.

Puerto Escondido was different than we expected. Outside was a small anchorage called The Waiting Room. There was only room for a few boats to anchor there, but it was a good place to wait for a favorable tide to enter the larger bay beyond. There were a few dilapidated buildings and a large deteriorating concrete pier near the narrow shallow entrance.

Inside, Puerto Escondido was completely surrounded by hills, except for a low area facing the Sea of Cortez. On the Baja side, there had been plans for a grand development that was now abandoned and in ruins after a French group invested ten million dollars. The nearest town was Loreto, fifteen miles away. Scattered throughout the bay were many anchored yachts, and we soon found our friends Norm and Danny on *Endeavor*, who had been our slipmates at the Duwamish Yacht Club. They left Seattle in 1980 and had been in Puerto Escondido several years. This would be our homeport for the next nine months.

Phyllis was scheduled for more reconstructive surgery in Seattle, so we left *Fram* and Katisha in the care of cruising friends. While we were in Seattle, I bought back our old Chevy from David. He thought I was crazy to drive such an old car all the way down the Baja peninsula.

"But Dad, it needs new tires." So I bought two new tires to calm his concerns. "But Dad, the brakes are bad."

"Oh, that's all right. I never use them anyway," was my response. He just couldn't talk me out of that car. It looked terrible but actually was in pretty good shape for an old car. The old Chevy fit right into the Mexican scene and was soon dubbed the Baja Beater.

We fell into an easy routine. The weather was a hot one hundred degrees and water temperature in the nineties. We didn't to do much but fish, read, swim, and eat. We lazily moved from anchorage to anchorage on the various islands. We dropped our hook in thirty feet of water over a white-sand bottom and were often all alone. The water was so clear we could count the links in our chain. Most of the time we didn't wear clothes, and at night, before going to bed, we went for a swim to cool off. When the moon was full, we could see the bottom as clearly as in daylight, and the shadow of the boat was there with crisp, sharp lines. The water was smooth as a sheet of glass. Time just drifted by.

We gathered our food from the sea to sustain our bodies, we played in the sea for refreshment and exercise, and we were surrounded by beauty to satisfy our souls. For entertainment, we watched the pelicans as they dove for fish near the boat. Even more entertaining was watching as flocks flew in formation, barely skimming the water with their wingtips. In the heat of the day, we stayed inside and watched movies or read while twelve-volt fans kept us cool. We were basking in the most perfect environment we could imagine.

Everything in our world was not perfect though. We started north to explore other islands but soon developed an engine problem, so we returned to Puerto Escondido. I found two broken engine mounts, and we spent several weeks waiting for replacements and then installing the new mounts. They had been broken for a quite a while and probably were what caused the roll-pin to break earlier. While we waited for parts, I finished several other jobs I had put off because we had become so lazy.

One day, when Phyllis and I were sailing fast in a twenty-knot wind, we hooked a large dorado. We were going too fast to stop, so we turned into the wind and discovered we could heave to, with all sails standing, and take our time bringing in the fish.

We adjusted the helm and sail positions, so they tried to steer the boat in opposite directions. This resulted in the boat coming to a stop with the sails trying to sail one way and the rudder steering the other. In this condition we were hove to. It worked perfectly. We would remember this important lesson later when we hove to for three days during a storm. There was always more to learn about sailing.

We wanted to take the train to the Copper Canyon on the mainland; we would have to take a ferry from La Paz to Topolobampo. Making the reservation from Puerto Escondido was not easy, but after much confusion, we seemed to be successful. With friends Norm and Margie, we drove to La Paz in great spirits for our big adventure. We knew that there were no sleeping cabins on the ferry, so we naively thought, *That's okay, we can just sleep in the car on the overnight crossing.* We drove to La Paz the day before the ferry was scheduled to leave, and it was a good thing we did, because it took five hours to buy the tickets and get an import permit for the car. Then we were told to be at the terminal at Pichilinque, outside of town, three hours before ferry time. We dutifully complied and were in line at 1700 for a 2000 departure. We didn't want anything to go wrong with our trip.

While we waited in line, the Mazátlan ferry was loading, but our ferry was not there yet. Later, when it pulled into the dock, we looked at each other with a sense of impending doom. None of us felt good about our coming adventure. It was not one of the big ferries we expected but a squat little ugly thing, rusty white and covered with red primer paint patches. Then there was some commotion at the other dock as trucks started unloading from the Mazátlan ferry. A guy in line ahead of us went to investigate.

When he came back we heard him say to his friend, "At least we are going." We didn't like the sounds of that, so Norm, who could speak some Spanish, went to investigate. When he came back, the news was disconcerting. Hurricane Debbie that had done so much damage in the Caribbean crossed over Mexico and was now a tropical storm located between Mazátlan and La Paz. That ferry was cancelled, but they were going to run ours anyway and just go north around the storm.

After much discussion, we decided that since we had come this far, we would keep going. Around 1830, they started loading vehicles—drivers only. That was when I realized we would not be sleeping in the car. They didn't load according to where you were in line. Men wandered through the crowd of vehicles, which were mainly large trucks, choosing which one to load next. When I was waved aboard the stern-loading ramp, I was directed forward by a crewman wearing a gas mask. That was unnerving, but upon boarding, I could understand why, as the exhaust smoke was so thick I could hardly see where I was going. Where I was going proved to be down a steep ramp into the forward bilge of the ship. The floor was laid directly on the ribs forming the bottom of the ship, and there was just enough height for my car. There was room for fifteen cars in there, and we were jammed in so tight the only way I could get out was by climbing through a window and over the tops of the other cars. As I walked up the ramp and out onto the lower deck, a large door swung down and sealed off the car hold that was now one of the watertight compartments. That seemed like an ominous state of affairs. All the rest of the vehicles loaded were trucks, except for the few cars buried with the Baja Beater in the bilge.

When the passengers were finally loaded, we began to understand how grim this night was likely to be. More passengers were being loaded than there were seats, and people were staking out space, wherever they could find it, to sit or lay down. We found four straight and narrow seats. Marjorie investigated the head and came back in a state of shock. She reported that only one toilet was working in the women's restroom; the other one was overflowing. There were probably three or four hundred people onboard, and we were going to cross the Sea of Cortez on the edge of the remains of a hurricane. The prospects did not look good. By now it was totally dark, and we saw lightning to the east in the clouds at the edge of the storm. The wind had picked up, and there were white caps in the enclosed bay. We gritted our teeth and sank deeper into our cramped seats. Departure time came and went, but we did not. At 2100, the lines were cast off, and we edged away from the dock and proceeded out into the bay but not very far. The ship stopped and then slowly backed up toward the dock, and the mooring lines were reattached. No explanations, so an enterprising passenger said he would go ask the *capitan*.

When he came back, he announced, "There's a crack in the stern, and one of the bilge pumps isn't working, but it should be fixed soon, and then we'll go."

Great! Here we were captives on a sinking ship about to sail into a hurricane loaded with people eating lots of spicy greasy food and with only one operating toilet. The cabin was already a pigpen, with trash and food scraps all over the floor along with dogs, crawling babies, and sleeping grandmas. And we hadn't even left the dock. We tried not to think about what it would be like in the storm with an overflowing toilet and vomit covering it all.

Finally, just before midnight, they announced the ferry was not going after all, and the four of us heaved a collective sigh of relief to escape with only the loss of our time and the price of the tickets. It was almost worth it for such a bizarre experience. This was the same ferry that sank a few months later on the run from Pichilingue to Topolobompo.

We left Puerto Escondido the end of January and made the run south before the wind and arrived in La Paz a couple of days later. We hauled the boat out for bottom painting and general maintenance before leaving on our long passage. The rest of our time in La Paz was spent buying provisions. Because of the high prices in French Polynesia, our friends in the South Pacific advised us to stock up on everything before we left, so we did. It was good advice. Here we bid a fond farewell to the Baja Beater. It served us well.

We sailed to Cabo with the engine doing the sailing in absolutely windless conditions. Where were the northerlies that plagued us so last year?

We finished the final preparations, getting the boat ready for sea. It had been a long time, and this time we were preparing to cross an ocean. We braved the fuel dock once again to top off our fuel and water tanks. No difficulties this time. We ate dinner at one of our favorite restaurants and said good-bye to our yachtie friends. We checked out and had our first Zarpe, the official document from customs/immigration clearing us out of the country to be presented when clearing into French Polynesia. We followed this process each time we departed from one country for another.

Phyllis received her general amateur radio license and then upgraded to an advanced license before we left Mexico. She was known in the amateur radio world as KF7SQ on *Fram*. Whenever we were on a passage, she would check into the Mobile Maritime Net (MM) with our position and weather conditions. We, in turn, received weather forecasts for our area and any messages or other information. We were placed on their roll-call list, and they will call us at the same time each day. The volunteer net controllers were scattered all around the Pacific, and most have sailed the oceans. It was a safety feature and our lifeline to the rest of the world.

Ralph's brother-in-law, Dick Borton, listened to the roll call every day and kept the rest of the family informed about our progress. He also made phone patches so we could talk to our kids. The most comforting presence in our lives from now on would be Dick, who we knew was always listening. We talked to him at least once a week on a regular schedule throughout all our cruising years.

Phyllis called the MM Net with our information and let them know we will leave Cabo San Lucas tomorrow. They now have complete information about *Fram* and her two passengers. Her new circle of fellow hams included Al in Seattle, Les on Moorea, Don in Australia, Bill in Raiatea, and John on Norfolk Island, plus several others, including Arnold in the Cook Islands, who gave the weather forecasts.

Tonight, we sat in the cockpit, anchored in the same place we first anchored sixteen months ago, and reminisced about our time in Mexico. We watched the brilliant Mexican sunset over the mountains behind Cabo for the last time. Our lives have certainly changed. It has been a time of relaxation and decisions for the future. We leave tomorrow, refreshed and ready to leap out over the ocean into the next phase of our odyssey.

The Baja Beater

Chapter 21

Living Our Dream

Tomorrow dawned as the morning of March 16, 1989. It did not seem much different from other days, with a couple of cruise ships anchoring nearby while I put the last touches on a repair of the anchor winch and Phyllis did the laundry. We made a final pilgrimage to town for fresh produce and breakfast at Papi's. When we returned to the boat, we made the rounds of the deck and below to make sure everything was lashed down. I deflated the dinghy and stowed it below and mounted the outboard on its stern pulpit bracket. We were ready at last, and as we brought in the anchor chain, I flaked it down flat in its locker. We were underway at 1400 bound for Atuona on the island of Hiva Oa in the Marquesas, with an intermediate stop at the Socorro Islands. As we passed Los Arcos, the sails were raised, and *Fram* was charging south at over seven knots in a twenty-knot wind. It was not long before Cabo disappeared astern in the overcast sky. However, we were not looking back. We were looking ahead to a long ocean passage and the adventures that would unfold.

This was our first night at sea in a long time and the first long passage with only the two of us. Phyllis put her new ham radio license to good use and checked us into the Mobile Maritime Net roll call.

"KF7SQ, KF7SQ. This is Al, W7EMZ."

"KF7SQ here. This is Phyllis on *Fram*."

"Are you ready with your report?"

"Our position is lat 22°45'09" N, long 110°12'87" W. Boat speed—six knots. Course—180 degrees, magnetic. Sea-state—three-to-four-foot waves from the west-northwest. Wind speed—eighteen to twenty knots west-northwest. Barometric pressure—steady. Cloud cover—overcast. Everyone aboard is okay."

"Thank you. You can expect the same weather conditions in your location tomorrow. Have a good evening. W7EMZ clear."

"KF7SQ clear."

Phyllis checking into the ham net

Night watch was often a time of beauty and serenity. Phyllis was enjoying the dark tranquil night with Katisha in her lap, listening to the soft *whoosh, whoosh* as the hull passed through the water. All of a sudden, there was a loud *WHOOSH* on our port side, and when she jumped up to look, there was another *WHOOSH* on the other side and the sound of air being sucked into a large chamber. With her heart pounding, she tried to call me. Just then, the backs of two huge black whales, longer than *Fram*, rose out of the water. She was trembling with fear when she grabbed the helm to turn away, but there was no place to go! We were sandwiched between the two behemoths. She remembered stories of boats being sunk by whales and thought it was really unfair to happen on our first night out. Katisha was scared too, but I slept peacefully through it, even after a shivering cat joined me under the covers.

In the morning, the wind died down until our speed was two knots. After an hour or so, I gave in and started the engine. The conditions did not change much over the next day and a half, and we spent part of the time sailing slowly and part motoring. The temperature, both air and water, increased as we made our way south. The following morning, we motored to Isla Socorro and anchored in Bahia Braithwaite at 1530. There we joined two other boats in the anchorage. Even though it was exposed to the open ocean on the south, with calm weather, we slept well to the gentle rocking of the boat.

We planned to spend only a couple days at Socorro but ended up staying nearly a week. This volcanic island was about 250 nautical miles south, southeast of Cabo San Lucas and belongs to Mexico. The only inhabitants were part of a Mexican Navy base. It was difficult to get formal permission to visit there, but we showed up with our papers in order, and they gave us an exceptionally friendly welcome.

As we approached the island, we saw many humpback whales. Whenever we looked out to sea from our anchorage, we saw several whales, often with one of their giant flukes raised vertically before slapping the surface with a great splash. Sometimes, this would be repeated many times in rapid succession. We watched two or three thrashing and rolling in the water in a swirling mass of bodies as they appeared to be mating. When we lay in bed, we listened to whale songs through the hull as they serenaded us through the night with their eerie sounds of communication. We couldn't hear them outside, but their haunting voices came clearly through the hull. After the first night, Phyllis asked if I heard a baby crying. The entire week we were there, the whales sang us to sleep.

One day Commandante Fernando, a rear admiral, arranged for us to visit the volcano. We arrived ashore early and were met by the admiral and several of his men. After introductions and pleasant small talk, we six yachties climbed into jeeps and set off up a rutted, dusty road. It wound back into the hills away from the sea, climbed steeply in places, and then ran along the crest of a hill. As we looked back, we saw our boats riding at anchor in the clear blue water of the bay, with leaping whales making white splotches on the smooth surface of the sea.

The sun was high in a brilliant blue sky with fluffy white clouds fringing the horizon. We drove through hills covered with sparse vegetation, but our guide said we would be into a forest before we left the vehicles. The road degenerated into a couple of ruts as we climbed higher. The radiator was boiling as we struggled up a particularly steep grade until we came to a wheezing stop in a small glade on the edge of a forest of gnarled trees. From there, we continued on foot.

Our guide was a handsome young officer in a spotless uniform, with a ready smile and good English. We hiked through the underbrush in the shade of small trees with knobby trunks and dense foliage. Overhead, wild parrots accompanied us through the forest with a cacophony of sound, scolding these intruders into their sanctuary. Occasionally we came across flocks of wild sheep that are all over the island. They were skittish around us, probably because personnel from the navy base hunted them for food. It was strange to see sheep with long tails.

The trail was faintly defined, and our guide cautioned us to stay together. I didn't see how we could get lost; after all, it was an island, and up went to the volcano and down went to the sea. Later we stopped in a small clearing to rest and pick some *limons* (small yellow limes). The young naval officer took off his dress shirt to climb the trees and threw the fruit down to us. Our packs were soon filled, and we were thrilled to have an abundance of *limons* for the rest of our passage. By now we were enjoying his company, and he seemed happy to have the diversion of our visit.

After leaving the *limon* trees, the visible trail became harder to follow through the rest of the forest. Now the only thing guiding our guide was the bright yellow paint splashed on trees or rocks about every fifty yards. The forest became unbelievably dense, and I could see it would be possible to get lost. Before long, we missed one of the marks, and six American sailors and one Mexican naval officer wandered around a volcano in the Pacific Ocean, looking for the trail. After that, we paid closer attention.

We continued to climb the steep trail through dry washes and over rocky banks. We sweat profusely in the heat of the day. It was time for another rest stop and drink of water from our packs. As we came around an outcropping of rock near the top, we were greeted by the sight of barren rock splashed in garish yellows and reds and greens, with steam wafting from cracks in the earth and the strong stench of hydrogen sulfide. We picked a path across the remains of the crater and up the final steep slope to the top. It was marked with a weathered monument and a bronze plaque at 3,707 feet.

Top of the volcano on Socorro Island

The view was well worth the climb. In all directions, the mountain sloped away to a vivid deep blue sea. It was flat calm and marked with the tiny white specks of whales at play. Our boats were miniature toys floating in the distant bay to the south. To the north, Isla Benedicto grew out of the sea. We were above the few clouds that drifted through the sky, and the ocean seemed to stretch forever into the distance. It gave us a sense of its vastness. I stood in silent awe at the magnitude of the world in which we had chosen to dwell.

The return trek was much easier, but before long, we were lost again. I think our guide was embarrassed, but by then, we were well acquainted and had a good laugh as we searched for yellow markers.

When we arrived at the end of the road, Admiral Fernando and his wife were waiting to greet us with a couple jeeps and cold lemonade. We were ready to pile in for a ride back. Living on a boat does not prepare muscles for mountain climbing, even small ones.

We held on for dear life on the wild ride down the steep rutted road. I rode in the back of the second jeep, which did not have any cushions. We bumped along until my behind was nearly as sore as my legs while our driver tried to keep up with the admiral driving the lead jeep. It was late afternoon when we arrived at the small pier. It had been a wonderful day, and we thanked our hosts for their kindness and invited them to visit our boats the next day.

As we were getting ready to leave in our dinghy, the *commandante* took me aside to ask me if I would take him out to visit one of the large tuna fishing vessels we had seen fishing south of the island. He said he needed to check their papers, and the only boats they had at the base were a couple of small open launches with old, old engines that cruised at about five knots. He saw my Callegari with the fifteen-horsepower Evinrude and knew it would be much faster, so we made arrangements to go out first thing the next day.

When I saw his jeep come down to the pier in the morning, I hurried in to pick him up. Life in Mexico does not hurry. Before our trip to the tuna boats, the admiral brought his family, who were visiting on the island, out to see *Fram*. Their two good-looking teens wanted to see what a sailing yacht was like and were excited to see our nautical home. Back at the pier, one of the navy men was waiting for us. He handed us a heavy plastic sack, and we were ready to go. From the shape and size of the sack, I guessed that it probably contained a large skinned lamb.

The tuna boat was just visible on the horizon as we headed out of the bay. Fortunately, the wind was calm, so we only had to contend with long ocean swells. The Callegari simply climbed up and down like driving over low rolling hills. It took us a half hour to reach the tuna boat, so I figured they were about ten miles away. It was a large vessel, well over a hundred feet, and as we approached, the *commandante* called them on his handheld radio. They drifted to a stop as we came alongside. We climbed up a steel ladder built into the side of the hull and tied the dinghy off near the aft rail, where they bring up their tender.

With the admiral off doing his duty, I was given a tour of the bridge of this well-equipped and maintained Mexican ship. Their capacity was six hundred tons of frozen fish. When it came time to leave, Fernando asked me, "How much do you think we can carry?"

It took me a moment to realize he was asking how many fish we could take back in the Callegari and still plane.

"How big are they?"

"About fifty kilos," he estimated.

"At least two and maybe three," I replied.

The crew came dragging two frozen hundred-pound yellowfin tuna across the deck, and we manhandled them into the dinghy, and then I told them we could take another. When the third was loaded, we cast off and headed for the island. One lamb had turned into three hundred pounds of tuna. I'm sure the admiral found their papers were in order. A generous chunk of tuna was delivered to *Fram* before we left the next morning.

Since this was our first long passage with only the two of us, it took a while to work out a satisfactory watch schedule. We maintained a twenty-four-hour watch while at sea. Because I had trouble sleeping in the daytime and it also took me a while to get to sleep, three hours on and three off was not a good schedule for me. Phyllis could sleep nearly any time and needed more sleep than I did. We experimented with various combinations and finally found one that worked well for us. I normally maintained the daytime watch, and Phyllis went to bed early after checking into the MM net and came on watch from 2200 to 0300. Then she went back to bed and slept until 0900 or 1000. Five hours is all the sleep I needed if I could get it all at once. This worked well for us.

We followed the same safety rules we established when we left Seattle: no sail changes without both of us on deck, and nobody went forward at night without the other one on deck. We wore safety harnesses at all times and were always clipped to the boat, night or day, even in the cockpit. We sail conservatively at night so we can avoid waking the sleeping person unless absolutely necessary.

Our daily routine was simple. Phyllis prepared our meals. She baked banana bread before we left port since we enjoyed if for breakfast and on night watch. Our main meal was midday when we were both awake. Since the boat was in constant motion, she cooked one pot meals in the pressure cooker on our four-burner propane stove. She clamped the pot to the stove and hooked the pot lid on so its contents would not be thrown out. However, cooking under pressure was only done when we weren't moving. The stove had a good oven, and she baked all our bread. The smell of fresh bread on a boat at sea was a special luxury. Cooking was challenging, but she always produced nourishing meals even in the worst of conditions.

We shared navigation duties. We kept a running record of our noon position in the ship's log and on our charts. Our position was plotted hourly if we were near land. I maintained the engine and all other systems. We usually charged batteries once a day to keep our electronics running and for lights. At night, we ran with a trimasthead light that was divided into three sections. It showed a red light to port and green to starboard. From the stern, the third quadrant was white. On the main mast, we had a white light that was visible forward. This was the internationally recognized arrangement that let another ships know our direction of travel. We had 1200-amp-hours capacity in two banks of batteries.

The wind vane steering was used most of the time to conserve battery power, but if there was any question about the vane being able to handle the conditions, we switched to the autopilot. We rarely steered manually in the entire three-week passage. *Fram* was a heavy stable boat, so we did not have much to do except watch out for other boats. We had ample time to read, relax, listen to music, and enjoy the water world around us.

As we neared the equator, the air and water temperature continued to rise. We liked to watch the flying fish travel great distances in their escape from predators. They often landed on our decks, where Katisha, the ultimate predator, gobbled these gifts from the sea. He ate everything but the wings, which were hard like quills. He knew instantly when one came aboard and bounded out to investigate.

The number of birds we saw surprised us. Even when we were a thousand miles from land, there were often small birds. Sometimes at night, they circled our masthead light, and when they passed through the aft white quadrant, they looked like ghosts flitting about.

If there was no moon and it was overcast, the night was blackest black. At those times, we felt protected in the cocoon of *Fram*. Other times, with a brilliant moon in a clear sky, it was bright and beautiful with the silvery flash of moonlight on the water. In the foaming radiance of breaking waves and the surging flow of the bow wave, we sat by the hour and never tired of the splendor around us.

Bow wave

On a small boat in the middle of the ocean, we were surrounded by dazzling beauty. One night, Phyllis was below asleep, and I was alone in the cockpit in the wee hours of the morning. The waning moon had just risen out of the sea and turned my world into a glittering wonderland. *Fram* was slipping along at five and a half knots, and the ballads of John Denver filled my head with music. I was at peace with the world. The feeling of contentment and well-being that filled me that night was a rare gift. It was a time to savor and remember. The last time I felt this way was many years before on a flight from New Orleans to Seattle as I rode first class in a nearly empty airplane. I listened to the stereo playing "The Age of Aquarius," as I watched the grandeur of the Rocky Mountains slide below us. I was in the middle of the Saturn/Apollo lunar landing program, and all was well with my world. I had been living a dream then, as now.

We enjoyed this ocean passage more than we ever expected and had become quite lazy. One day, we were both in the cockpit reading as *Fram* sailed herself at five knots, when a loud clear voice broke into our solitude. We always left our VHF radio on channel 16 whenever we were at sea, but with no other ships around, it was silent.

The voice was calling "the black ketch off our starboard bow." That was us.

"To the vessel calling a black ketch, this is *Fram*," I answered. "I see you at half-mile range, crossing our bow."

"This is *Wind Dancer*. We are a fifty-one-foot ketch bound for Atuona," the voice came back to me. "Where are you going?"

Since they were crossing our track at ninety degrees, I was puzzled. "We are also headed for Atuona. Why are you on a westerly course?"

"We talked to a ship west of our position, and they told us that the wind was good where they were. We decided to take advantage of the wind and stay north of the equator heading west, until we reached the longitude of the Marquesas and then turn south." They thought it would be faster on a beam reach than running as we were.

We were following the conventional wisdom of setting a course to the east of your destination in order to take advantage of the northeast and southeast winds. They had a fast sail but never did reach Atuona because they were too far west. This incident reminded us to keep a better watch during the day. This was a lesson we later forgot that nearly cost us our boat.

Each day when Phyllis checked into the MM net, other hams from around the world often wanted to talk to her. One evening, she talked to a young man in the U.S. Navy, stationed in Antarctica. Then another ham, also in the navy, joined them from Alaska. It was the highlight of our day. A woman sailor on a small sailboat in the middle of the Pacific Ocean had a conversation with two U.S. sailors stationed at both ends of the earth. Amazing.

As we approached the ITCZ (Intertropical Convergence Zone), we ran into more and more squalls, some with strong winds. They didn't last very long, and it was a nuisance to lower the jib for a short time and then put it back up. We soon found that if we kept at least one reef in the main, we could carry all sails in the squalls and avoid lowering the jib. It was exciting for a few minutes, and when the wind vane could not handle the higher gusts, I took over the wheel for the few minutes it took to pass.

It was always exhilarating as I stood in the warm driving rain in my birthday suit, with *Fram* charging before the wind at eight and, sometimes, nine knots. At that speed, I began to worry, because it meant the wind was blowing at least forty knots, with a relative wind of thirty as we ran before it. The bow wave was awesome as *Fram* tried to dig a hole in the ocean. Fortunately, the squalls didn't last very long, but they were exciting. We appreciated our big heavy boat and strong sails to match. Many of our friends in smaller, lighter boats were constantly changing sails in similar circumstances.

The evening we approached the ITCZ, I saw the green flash for the first time. I heard about it and read about it but didn't really believe it existed. I was in the cockpit watching the sunset while Phyllis was talking on the ham radio. The orb of the sun settled on the horizon and gradually sank into the sea. When the top limb reached the horizon, it flashed a brilliant emerald green, and I could hardly believe my eyes. The green flash does exist. This event occurs when the yellow sun touches the blue sea and momentarily creates the green color. I was sorry Phyllis missed it, because, as a believer, she spent many hours watching for it. Now that we knew what to look for, we observed this phenomenon many times. It was an unforgettable sight.

As we entered the Intertropical Convergence Zone (ITCZ), the weather changed from frequent squalls to bright sunshine, very little wind, and seas as calm as a lake. We started the engine and dropped the sails and let the W-H autopilot take care of us. There was nothing to do except relax, enjoy the ride, and enjoy each other. Always on the horizon were fluffy clouds hanging in the heavens, sometimes white and other times painted in soft colors from an artist's pallet. At the end of a tranquil day, we enjoyed cocktails as the sun was extinguished by its plunge into the sea. After twenty-two hours of motoring, we shut down the engine and ghosted along with the jib alone at three knots through the rest of the night. It was a perfect night, and we each enjoyed a relaxing sleep with the boat hardly moving. This probably wouldn't last.

The next morning, we were greeted with a sky that warned of squalls. I was prepared. I had modified our cockpit awning to catch rainwater, and this would to be its first test. The wind always appeared first, so we hung on for a five-minute sleigh ride across the waves before the rain came. When it arrived, water gushed down through the new drain fitting in the awning, and we soon collected five gallons for our water tanks. After the squall passed, the wind set in from the southeast. We were through the ITCZ and into the trade winds of the southern hemisphere, even though we were still at four and a half degrees north latitude. We put up all sails and were soon galloping over the waves for the Marquesas at seven and a half knots.

April 6, the fourteenth day out of Socorro, we crossed the equator. We toasted King Neptune with a bottle of champagne and gave him a little sip. We drank the rest while cavorting in the sunshine to the music of Neil Diamond at our party for two and a half. Katisha had a special kitty treat, and we had a special dinner, topped off with apple pie. We were official shellbacks (one who crossed the equator by boat), sailing with a shellback kitty. He seemed extra mellow to have been awarded that distinction. Ralph determined that we crossed at 1015. Mountain Standard Time (the time we were using on the passage) at 124°58'20" west longitude. We had missed our target crossing position of 125 degrees by 1.8 miles.

It didn't seem any different south of the equator than it had north, except we could no longer see Polaris. Each night we looked for the Southern Cross and enjoyed the new appearance of the sky. Our constant heavenly companion, both north and south, was Orion, lying on the equator with his belt turning around the sky. We could actually steer by the stars as did the ancient navigators. Often on a clear night, we took down the Bimini cockpit awning and enjoyed the splendor of the heavens.

It was now more than two weeks since we left Socorro Island, and we were well into the routine of passage making. The southeast trades kept us moving at a steady pace with an occasional squall to get our attention. I never tired of sitting in the cockpit, watching the water flow by as *Fram* rode down the face of the waves and then rose as she surged forward, with the power of the wind driving her relentlessly on. This was what I dreamed about during all the long years of work, sacrifice, frustration, and yearning. We are rewarded by the majesty of creation, the universe, and the endless multitude of stars. This passage gave us the time and opportunity to see and absorb this spectacle day after day and night after night. For many years, we struggled to keep the vision alive, and now are being repaid in full by this trade wind passage to the South Pacific.

We were getting closer to the Marquesas and anticipated our first South Pacific landfall. The navigation marks continued to march across our chart. We crossed a big ocean and were excited and nervous to arrive at this wee speck due to the miracle of modern electronics and good planning by the navigator. But at the same time, we were sad for this passage to end. *Fram* took us safely and comfortably across the sea (well, comfortable except when it wasn't comfortable). We had time to focus on simple pleasures: enjoying the beauty around us, sunrises and sunsets and clouds and waves and the moon and the stars; eating tasty meals; listening to music and reading books for endless hours without interruptions; and being together alone and dependent on each other for the safety of the ship and ourselves.

As the day of our arrival approached, our radio contacts were filled with the excitement of a whole fleet of yachts nearing the same destination. We made friends with several hams along the way on land as well as at sea. Throughout the South Pacific, we looked forward to meeting several land-based hams, who followed us on our passages. There will be a great gathering in Atuona from our various courses across the sea, and it looks like several of us will be coming into port the same day.

Michael, on *Ishara*, out of Boston, became one of our radio friends, and he and Phyllis talked almost every day. They were on passage from the Galapagos Islands with a family of four plus two crew. They were 192 miles out of Atuona at noon and were trying to beat us in. They were eighteen days out of the Galapagos and doing about ten knots when we talked. It is about the same distance as from Mexico, and we are twenty-two days out. We were impressed and can't wait to meet this family.

Our last day out was turning into one of best sailing days of the whole passage. We felt like we could go on and on. *Fram* has proven to be an ideal cruising boat. There are few things I would change. Running all the lines aft to the cockpit worked extremely well. We could reef the main from the cockpit on any point of sail without changing course. We could bring the jib down with my refined down haul and, of course, raise the jib and the main from the cockpit.

Since leaving Seattle, Phyllis was the one that went forward on the bowsprit to handle the jib. She volunteered for this since she was afraid if I fell overboard she would not be able to get me back. She had a lot of confidence that I would be able to get her back onboard. Actually, anyone falling overboard at sea is nearly always a tragedy on a fast-moving boat under full sail. Of course, she was always clipped on to the jack line (a rope that runs forward from the cockpit to the bowsprit) and various fittings as she moved forward. We are beginning to think we should put roller furling on the jib, which would be much safer since it would be handled from the cockpit.

The wind was up again, and we were experiencing the biggest seas yet. They remind me of the huge following seas we experienced off of Cape Mendocino in 1987. We're sailing at seven knots, so the island of Hiva Oa was really getting close. We expect to make landfall tomorrow. I'm looking forward to my last night watch. I will miss my faithful stars, which I came to know so well these last few weeks. It will be a welcome change to sleep together again in our great big bed with Katisha snuggled between us. *Fram* surged along, and we watched the seas roll up behind us in a never-ending procession. Some so large they looked like they would break over us, but the boat lifted her stern gracefully, and then we were on top looking down into the valleys. It was wonderful fun. We were reminded of our circumnavigation of Vancouver Island and the big seas that appeared to bury the fishing fleet.

The evening before landfall, we slowed down so as not to arrive before dawn. When Phyllis woke me for my watch at 0245 the weather didn't look good. The wind was back up to twenty knots, and we were moving too fast. The sat nav position showed us thirty-eight miles from the entrance to Atuona harbor and twenty-five miles from the nearest land. The sky was heavily overcast, with dark clouds hiding the horizon. A small squall came by, with extra wind and a little rain.

The next sat nav fix placed us north of our desired course and heading straight for the tip of Hiva Oa. I wondered if we had been pushed off course by a current. I was not about to take a chance, so I altered our course to take us further south. It was so dark I couldn't see a thing, so when the sat nav said we were eighteen miles from land, I turned on the radar at twelve miles range. What a shock! Four miles off our port beam, it indicated two islands, but there wasn't anything on the chart at that location. Since we were not in danger at the moment, I kept going. After watching for a while, I realized they were dense rainsqualls. This was the first time I had radar on during squalls, so I didn't recognize them at first.

These two were just the first of many that marched by. We were surrounded by lightning, so I disconnected all the radios and electronics, except for radar and sat nav. They were going to have to take their chances. On a boat with tall masts and rigging, lightning scares me, but there was nothing else I could do. The radar flickered with each flash, and then with a particularly close strike, the radar screen flashed into a disc of solid yellow light and stayed that way. My gut twisted. It was positively the worst time for the radar to stop working when we were in the middle of a squall line and coming up on our first landfall in 2,400 miles. We were less than fifteen miles away and going over seven knots with all sails up, which meant we were two hours away from crashing into Hiva Oa, and daylight was still three hours away. We were caught in nature's fury.

Nothing was visible in the dark night except the squalls appearing as denser black against the blackness of the sky. Conditions were wild. The wind was howling, and the boat surfed down the wave fronts. When Phyllis woke up and came to see why it was so crazy, she took one look at the radar, which was now working again, and went into a panic. It looked like we were in the middle of a cluster of islands.

"Ralph, where are we? What are you doing?"

"I had a terrible scare a few minutes ago, when we lost radar completely in a lightning flash."

"Where are we!" she shouted, peering into the darkness and then at all the targets on the screen.

After calming her down, I showed her the real island that was then only five miles away. Now she was wide-awake and panic-stricken.

"We are going way too fast," she demanded. "Aren't we going to get some sail off?"

We lowered the mizzen and jib and were still going almost six knots with only the double-reefed main. At least it would be light when we arrived at the harbor entrance. Our stomachs relaxed when we were two miles off and caught our first glimpse of green land through a break in the clouds. After we turned toward the anchorage, which was still a black wall in the distance, behind us the rising sun's rays shown through the clouds with the promise of a new day. We followed another boat in, and we were relieved to see all the masts tucked in around the harbor, looking like matchsticks against rich green mountains towering over the anchorage.

We had arrived in paradise! Sitting in the quiet cockpit, we gazed around in wonder at the fabled Marquesan Island of Hiva Oa. It jutted out of the sea in rank green majesty with soaring cliffs and pinnacles that reached into the sky seeming to hang from the clouds. Who could ever envision these thrusting, rugged mountains encased in their clinging shroud of living deep green vegetation, with small rivulets and waterfalls tumbling down their sides to join the frothing surf far below. Not even in our wildest imagination could we have dreamed of such a place.

During our approach to the island, we had just come through the worst weather of our entire passage, but we were here safely, and it was an enormous relief when the anchor went rolling out at 0930. We were squeezed into a small space among sixteen yachts from all over the world. They were German, Dutch, Kiwi, Canadian, English, French, and American (both East and West Coast). We were part of a community of serious sailors, all of whom sailed many miles across an ocean to get here. There was no other way.

Beside us was the boat that we had followed into the harbor. It was a forty-five-foot German ketch fifty-three days out of the Galapagos, the hull sides covered with sea growth—barnacles and weeds—gathered as they rolled their way across the Pacific in light airs near the equator. This was in marked contrast to *Ishara*, who came in about an hour later and were only nineteen days out of the Galapagos after going south to meet the southeast trades. They had made the last 192 miles in less than twenty-four hours.

Unknown to us at the time, another boat was approaching Hiva Oa behind us in the early morning hours. Running without lights to conserve battery power, they followed our masthead running light until we disappeared in the squalls. They dropped all sails and waited until morning light to make their entrance. They arrived about two and a half hours after we were at anchor. Monica was at the helm and rounded up in a good anchoring place in front of us. Jack went forward and threw their anchor over the bow but forgot to attach it to the boat. Thus, we met Jack and Monica on *Island Breeze* from Canada.

After retrieving Jack's anchor with a grappling hook, we took time to get the boat and ourselves settled into the anchorage. Along with Michael and Jesse from *Ishara* and Jack and Monica from *Island Breeze*, we made the one-mile trek into town to check into French Polynesia. Jesse and Monica both spoke some French, so I stuck close as my French began and ended with *merci* and *oui*. We arrived at the gendarmerie's office as he was getting ready to close for lunch, so he told us to come back in a couple hours. Since it was Monica's birthday, we celebrated her birthday and our safe arrival with hamburgers, beer, and ice cream cones. That day began a close friendship among our three boats, which grew as we sailed on across the South Pacific. We did not often sail together, but we seemed to end up at the same place at the same time. We were all part of the extended families we found among yachties throughout the South Pacific. With the formalities of the check-in complete and six months in French Polynesia ahead of us, Phyllis and I had a chance to stop and evaluate our lives and our dream

Our odyssey began a long time ago. Our dream developed gradually until it had the vitality to capture our imagination and influenced the direction of our lives. Finally it became the driving force of our lives. Everything we did was influenced by this goal. We abandoned many conventional pleasures. I did not strive for career advancement, which would have meant a long-term job commitment. Phyllis gave up a music career. We sacrificed nice homes and committed ourselves to endless hours of arduous, difficult labor. We tried to accelerate the achievement of the goal and failed. Once, in a time of serious trial, we nearly gave up but worked our way through and were much stronger, because if it. When Phyllis developed cancer, there was no thought of giving up, only modifying and rescheduling.

At last we were living our dream. Was it worth it? The simple answer is *yes*. We are living new exciting lives that can go on as long as we want. We visit places we would never see any other way, except in a small boat. The cruising people we meet along the way are some of the most interesting people we have ever known. Our friends come from all the nations of the earth.

We enjoyed the simple pleasures of life by stepping out of the fast lane and into the homes and hearts of simple, gentle, giving people in remote places. We take time to stop and smell the roses along the way. We lived in some of the most beautiful places on earth for weeks on end and only moved to go to the next bit of paradise.

We developed the confidence to be alone and responsible for our survival, with nobody to come and help. We learned how to make our way in foreign lands with strange languages and, sometimes, stranger foods. We were able to maintain our boat in remote places, where there were no mechanics or parts stores. All our power came from our own generators. Keeping a cruising yacht operating is equivalent to maintaining, on a small scale, all the systems and utilities of a modern city: water, sewage, electric power, garbage, communications (two-radio stations), weather forecasting, entertainment, and some things a city does not need—navigation, for example. Keeping it all in continuous operation was a satisfying achievement.

The most rewarding and thrilling aspect of all was passage making. Using the power of the wind to take us great distances. Feeling the boat surge through the seas and watching as the bow smashed into a wave, sending sheets of spray flying high into the sunlight in a thousand flashing drops. Having dolphins come alongside and leap into the bow wave to play as they escorted us on our way. Looking back as we ran before the wind with the waves building higher and higher behind us until it seemed they would crash and bury us, suddenly the stern lifted and we were once again surfing down the face of the wave in exhilarating abandon.

It was quiet nights alone on watch, when there was no one else in the world, except you. Then the fearful times when the wind and the seas created a living hell and you wondered, *Will we make it? Is the boat strong enough to take the terrible punishment? Are we?* But when it was over and you were alive, only the thrill of danger was remembered.

Was it worth all the effort and sacrifice? We shout a resounding, "Absolutely!" My first great dream was fulfilled when man stepped on the moon. Now we shared a dream, Phyllis and I. It took vision and commitment and hard work. If you want to live on the high side of life, get out of the fast lane and follow your dreams and visions.

Laundry day after our long passage

Chapter 22

A Turtle's-Eye View of French Polynesia

Turtle: a creature that lives in the sea and carries its home on its back.

This is Phyllis, and I want to tell you what it was like living our South Seas adventure. When I think of the many ocean miles we traveled, it's not the passages I remember. By now they have become somewhat routine, but rather, the rare opportunity to visit so many different cultures in a way that was both ancient and natural for all these seafaring nations. Arriving by sea in a small sailing vessel immediately opened the door of communication and friendship. Living among the natives, eating their food, walking their shores, even adopting their clothing customs gave us a unique insight into their world.

I often dreamed about what it would be like to sit on a beach under the palm trees on an island in the South Seas. I had romantic visions of sailing the oceans in our own boat. I tried to imagine how we would be accepted by people we met along the way. Sailing among these islands in French Polynesia introduced us to the warm and generous people we would meet all across the South Pacific

Hana Menu was our first Polynesian feast on the beach. All the yachts were invited and Osanne and his family prepared roast pig, breadfruit, spinach, taro, poisson cru, and fruits while we brought various desserts, salads, and rum, which was a big hit with our hosts. The fact that we heard the pig squealing earlier in the day while being dispatched by the dogs did not diminish our enjoyment of this succulent meat prepared in an *omu*. Pig, fish, sweet potatoes, onions, and spinach were all cooked on the beach in a hole in the ground filled with hot rocks and covered with leaves and sand.

Served with coconut cream over all made this delectable food worthy of the highest rating for fine food anywhere.

After the feast, the instruments came out, and we all sang and danced on the sand under the palms with a full moon shining on our joyous celebration. These simple people managed to bring together people from many different countries for one of our most memorable evenings ever. It didn't matter that many of us were dumped in the sea by the surf as we landed and dumped again when we launched through the waves after the party was over. I can't remember when we've had so much fun.

Each anchorage and village was different. Sailing between the islands was often vigorous, and all the anchorages were plagued with sea swells, so it felt like we were riding a galloping horse even at anchor. We perfected our technique for bow and stern anchoring and continued to make improvements to *Fram* as we learned how to adapt to our new life.

We met handsome, tattooed Eric when we walked through his village of Hana Iapa on Hiva Oa, who, at age twenty-five, boasted of five wives and several children. He seemed to have a casual attitude toward marriage and children. Eric loaded us down with heaping baskets of fruit and vegetables and armloads of fragrant flowers all in preparation for our mutiny on the Bounty party that night. Eric was our guest as we celebrated the two-hundredth anniversary of that event with a potluck dinner on four boats. When we later watched the movie by that name onboard *Fram*, Eric found the Polynesian dialogue strange and amusing.

Ralph became known in the yachting community as "Ralph Can Fix It" from *Fram*. He helped many boats repair broken and nonfunctioning systems from his many pieces of junk carried in our bilge. He provided an alternator for the ailing electrical system on a Dutch yacht approaching the end of a circumnavigation begun in Australia ten years ago. He found just the right piece of stainless steel in his bilge junk to fabricate a piece of rigging for an expensive luxury yacht in need of a new fitting for their rigging after their strenuous passage from the Galapagos. I constantly complained about all the junk he carried around for years and asked why he didn't get rid of it. Then he found the perfect piece of junk in the bilge and used his cockpit-mounted vise to create something important for *Fram* or another boat.

Our yachting community was always ready to help each other in many ways. One dark night, we were awakened by a call for help from a young Canadian couple we met previously in the Socorro Islands of Mexico. Their dinghy had come adrift, and they asked Ralph to help them search the open sea outside our anchorage with flashlights in the dark. The search was unsuccessful, and we loaned them one of our dinghies until they could replace it. Fortunately about a week later, they found their dinghy washed up on the beach. Rescuing dinghies was an ongoing event.

One evening, Ralph responded to a call for assistance from a large California yacht becalmed outside our anchorage at dusk. At the end of a long passage from Mexico, with an engine that wouldn't start, they found themselves rolling from side to side in ten-foot swells. We were surprised at how often Ralph was able to use our twelve-foot inflatable with its fifteen-horsepower outboard as a tug to help others. This, the same patched dinghy and engine that were stolen and then found months before in Mexico.

Calligari in Mexico

One of the challenges we faced while far from grocery stores and markets was provisioning. We all had our own system of keeping track of our needs to keep the ship running smoothly and with adequate supplies. I maintained an inventory of all the stores on *Fram* and kept it up to date. When living in a home on land, it was simply a matter of getting into a vehicle and buying whatever was on my shopping list, a relatively easy task. It was another matter when many things were unavailable for months at a time. Before we left Seattle, I kept a daily log of everything we ate and used for several months. This included meat, flour, fresh fruits and vegetables, butter, paperclips, detergent, toothpaste, toilet paper, etc.—everything. Besides being an interesting exercise on how we spent our money, it formed the basis of my onboard inventory.

One day, several women from the yachts went shopping at a small Chinese grocery on one of the islands. Rita, from a large expensive yacht, bought all the available potatoes to add to her ample storage bins while the rest of us did without. In the aisle with cake mixes, she opened every box of cake mix, checking for weevils that of course were there. Not finding any weevil-free, she took all the opened boxes and inner bags of mix to the counter and let the proprietor know there were weevils in all the boxes. The rest of us were embarrassed at this crass behavior by one of our own. One of my most important tools was a vacuum-sealer system with both bags and jars. Whenever I bought things that could contain weevil larvae, such as flour, powdered milk, spices, cake mixes, etc., I used my vacuum sealer before putting them in my storage lockers. We all had the same problems with provisions, and many weevils died in my vacuum-sealed bags, and we forgot all about them.

The Tuamotus, the dangerous archipelago—its very name strikes fear in the heart of all ships that must pass among the coral atolls lying between the Marquesas and Tahiti. We studied the charts, read other people's experiences, studied sailing directions, and still had a hard time deciding whether to take an easier passage and follow in the wake of most of the yachts or be brave and visit some of the lesser-known atolls. We wanted to visit villages least exposed to outside influences. Even though the sailing directions discouraged us, we decided to visit the atoll of Kauehi in the center of the archipelago anyway.

So in the company of friends on *Footloose*, we left Daniel's Bay on Nuka Hiva for the next phase of our sea journey. We sailed five days and nights in perfect conditions past several dangers we avoided by using our sat nav and trusty radar eyes to see what we could not.

From now on, we traveled among coral reefs and atolls while in tropical waters. This is a simplified explanation of how coral atolls are formed. A high volcanic island arose out of the ocean, and over time, living coral formed a fringing reef around it. Then the island gradually sank back into the sea, leaving the coral reef surrounding either the top of a high mountain (like Bora Bora) or a lagoon with no mountain remaining in the center, like Kauehi. Eventually, small low, flat islands called *motus* formed on the fringing reef. A safe deep passage into the lagoon was recognizable by darker-colored water while the coral lying just beneath the surface was covered with shallow light-colored water. Not all gaps between the *motus* were safe passages, and this was the challenge—finding the safe pass. Many times during all our sailing in tropical waters, we had to find safe passages, and it was always nerve-racking since running into a reef usually resulted in a shipwreck and was feared by all sailors.

More than 530 miles after leaving the Marquesas, morning revealed several spiky-looking things on the wave tops right where our chart said they should be. These spikes stretching out along the horizon soon became the tops of palm trees. Kauehi. We had sailed safely past the dangers, and now our problem was to find the pass through the reef into the lagoon.

At this point, we were painfully aware of our inexperience with coral reefs. We remembered with fast-beating hearts how many ships came to grief on reefs such as those lurking below the surface off our port bow. Now we had to decide which gap was the pass and not just shallow reef between the small *motus* of land and palms. Ralph and Fred compared notes, and both decided the same gap was surely the pass. With two skippers in agreement, we aimed our bow at the gap.

Finding the safe pass into the lagoon wasn't the only problem. Once inside, scattered coral heads were growing just under the surface of the water and had to be avoided. The only way to see these was by the change in water color. Ralph was going to be polite and let *Footloose* enter first, with us following. We were such chickens, but Fred outchickened us and held back at the critical moment, so *Fram* entered first and led the way across the lagoon. With Ralph in the spreaders, remote steering control in hand, and me on the helm in case of urgent instructions to slow down, speed up, or stop, we inched our way across the five miles to the anchorage. With the sun at our back, Ralph was amazed at how easy it was to see the coral heads in the crystal clear water. We were relieved that our first experience was successful. Everything was exactly as the books described. Fred followed with confidence behind the cement-battering ram (his words).

Each day, the sun awoke us to another perfect day. We found incredible white coral-sand beaches with whispering palms beside a turquoise lagoon that is everyone's idea of tropical isles. We swam and snorkeled, raced sailing dinghies, explored deserted *motus*, and enjoyed beach fires and potlucks with the other yachts sharing our new neighborhood. Jack and Monica painted, inviting Jessica and me to join in. Michael, Jake, and Fred scuba dived, looking for sharks. Ten-year-olds Matt and Jason, in young boy heaven, explored the beach and learned to scuba dive. Dave and Karen went spearfishing each day to provide fresh fish for their Old English Sheepdog, Buckingham. More important, we became part of the lives of a community of seventy-five Tahitians, who welcomed us with gifts, friendship, music, and feasting. We invited them to our yachts, where we had music, dancing, singing, and movies, which they loved.

Ralph helped build a fish trap with William and Jean. We stood with the women and children and watched as they brought in the fishes each day and cleaned them before putting them on strings made from coconut fibers to take to the rest of the community. We admired their pet baby frigate bird, and when it disappeared one day, they simply said it died. They always fed a few fish to the bird as a quick test for ciguatera (a poison). Small toddlers and babies were everywhere, following the women who helped the men. It was a strange sight to see a naked two-year-old playing in the sand, sucking on a small raw fish. I took special delight in holding Irene's baby, Raphael, who was the same age as our grandson Nicholas. I thought of Nicky so far away and delighted in the feeling of a little one in my arms. Since this was twenty-four-year-old Irene's fifth child, she was always glad to see me coming.

We met Xavier, who invited us to his modern and comfortable home, where he served juice and cookies. Soon his wife, Tania, who was the schoolteacher, came home for a break; and we were warmly welcomed with shell necklaces and a *pareau* for me. Xavier had been the village chief for many years and was the lay reader for the Catholic Church that was without a priest.

The following Sunday, we all attended church, where we were welcomed in Tahitian. The singing was a wonder. No instruments—just voices raised in eloquent, complex counterpoint and harmony. When they sang "The Battle Hymn of the Republic" in Tahitian, we added our voices to theirs in a great chorus. I have goose bumps now as I remember how moved I was by this profound experience. We have worshipped in English, Latin, French, Spanish, and now Polynesian. We will not forget the good people of Kauehi and this special church service.

Grandmère

One day, all the ladies were invited to learn basket making with *grandmère*. This charming lady, shriveled with age, surrounded by her many grandchildren and great-grandchildren, met us under a palm tree. Sitting in the sand, her gnarled and skilled fingers quickly fabricated a basket from palm fronds. Then she patiently showed the *popaas* (foreigners) how to prepare the fronds and weave them together to form, what for them, is a simple disposable container for whatever they need to carry. I couldn't bear to throw it away. I still have my basket.

Meanwhile, Irene and her sister Ida prepared coconut bread for all the yachts. This was formed into small loaves and wrapped in clean cloth to rise on a bench under a tree. The "oven" was ready for baking when our baskets were finished. We watched in amazement as they baked twenty loaves in a barrel heated by hot rocks with a lid of corrugated metal on which they built a small fire. After this time-consuming, labor-intensive way to bake, we each took home two warm loaves in our new baskets.

Arrival of the copra boat was an important event. We, like the villagers, needed some basic supplies; and with no village store, we anticipated shopping on the boat. All the villagers and yachties alike tied up to the anchored ship and waited our turn to buy from the surprising variety available at the "store." This was a typical market day with laughing and gossiping among the women (that by now included us) while the children enjoyed a rare ice-cream treat and the men loaded filled bags of copra. Copra, a labor-intensive cash crop in the tropics, was the dried meat of coconuts that is used in many products, such as soap, coconut oil, etc.

By now we began to feel overwhelmed with the generosity of these simple people, who at first glance have so little by our standards. We reciprocated when our men helped the village chief, Koko, build a fishing boat and then rebuilt an outboard engine of great age from spare parts. This was a fun project for Ralph and the other yachties. Ralph Can Fix It earned another name—Monsieur Panneau Solaire. Bald heads are unknown among the Polynesians, and they laughed and thought his head was quite funny. On the day he took his battery-powered electric drill ashore, their eyes grew big in wonder when it ran with no electricity. They laughed and said, "Monsieur Panneau Solaire charger le batterie!"

In appreciation for the yachties working on his boat and fixing his engine, Koko invited all of us to a feast at his home. By now our neighborhood had grown to an astounding nine boats, the most they ever had at one time. We dressed in our finest and arrived at Koko's home in the dark after navigating over and through the coral heads in our dinghies. *Clunk—scrape—bang*! Upon landing on the beach, the family greeted us with special shell necklaces and carried our potluck offerings into the kitchen.

Koko must have borrowed most of the dishes in the village and set an impressive table for thirty. It was the custom for the guests to eat first and the men second. The women and children ate last. Since he was the important host, Koko ate with us. Again, we had roast pig—tasteless fatty chunks floating in grease. Much more to our liking was the lean meat in a spicy sauce, a delicacy reserved for special guests. Rice, bread, and poisson cru completed the meal.

His wife and family served the table and retreated to the kitchen for their own feast. Our beef, chicken, casseroles, and desserts remained there, not to be seen again by us. After the meal, the table was cleared away, and out came the instruments. We danced together until we could dance no more. The next day, we were sad when we missed the two scrawny dogs that used to follow us around. This feast has since been referred to as the infamous Koko dog feast by all who were there.

After a month, we bid farewell to our new friends and crossed the lagoon on our way to Papeete on the island of Tahiti. How could we possibly find anything to compare with the paradise we just left?

On the morning of the third day, we sighted the Tahiti in the Society Islands off our port bow with dramatic Moorea to starboard. Palm trees waved their welcome under a blue sky, filled with piled-up mountains of clouds reflecting the rising sun in gold and peach and mauve as Papeete beckoned to us from behind the reef. Our senses were perfumed by the fragrance of frangipani and assailed with the bright colors of a turquoise lagoon and red and orange and pink hybiscus when we arrived at our most anticipated destination.

What a thrill to finally arrive at this fabled South Sea Island, where we tied to the famous quay before noon. We found a place in front of a small park, and *Fram* was once again in the same neighborhood with Jack and Monica from *Island Breeze* and Michael, Jessica, Jake, Matt, and Scott on *Ishara*. Many other friends soon arrived, and we were ready to be charmed by Papeete.

We were still tying our lines, when a statuesque blonde standing in a speeding dinghy roared up to our deck, thrust a long baguette toward me, and said, "Hi, I'm Maria from *Countess Maria*. Welcome to Tahiti."

With that, they turned and sped off. Maria, from Nebraska, and I were ham radio friends but had not met until now. Yes, welcome to Tahiti indeed.

Our new home was a modern bustling city—very French and yet uniquely Polynesian as well. We were warned that French Polynesia would be expensive, and it was. Yet how could one put a price on the experience of visiting in the wake of many historic sailing ships to this exotic port of call? We understood the famous mystique of these islands when they were discovered by Europeans so many years ago.

The men were muscular and handsome and the women extraordinarily beautiful. I would not have believed how sexy a man looked wearing a flowered lava-lava (skirt) around his waist and a flower tucked behind his ear. As a contrast, one had to be vigilant against being run over by a big mama in her snow-white brassiere as she barreled down the street on a moped. Alas, beauty can be a fleeting thing.

French sophistication was evident everywhere, especially in the food shops and the public market, a gazebo-like, light-filled structure vibrant with color. The people laughed and chattered behind their counters, dressed in vivid colors and patterns. It was a feast for the eyes with exuberant flowers; exotic fruits and fresh vegetables in red, purple, green, and yellow; breads, pâtès, and cheeses; wonderful wines; colorful fishes, and meat from every edible part of every creature (including some that didn't look edible to my *popaa* eyes). Here I bought a hat woven by brown hands, to protect my pale skin from the sun, and another colorful *pareau* to add to my wardrobe.

Fete celebrates French Bastille Day, and the carefree Polynesians managed to make it last three months. We joined in judging dancing and singing competitions and cheered for outrigger canoe and sailing races in the lagoon off our stern. We held a special feeling for this seafaring race that eventually explored and populated the far-flung islands of Oceania, from New Zealand to Hawaii.

Sailing race in Papeete

We were in a party mood when the Fourth of July came along during the festivities. By now, our neighborhood had grown to an impressive group, and we had a party. We moved the boats together and prepared an all-American meal for our friends from 5 countries, ages 10 to 57, and boats 25 to 102 feet long. We were exhausted after celebrating far into the night with singing and dancing.

An interesting addition to our community was Edwardo, from Argentina. His rough, battered, dugout canoe, with a tattered lateen sail, was first spotted west of the Galapagos Islands. He had been rolled over in a large wave, losing all his provisions, clothes, and compass. Our friends found him and offered bare necessities that he gratefully accepted but refused the compass, saying he didn't need it. We didn't see much of Edwardo. Wherever he went, with his long bleached-blond hair and his movie-star good looks, there was always some equally gorgeous woman who took pity on him and took him home.

The jagged peaks of Moorea, intriguing under its cap of clouds, rose out of the ruffled cobalt-blue sea. From our deck at sunset, we watched the drama of brilliant colors setting behind its stunning outline while the rays of the setting sun called to us across the water. The celebration of fete was reaching a climax in Tahiti, so it was time to change our scenery and answer the siren call. After a short boisterous sail to Moorea, we found the pass leading into an unbelievably beautiful anchorage nestled beneath the soaring peaks in Cook's Bay.

Words fail to describe the beauty of our setting. Resting near the reef, on still water the color of champagne, over white sand in fifteen feet of water, backed by shimmering green palms and towering mountain heights, *Fram* had reached what surely must be the ultimate destination of all our visions and dreams. We played in the warm water and had picnics on the white-sand beach. We hiked around the island and marveled at the bounty of fruit and flowers growing in wild profusion everywhere. Neat little homes nestled against the mountains, facing the sea.

We visited a ham friend, one of the Mobile Maritime Net controllers who lived on Moorea. Les and his wife, Gloria, sailed here from California several years ago and stayed. Les followed our long passage across the Pacific and on all our other passages as well. During our time in the tropics, I joined his Saturday Coffee Klatch Net, where we heard news of world events and discussed what was happening in our various locations.

One of my favorite hams on the Coffee Klatch was Meralda, on Pitcairn Island. In her lilting English / New Zealand accent, she described life on that isolated rock of an island, famous as the final destination of the sailors from the HMS Bounty mutiny and their Polynesian women. One morning, she told us they were expecting a bulldozer the following week. That raised my curiosity, because I knew there wasn't a good harbor on the island, where a ship could land. Meralda explained that the bulldozer would be dropped by the New Zealand Air Force. It created an unlikely picture in my mind of that huge machine falling out of the sky. I couldn't wait until the following week to ask if it arrived safely.

"Oh, yeh," she said. "No problem, nothing broke, and we have been using it to build a road."

Reluctantly, it was time for us to move on, so late one day, we sailed into the sunset for an overnight passage to Huahine. After a fast sail with twenty-five-knot winds on the beam, we arrived in time to assist in a hapless yachtie's misadventure. It seems that anchoring in the strong current caused him to drag back on another boat, and now their anchor chains were tangled. Ralph, along with Fred and Jack, finally had the situation sorted out.

We found a stunning anchorage inside the reef on the south end of the island and spent an idyllic few weeks at another special discovery in the Societies. We bicycled around the island, stopping to refresh with drinking nuts provided by an agile young man who climbed a palm tree when he saw we were tired. We hiked to several ruins of ancient *maraes* that were old Polynesian sacred grounds. Throughout Polynesia, we saw these remainders of the old culture. Most were in ruins but were still held sacred by the people.

Bicycling on Huahine

When we were greeted by a handsome little family bearing gifts of fruit, we invited them to return the next day for juice and cookies.

"Oh, oh," said Deborah on *Footloose*. "We invited them onboard the other day for a movie, and the baby peed all over the settee and the carpet."

Forewarned was forearmed, so I composed a sentence using my French dictionary: "On the yacht, it is the custom for the baby to wear a diaper" was my planned greeting.

We carried disposable diapers in case of an oil spill, so I had one ready when they arrived the next day. Our ready diaper was put away for another day. That poor little baby's bottom was swaddled so tight, I worried it would strangle an important appendage, rendering him impotent later when those things mattered.

One day, Jack and Monica and Jessica went to a nearby sandy beach to paint. Ralph and I followed a bit later, but there was absolutely no painting going on. Monica and Jessie couldn't get Jack interested, because all he could do was sit and stare at the beautiful French girls sunbathing in the nude. He claimed he couldn't focus on his art, and Ralph was only too willing to help him keep watch over this spectacular scene. It was a lost day for art, but the guys thought it was wonderful and important for their well-being.

Receiving devastating news from home was made less difficult by being in such lovely surroundings. An arsonist set fire to our storage unit in Seattle, which destroyed many irreplaceable belongings, including all Ralph's important papers, our family photos, and my extensive music library, among other things. Normally a cause for weeping at such a loss, the message was greeted with a benign, "It's only stuff." Later, the loss of this stuff would be sorrowful indeed.

It was now August, and we had a deadline when we must be out of the tropics. December was the beginning of cyclone season, and we have decided to spend those months in New Zealand, which was still a long ways away.

So we set sail for the islands of Raiatea and Tahaa. The two islands share a lagoon inside a reef, and after a long day, we sailed past the ever-present coral fangs and tied to a mooring buoy off a small hotel. The next day was market day, and we took the dinghy several miles to the main village on Raiatea. The town was alive with men talking over beers and women and children gossiping and selling their wares. They came from all the villages on both islands inside the lagoon, arriving early in overloaded small boats of every imagination. They brought their fruits and vegetables, also their pigs, fish, baskets, and other commodities. In turn, they loaded the boats with necessities until the next market day. They also managed to have time for visiting, making music, and having another beer and a meal before heading back to their homes. We were delighted to walk among them and share a part of their day.

We moved *Fram* and anchored behind a *motu* just inside the surrounding reef near the pass. The constant crashing of waves on the reef did little to diminish our anticipation as we gazed across the sea to the island of Bora Bora. Oh, how the very name promised romance and excitement, adding to the lore of this fabled destination. Our spirits were buoyant the next morning, when we sailed through the pass toward our final destination in French Polynesia. Squalls filled the air, but we were drawn as if toward a grand love affair, and wind and big seas could not keep us from beautiful, enticing Bora.

Bora Bora

Bora Bora was an ancient sunken volcano surrounded by an extensive coral-filled lagoon. Our first challenge was to find the reef between us and the entrance to the lagoon. In a squall, we couldn't see a thing.

"Ralph, can you see the reef? The chart shows it extending quite a ways out from the island."

In these rough seas, it would be hard to see the breaking surf. "The chart shows a marker on the reef, but I don't see it. Can you see it yet, Phyl?"

Cautiously, we approached. "There, Ralph, do you see the inner lagoon?"

"Oh yes, I see it now."

Clearly, the white surf line separated the cobalt blue of the deep ocean from the pale aqua of the outer lagoon. In the middle of the deep inner lagoon, like a beauty queen in the center of a parade float, sat dramatic Mount Otamanu, with its dark spire pointing to the heavens. As we searched ahead for the pass through the reef, the sun disappeared in another squall, and we were lost in the mist. With nerves of steel, Ralph maintained our course, and we continued along the breakers until, at the critical moment, the rain stopped, and there ahead were the lead markers. Inside, we saw boats at anchor. A friend watched us enter the pass and was waiting at a vacant mooring buoy to help us tie on.

Oh, beautiful majestic mountain, why did the allure disappear now that we finally lie at the feet of our goddess? We cowered in the shadow of that gigantic peak, hovering over our position like a brooding menace as we sat for several days through strong winds and squalls and torrential rain. We hung there, confined to the boat by waves sweeping through the anchorage while we clung to that buoy with great faith that it was well secured to the bottom, 125 feet down. At last the squalls moved on, and we explored the village that seemed indifferent to how and why we were there. Here at this crossroads, we said good-bye to many friends as we went our separate ways. Some, we would see again soon, others, not until New Zealand; and the rest, traveling a different path, perhaps we would not get to meet again at all. We, on *Fram*, prepared for a pilgrimage.

After clearing out of French Polynesia on August 28, we watched Bora Bora fade slowly in our wake and remembered the marvelous Polynesian experiences we were leaving behind. We were given gifts of handmade ukuleles from young men, who spoke music as a second language and taught us how to dance the seductive *tamarae* on *Fram*'s foredeck. We discovered a fascinating combination of French-speaking people with Tahitian, their second language, who traced their Polynesian roots back many centuries and became part of a modern world without losing their ancient culture.

We won't forget these beautiful people, and our memories will be forever imprinted with the fragrance of frangipani, always in the air, and the awesome beauty of islands that can never be lost to civilization and tourism.

Indelibly etched in our memories is the courtesy of French officials, having to deal with us in our halting and poor use of their beautiful language. I still remember the polite French veterinarian in Atuona, when I took Katisha to be wormed. Using my trusty French dictionary, I carefully prepared my phrase, explaining the problem; and after blurting it out, the smiling vet said, "But Madame, I speak English."

I won't forget the friendly banker in his colorful lava-lava with a red hibiscus tucked behind his ear, returning our bond money as we checked out of the country. But most of all, I will remember the music everywhere we went. We long to return to these gentle shores. But now we sailed to a place of destiny.

Learning Polynesian dances

Mopelia, an isolated coral atoll 120 miles west of Bora Bora was the graveyard of our sister ship, *Aura*. Recently, we heard rumors of a strange discovery there. It seems a couple of months ago, a yacht stopped and found the place abandoned. Food was left uneaten on the table, dishes and pans and children's toys were scattered around the yard, clothes were in disarray, and there was other evidence of a hasty exit. No boat or any other means of travel was in sight. There was no indication of foul play, and nobody could explain what happened, but it cast an ominous spell over our anticipated visit. We didn't know what to expect.

This atoll was typical, with a surrounding reef dotted with low-lying *motus*. The current was strong in the only pass into the lagoon, and we were swept helpless through before we realized we had actually found it. We dodged many coral heads until we reached a small clear sandy place, where we anchored in front of the village.

We were surprised to see fishermen inside the pass and saw others on the beach. We launched the dinghy and motored ashore. Several dark-skinned men with wild hair lay around watching us with what appeared to be a menacing manner. A vicious-looking dog was tied to a tree, and they offered no words of greeting. We weren't sure what to do and walked away along the beach, discussing the situation. Ralph decided to approach and ask for the village chief.

About then, the fishermen returned and emptied their catch in the surf. Ralph asked for the village chief. A small man with Asian features introduced himself and spoke to us in English. We explained our mission to him, describing *Aura*'s shipwreck. At the mention of this, one of the men ran toward a small building and returned with a guest book open to a photo of *Aura* in all her glory under full sail.

It was heartbreaking to read the account of the wreck as written by friends who were waiting for Thom and Karen's arrival, only to find they would be involved in a rescue mission instead. *Aura* struck the outer reef in the middle of the night while sailing at seven knots. The impact holed her, and she began breaking up, eventually slipping down the face of the reef into the sea. They jumped off their stricken yacht into the inner lagoon and swam for help.

The men described for us where she wrecked, and we asked permission to visit the site. With gut-wrenching memories of our friends and their exquisite *Aura*, we toasted her memory with a glass of champagne and threw a piece of stainless steel from *Fram*'s construction into the sea to mingle with her bones. After seeing the unbelievable force of the waves on the reef, we understood how a boat caught in its clutches could be bashed to pieces with no hope of survival. We walked the *motu* that was haunted by pieces of her teak scattered among the trees and brush. We saw Thom's skilled hands forming each piece and Karen lovingly finishing them. Our hearts were heavy, but now our sadness was purged, and we could leave her to live in our memory.

After this, the men became quite friendly, and we spent several days with the nine who were there. We did not ask about what had happened, and it remains a mystery to this day. They told us they were from the Austral islands, the southernmost islands in French Polynesia, and were sent here by the government to work copra. It was a lonely existence with their families far away. We invited them to the boat and showed a movie, and they entertained us with Polynesian songs.

They seemed to enjoy our little diversion from their boring existence. In a gesture of friendship, they invited us ashore for lunch. They had prepared a feast. The tables were covered with woven coconut fronds and fresh flowers and, at our places, drinking nuts. The food was overwhelming in its abundance and variety, which was particularly amazing considering their isolation and lack of supplies. They were childlike and watched as we sampled each dish, delighted that we liked what they had prepared. Considering that they were the wildest-looking people we had seen in all of Polynesia, their simple pleasure in our company was touching, even though I felt a bit anxious, being the only woman for hundreds of miles. The next day, we left for American Samoa, but I took more than memories with me since I was sick to my stomach for the entire nine-day passage.

We were still experiencing unsettled weather patterns, but it was time to move on, so we crept across the lagoon under overcast skies and once again approached that fearful pass. This time, we were going with the current that spit us out the other side before we had time to worry about the coral. The winds were fifteen to twenty knots with confused seas. The boat was being thrown around as if in a gigantic washing machine, and that didn't make me feel any better. We had four days of miserable, dreary, squally weather with big uncomfortable seas.

One night, I was on watch when we had a knockdown while we were on a beam reach. I was sitting in the salon on the settee, when a rogue wave broke over the boat. The wave hit the port side with a loud boom, and the boat lay over on her side. The next thing I knew, I was on my back, looking up, as books, dishes, and pans fell on top of me. Ralph, sleeping crossways in the aft bunk, was now standing upright on the side with our Fibber Magee's closet of stuff falling out of the side bunk on top of him. All I could think was, *Oh my goodness, this is really happening*! I don't remember being afraid, just surprised. Fortunately, we righted again and all was okay, but we realized it was not a good idea to be sailing on a beam reach in these big seas. With a slight change of course, we continued on our way. The next day was beautiful, and for five days, we had perfect sailing conditions. By the time we arrived in Pago Pago, my stomach was back to normal. Reflecting on this incident, I realized how fortunate it was that I was sick and down below; otherwise, I would have been sitting in the cockpit and might have been thrown overboard.

On the quay in Papeete with dugout boat

Chapter 23

On the Way to New Zealand

Pago Pago, American Samoa, had a bad reputation with the yachts—dirty, smelly, theft, excessive harbor charges, and Samoans who took things. We came here to take advantage of good inexpensive provisioning of American brands and cheap diesel fuel. Friends spent cyclone season here last year and enjoyed themselves. Certainly our first view was of a lush tropical island with a perfect landlocked harbor sparkling in the sun. Once we cleared in (an all-day affair with friendly officials in skirts) and anchored, we began to understand why it was considered such an unpleasant place.

Tuna-processing plants were surrounded by derelict fishing boats, and the stench was exceeded only by the bloody tinge in the water from the effluent dumped in the harbor. Added to this was the twenty-four-hour-a-day roar of the diesel-generating plant at water's edge. Coupled with a poor anchoring bottom, we began to wonder at the wisdom of coming to this place.

A bus tour of the island of Tutuila gave us a different impression of American Samoa. It was a beautiful island. We visited the outer villages and saw how the Samoan people lived in their open-air oval *fales*. They were high cone-shaped thatched roofs supported by posts over a floor covered with woven pandanus mats and having no walls. Woven shades could be dropped for protection against the weather or for privacy—a perfect design for a hot and humid climate.

It was also their custom to bury important family members in huge tombs built above the ground in front of the *fale*, so it was an interesting sight to see children at play on Grandpa's tomb while parents took a nap on the floor of the *fale*.

Theirs is a social system based on the extended family group of many relatives closely dependent upon each other. Christianity was part of *fa'a*

Samoa (the Samoan way). Each village has a *matais* (chief) and a talking chief of lesser rank, who speaks for the chief. The symbol of this position is a staff and fly whisk. We acquired those symbols for the *Fram* household, so there was no question who was *matais* (Ralph) and who was talking chief (me). In this communal society, if you had something they needed, they just took it. We called it stealing, but in their culture, it was acceptable. We were all careful to lock our dinghies, outboards, and boats.

We had quite an adventure on our tour of Tutuila. We started out on a paved road that soon deteriorated into just a sandy track in some of the remote villages. Halfway around the island, the modified truck, in which we rode, became stuck in the sand on a lonely stretch of road. It was hilarious watching nine yachties, who each had advise for the poor driver about how to get unstuck. Spinning the wheels only succeeded in digging himself a deep hole until the back tires were buried up to the truck bed. We women—sailors, first mates, navigators, watch keepers, provisioners, and cooks, among other things, kept our silence and tried not to snicker out loud, when our captains argued about the correct solution to the dilemma. Finally someone had the bright idea of cutting some palm fronds, which were certainly plentiful, to put under the back tires. Could that have been one of us, the fairer sex? The rest of the trip was uneventful.

Touring America Samoa

We ate at the famous Sadie Thompson restaurant at reasonable prices. We also discovered a New York-style pizza parlor and tried to eat our way through their menu but, after a valiant effort, didn't quite make it. After expensive French Polynesia, we all went a little crazy here. Following a week of nonstop shopping and pizza, with *Fram* full of cheap diesel and us full of yummy food, we were ready to visit Western Samoa.

An easy overnight passage brought us to Apia and the independent nation of Western Samoa. The contrast was dramatic between the two Samoas, with the same ethnic race and culture but one dependent on Uncle Sam's largesse and the other responsible for their own economy. Western Samoans showed pride we didn't see in Pago Pago, and their government has done a remarkable job of building an economy based on their own resources.

Robert Lewis Stevenson spent the last years of his life here. Called Tusitala (teller of tales) by the Samoan people, he was beloved, and when he died, a great procession carried his body up Mount Vaea, where he was buried on the summit.

Aggie Grey's Hotel, another famous watering hole, had a healthy tourist business; and we played tourist on one of their island tours. We traveled into the interior jungle with its huge banyan trees and great "Tarzan" vines, where waterfalls plunged into the depths below. It was dark and wild, with valleys and ridges, astonishingly different than the ocean scenes we were accustomed to. On our drive along the beach, we had our photo taken sitting on a palm tree, leaning over the reef—a picture postcard scene to remember this spectacular island.

Here we had the unique experience of being the only yacht in the harbor flying the stars and stripes, and we realized how far from home we were. We added to our growing list of international friends on other yachts and even made friends with a couple of delightful older ladies from New Zealand, who were guests at the hotel. After they visited *Fram*, we exchanged addresses, and later, they introduced us to an interesting cruising family we met later in New Zealand. After a week, we reluctantly left. Time was running out, and we wanted to visit Tonga before we left the tropics.

We sailed from Apia at 0300, worrying our way past the extensive reefs surrounding the harbor and past the tip of the island at daybreak. We beat into the wind and waves as we fought for enough easting to clear the dangers and set a course to the tiny Tongan island of Nuiatoputapu. This was a tough trip for Ralph, as he had a touch of mal de mer and was unable to spend any time down below. The boat was under-canvassed, but with him feeling so bad, we did not want to carry too much sail. In hindsight, we learned two lessons. First of all, Ralph has to wear a transdermal patch at the first hint of seasickness, and we would have been more comfortable with a little more headsail. We were still learning. Old cast-iron-stomach Phyllis had no problem, but we were both glad when this passage was over. New Potatoes, as we all called this charming island with the unpronounceable name, was in sight the next morning; and after a little difficulty locating the entrance to the pass, we lined up the markers from our hand-drawn chart and entered one of the best lagoons we have seen anywhere.

Four friendly officials, again wearing skirts, boarded us and, after a pleasant visit, cleared us into the Kingdom of Tonga. This was probably the poorest island we have visited. Even so, this did not preclude the generosity of the people, as they shared with us their abundant fruits. We soon met Ofici, who invited us to his home for lunch the next day.

"How will we find you?" we asked.

"Just ask the village children," he said with a smile.

The next day, we soon accumulated quite an entourage of delightful children, dressed and undressed, who accompanied us to Ofici's home. We were bombarded with "What's your name?" "Where you from?" "Where you go?" "How old are you?" etc. We soon realized they couldn't understand our answers and were repeating the English phrases they were being taught in school. They brought us mangos to eat, and of course, eat them we did as we walked along feeling like pied pipers. They giggled and laughed, and if you ever ate an unpeeled ripe mango out of hand and know how messy this can be, you will understand why they thought it was so funny watching the *palangis* (foreigners) with juice running down their elbows.

Soon we arrived at a hut made of woven palm fronds, sitting on a platform about five feet off the ground and supported by poles stuck in the ground.

"Ofici," we called.

"Come," he said.

Inside, we were invited to sit on a raised platform covered with mats and tapa cloth that was probably his bed. We were followed up the ladder by several of our new small brown friends, who were soon shooed away by our host. We were then joined by a young man, who was introduced as a new father because his wife recently had a baby. She was unable to nurse, and he asked if we had some milk. I had several cans of wonderful New Zealand powdered whole milk onboard *Fram* and offered them to him. Suddenly, he jumped up and ran away. I was afraid I had committed a cultural faux pas until he returned with a large five-by-four-foot tapa cloth as a thank-you gift. We were touched.

We sat on mats on the floor and enjoyed a delicious lunch. We had papaya prepared several different ways, also poisson cru, taro, spinach, banana, mangos, and a dessert of cooked papaya thickened with manioc (tapioca). This was a bachelor pad, and from what I've seen, native men cooked as well as the women, and Ofici created an amazing variety of tastes from the same ingredients. You may notice that we ate poisson cru everywhere. They marinated raw fish in lime juice to cook the flesh and then added onions and seasonings and coconut cream. Everywhere, it was prepared the same and was delicious. Spinach was also interesting. Natives everywhere called the greens they cook spinach, and often it was taro leaves, but at Nuiatoputapu, it was leaves from one of their trees. In all cases, it was always served with coconut cream, which made it tasty and rich. Coconut cream is a staple throughout the South Pacific. Coconuts were plentiful, and we watched as the husk was stripped off, the meat grated and strained, and then the rich cream was wrung out using the coarse fibers of the husk.

Once again, we came to visit people in a remote location and were welcomed with warmth and generosity. It was a joy to be accepted into a small part of their lives, and we were happy to invite them into our home. They were curious about how we lived and accepted our mode of travel as normal. They always appreciated being invited to the yachts and were proud when we shared a part of our life with them.

The Vava'u group in Tonga was a destination we anticipated with high expectations. It was always a favorite with yachts, and after a pleasant thirty-hour sail, we entered the island group with a great sense of déjà vu. Here we found many beautiful islands in calm waters that looked a lot like our own San Juan Islands, except they were covered with palm trees instead of evergreens. If only the waters of our islands were also eighty-five degrees!

Can you imagine such a wonderful cruising ground? We spent three glorious weeks enjoying several different protected anchorages and getting acquainted with the friendly and enterprising people, who welcomed us wanderers of the ocean to their special piece of paradise.

The native dress was the most distinctive of any we had seen. Women wore long, ankle-length dark skirts over which they wore colorful dresses with long sleeves and long skirts, most of it polyester. Long ago, The London Missionary Society taught them the body was to be well covered, and in spite of the hot climate, this was proper and the custom. We saw some Western dress on a few young people, but it was always modest. Schoolgirls wore red or blue uniforms with midcalf-length skirts and short-sleeved white blouses. The boys wore long pants and white shirts. Both men and women often wore a woven mat tied around their middle called a *tavala*. This was a sign of respect for ancestors or in remembrance of someone who died and was always worn in the presence of the king.

The men wore dark plain-colored skirts to the middle of the calf and always wore shirts, as it was not proper for a man to show his bare chest. The officials were dressed in black. Out of respect for their customs, we dressed modestly with our arms covered so as not to offend our hosts. It was against the law to swim on Sunday, and women rarely went into the water at all and, even then, only when fully dressed. By contrast, the lessons of the missionaries were lost on the French Polynesians.

Our senses have been inundated with exotic experiences in all the South Pacific, but this was the ultimate in easy living. The earth was rich and the climate perfect to grow many foods. At birth, each male was given a plot of land on which to grow food. These plots were called plantations regardless of size.

Tongan market

Each morning, we looked forward to John, who came around the anchorage in a small boat with fruits and vegetables for sale. Once, he even had lobsters. One day, I bought a stalk of bananas, six papayas, six mangos, and a taro root for $3. He also threw in a couple more papayas and a handful of mangos. The only drawback to this type of shopping was the early hour of his arrival. Sometimes, before we learned to be careful, we would look up at some awkward moment to see a face pressed against a hull porthole looking at us. In this hot climate, we didn't wear clothes inside the boat. We must have been a shocking eyeful for such modest people.

Most tropical locations did not have laundry facilities, so I washed our clothes by hand. I had a big plastic tub and a scrub board, with large buckets for rinsing. My washing machine was named Phyllis. One day, I was sitting in the sunshine on the foredeck, washing clothes and feeling sorry for myself. When I looked around the boat at the beautiful turquoise water and the lush green trees behind a white-sand beach and thought about all our dreams and plans to get here, I remembered how lucky I was. I never thought of laundry day as drudgery again and relished the extraordinary pleasure of stacking folded, fragrant, sun-dried clean clothes in our lockers.

We went to Aiseia's Tongan feast on Lisa Beach, shopped for beautifully made baskets and carvings, sailed in brilliant turquoise waters, dove in underwater caves, and swam and snorkeled and walked miles around the villages. We spent our days in the wonderfully warm waters and visited many anchorages, which we knew by their number. We even went to an anchorage where the pigs on the beach waited expectantly to be slopped, as the yachties brought their food scraps ashore for them and macheted open a few coconuts as well. It was hard to say good-bye to this special place when we left for our long trip to New Zealand on November 1.

We carefully prepared *Fram* for this passage since we expected heavy weather with at least one gale. The high latitudes of the Southern Ocean have a deserved reputation as a tough test for men and ships. We set a course west to clear the many dangerous reefs, volcanoes, and reported dangers of Tongan waters. We sailed in perfect conditions for nine days. The winds then became so light we spent the last forty-eight hours motoring. In the clear dawn light, our first sight of land looked like a golf course of emerald-green hills covered with puffy white dots. We arrived in Whangarei, New Zealand, the morning of the eleventh day, after a voyage of 1,376 nautical miles. We have visited twenty islands, flown the courtesy flags of six different countries, and sailed more than twelve thousand nautical miles since leaving Seattle in August of 1987. Along the way, we formed many friendships among the yachting fraternity and visited and welcomed many friendly native people aboard *Fram*.

Land of the long white cloud

Each day we sailed away from the tropics, we had to add a few more clothes and quilts to the bed. We were bundled up in long johns and wool hats and gloves the morning when the New Zealand officials, dressed in shorts and short-sleeved cotton shirts, came to check us in. We nearly froze to death just looking at their bare arms and legs. Hardy folks, those kiwis! They were thorough and efficient. We expected a careful check by their agriculture inspector, and after examining our Tongan baskets and carvings, they took two drums to be fumigated. They also took popcorn and honey, but our nuts and seeds were declared vermin free. Since this country was an island, they were extremely careful about imports that could cause great losses to their agriculture. Knowing this was the case, we did not have any meat products or eggs and egg cartons.

The biggest problem was Katisha. We knew he would be quarantined to the boat, and we were required to sign a $1,000 U.S. bond to this effect. In addition, we had to pay for three visits a week to make sure he was onboard and healthy. We now have a very valuable cat after being in New Zealand almost six months. Agriculture gave us a green flag to fly at the spreaders, indicating there was an animal onboard. Whenever we went to a dock for fuel, we shut Katisha inside so he couldn't escape. We flew home for Christmas and left him on the boat, with a friend taking care of him. As long as he was available for the cat inspections, we had no problem.

Shortly after arriving, we bought a Ford Cortina station wagon with right-hand steering, and it took a while getting used to driving on the wrong side of the road. We had a funny, but not-so-funny, experience shortly after buying the car. Our nephew Todd came for a visit, and we picked him up in Auckland after telling the cat inspector we would be gone a few days for sightseeing. We stayed several days longer than we planned, and when we arrived back in Whangarei, the inspector came by the boat and said, "You're here! I'll be right back."

He hurried off to let the government officials know that we were safe, and they could call off their nationwide search for us after he reported us overdue. He later told us that they lose a lot of tourists, who aren't used to driving on the left-hand side of the road. We were embarrassed but also humbled that they cared about their visitors that much.

With Todd, we visited caves, thermal hot springs, and geysers and were entertained at the Agridome, where we learned about different breeds of sheep and the dogs that herd them. After visiting the giant kauri trees, we had an unexpected adventure when our car broke down in the mountains on a Friday and refused to go. Ralph and Todd agreed it was the timing belt, and that meant we weren't going anywhere for a while. An attractive young lady picked Todd up and took him to the next town for help. Help arrived and towed us to a lovely resort on the Tasman Sea, where we waited for parts and the auto mechanic who would be back at work on Monday.

We moved to Auckland, the sailing capital of New Zealand, in January to haul out, where it was easy to find most things we needed for the boat. We added a roller furling system to handle our large headsail and a Heart inverter so we have 110-volt AC power from the batteries at the turn of a switch. We also added a computer program that used our ham radio receiver to pick up weather fax signals. Probably the most practical addition for daily use was a kitty outhouse with a view window that Ralph built for Katisha.

Once we left the United States, kitty litter was no longer available. We carried a big supply onboard when we left, but clearly, something more permanent had to be done to keep our fuzzy crew member on his best behavior. Some boats use sand—not acceptable on *Fram*. Others use torn newspapers—also not practical with no newspapers. So Ralph, a rocket designer for Boeing, became a kitty-litter washer. He devised a three-step process of washing litter in batches. Katisha never, ever did his thing anywhere else on the boat besides his litter box. This was not a problem at anchor, but on a bouncy boat in big waves, he was a pitiful sight. Many times, the rocket engineer had to hold him in his box so he wouldn't fall out while doing his business. Also, sometimes in his enthusiasm, litter flew everywhere. Thus, a carefully engineered covered container for cat and box came to live behind the cockpit. Now he couldn't fall out, and litter was not scattered every which way. Engineers solve problems.

We didn't know much about the Land of the Long White Cloud or Aotearoa as it is known to the Maori. We traveled extensively by land to both the north and south islands and developed a special feeling for this beautiful land that reminded us of home. Auckland was a vibrant and lovely city built on many hills, like Seattle, overlooking the sea, both the South Pacific Ocean and Tasman Sea. I was especially happy to be in a city again with its many cultural events. I particularly missed classical music and the theater. When we moved *Fram* to Auckland, our moorage was bow and stern tied to pilings. We were in the middle of the sailing activities, and we watched them race and sail in all weather conditions, even though sometimes it was decidedly boisterous.

We were curious about the Maori people. Polynesian by ethnicity, civilization has been hard on their culture, as they have been absorbed into the *pakiha* (foreign) ways. They were struggling to preserve some of their traditions for the benefit of their young people. We went to traditional Hangi feasts and enjoyed their music and dancing. We tried to learn about their present lives and understand their problems. They were justly proud of Keri Te Kanawa, the internationally famous opera star, who was Maori and who returned to her people often to give concerts and honor her heritage.

I went with friend Jessica to the celebration of the 150th anniversary of the signing of the treaty of Waitangi. This was like our Independence Day, and since New Zealand was part of the British Commonwealth, this important event was attended by Queen Elizabeth of England. We began to understand how the Europeans settled here and took the land from the indigenous people. In honor of the anniversary, the government gave all the Maori settlements funds to build traditional war canoes. Jessie and I wandered among the impressive canoes, visiting with the people and learned of their problems and heard about their lost culture. Their stories reminded me of how we treated the American Indians in the settlement of the United States.

We met many New Zealand people who invited us into their homes. We were introduced to a delightful sailing family by the two ladies we met in Apia, Western Samoa. Eric and his wife, Jessica, invited us to bring our dirty laundry and come for dinner in their home one evening. What an original and greatly appreciated invitation. Those folks understood what cruising vagabonds needed.

While we were in Auckland, the Whitbread Round the World racers arrived to prepare for the next leg of the race. For a grand adventure, we loaded *Fram* with friends and took them out to watch the racers leave on the next leg around Cape Horn on their way to South America. We were directed by the officials in Hauraki Gulf to anchor near a tall ship near the turning buoy. It looked like we would have a great view as the racers made their turn toward Cape Horn. A last-minute wind shift caused the boats to change course, and we had more of a great view than we counted on. *Fram* became the turning buoy for the whole fleet, going at least twelve knots past our stern before turning to cross our bow. The sight of a big, powerful maxi-racer headed straight for us; going full speed in restricted waters was way too much excitement. (*Fram* wasn't the only boat anchored there.) When it was all over, our stomachs were clenched in knots, and even though our guests had a great time, we pondered how foolish it had been to place our boat in such a vulnerable position. It was exciting though.

Whitbread racer off *Fram's* bow

Doug and Lisa were welcome visitors. Our travels in the little station wagon took us from the North Cape, where the Tasman Sea meets the Pacific, through the Kauri forests, over the hills, past fluffy white sheep in the fields and herds being moved along the main highway. We saw deer being raised for export, but we did not find any venison for sale in New Zealand.

Later, Ralph's brother Earl and sister Veda, with husband, Dick Borton (my ham radio buddy), spent a week with us. Dick, a former orchard man, was interested in local apple varieties, and we visited an orchard owner on the South Island and sampled his apples. The South Island looked like a huge English garden with gaily colored flowers everywhere. We traveled by bus to Milford Sound in the fiord land, awash in waterfalls, where we took a boat trip to poke our nose into a gray and threatening Tasman Sea. We were charmed by Dunedin and Christchurch, looking like postcards right out of Scotland and Old England.

This beautiful country boasted sixty million sheep and three million people. While there, we enjoyed good beef and exceptional lamb that was reasonably priced. The cost of food was quite high, but the quality was outstanding. Their dairy products were renowned for high quality. Throughout the South Pacific, we bought wonderful New Zealand canned butter and canned dried whole milk, but when we tried to buy it there, we were told it was only canned for export.

We took *Fram* to the Salthouse Boatbuilders facility, just north of Auckland, for a haul-out and bottom painting. The last haul-out was in

Mexico, and much water had passed beneath the keel since then. Keeping our teak varnished in good condition was a relentless battle with salt spray and the tropical sun, so we covered our beautiful railing with a coat of gray paint. We tried to like the change but will be happy to again have varnished teak when we return to the more temperate climate of the Pacific Northwest.

A yacht cruising on the ocean is in constant need of maintenance. We were fortunate that Ralph was able to fix just about everything. We have had few breakdowns, but *Fram* was now twelve years old. Much of our equipment was getting old, and most of our maintenance involved rebuilding systems before they became a problem. So far, we have kept everything working, but once in a while, when I watch Ralph fixing a pesky problem, I ask if he wouldn't rather have his feet up on a desk at Boeing with a cup of coffee instead of his head in the engine room with a greasy wrench in hand. Sometimes he doesn't answer.

Our six months in New Zealand passed too fast. We enjoyed being in a country that spoke English, or at least a variation of it (our ears eventually sorted out what they were saying). It was fun just being tourists, returning to our floating home between excursions, but now we were looking forward to returning to the tropics.

Sheep on the road in New Zealand

Chapter 24

Cyclone Season near the Equator

In May of 1990, we joined the Russell, New Zealand to Tonga race—a first for us—because we hadn't raced before. Since this was a race for cruisers with rules designed for yachts that were overloaded and overweight with stores and spares, *Fram* certainly qualified. There were twenty-three yachts entered—five Americans, three Australians, one Brit, and the rest Kiwis.

All was going well, and we were making a respectable track across the chart, when the weather decided to give us more of a challenge. Four days out, the entire fleet was caught in a gale with fifty-knot winds. We weren't having any fun trying to sail, so we hove to for three days. The motion became easy as we heeled over about twenty to thirty degrees, and the boat only moved up and down. We just closed the hatch and left *Fram* to take care of herself while we went below to eat, sleep, and read. We wedged ourselves in the dinette, and except for the screaming banshee noise and horrendous crash as the waves dropped tons of water on us, we were comfortable in our peaceful cocoon. All things are relative, I guess.

We were located over the Kermadec trench, one of the deepest parts of the ocean, far from any land, and could just wait out the storm. This was our first experience with these conditions, and we learned two things: the boat had no problem with this situation, and we could handle it. However, we had leaks that we had not seen before or since. Water was forced through watertight portholes and hatches and cascaded into the galley, thoroughly bathing my beautiful stainless-steel propane stove with saltwater. It just proved that a dry boat could be a wet boat in the right conditions, and never underestimate the tremendous force of waves at sea.

English friends not far from us had a wave break out two windows and dump tons of saltwater in their bunk. Other friends in a twenty-eight-foot boat just hung on for dear life, dreaming of becoming farmers if they ever set foot on dry land again. We maintained radio contact with each other for moral support. Like most things, even this came to an end, and we were happy to set sail once again—wet, wiser, and safe.

We arrived in Nuku'alofa, the capital of the Kingdom of Tonga, and were welcomed at the finish line by the Tongan Navy, who escorted us to the anchorage at the Royal Sunset Beach Resort, where we enjoyed the festivities as we all compared war stories and licked our wounds. One of the planned events was a race in the lagoon for all the boats. The crew of *Fram* was inexperienced with the nuances of competitive racing, and when a kiwi boat cut us off as we were nearing the finish line, forcing us to choose between a collision or hitting a coral reef, we turned way and lost the wind and all headway. Racing with Aussies and Kiwis was not for the faint of heart.

We intended to stay in Tonga about a month before going on to Fiji since we were here last year. We stopped at the Hapai'i group that lies between Nuku'alofa and Vava'u. It was absolutely essential to have good charts and good weather to safely visit these low-lying atolls surrounded by many reefs. We had to be ready to leave immediately when the wind shifted to the west. We anchored at Ha'e'feva atoll with several other yachts. One day, we decided to visit a distant island that had no good protected anchorage. Since *Fram* was the largest boat, we took everyone onboard to visit the village and the school. With about twenty-five people from eight other yachts, we left the anchorage towing several dinghies. With Jeannie from *Northmoor* at the spreaders, conning *Fram* close to the beach, we dropped our anchor on a sandy spot.

Waiting for us on the beach were many children dressed in red school uniforms or in nature's uniform. The adults watched cautiously as we came ashore and shyly bid us welcome. Bringing gifts, we visited the school and were charmed as the children sang and danced for us. Our friend Chris, who was a teacher, listened to their ABCs while the mothers in the background (typical of mothers everywhere) urged their children forward. The innocent charm of the children as they responded to this army of *palangis* was touching. Some of the younger ones, coyly hiding behind mama's skirt, had never seen white people before. The villagers were poor and lacked most basic essentials in the classroom, but their teacher was a gentle young man, who made up in creativity for what he lacked in materials. This was typical of all the schools we visited in Tonga. We left many school supplies behind.

Tongan school children with Chris

After idyllic sunny days on white-sand beaches, the inevitable wind shift to the west forced us to bid farewell to these isolated islands, and once again, *Fram* was heading for the Vava'u group. We made landfall after dark, using radar and trusting it and sat nav positions to keep us safe from the reefs and small islets between which we had to pass. It was a nerve-racking trip, and we were thankful when the anchor was safely down at 2200, and we could relax the knots in our stomachs.

Tonga was a temptress, and we allowed ourselves to be caught in her enchanting trap. Fiji's voice beckoning to the west became dim, and we made the decision to stay three more months for two reasons: for Ralph to finish the book he was writing and to have a chance to get to know the Tongans on a more personal basis. We accomplished both goals.

However, this decision created a financial dilemma. Throughout our travels, we were able to get cash through most American Express travel agencies and this worked well with some advance planning. We would write a check from our personal U.S. bank account that was guaranteed by our American Express credit card. We were limited as to the amount available, but most of the time, we did not need much cash, so this had not been a problem. Before leaving New Zealand, we cashed the limit and spent most of it provisioning before leaving for Tonga. We expected to be in Fiji after a month, where we would cash another check.

We were in Naiafu when we decided to stay the extra three months. We only had $200 left and went to the American Express agency to get cash as usual. Unfortunately, it didn't work in Tonga. We went to the Bank of Tonga to see if we could have our U.S. bank wire funds for us, but that didn't work either. So we had to go on a strict budget. We had provisioned well in New Zealand, so we had most basic needs onboard. We set aside half ($100) for beer and the rest for fresh fruits and vegetables.

This turned out not to be a hardship, because most of the time, we were conveniently anchored in front of Gunter's Bellevue Restaurant. Gunter was a German gourmet cook, who married a Tongan wife and opened a fabulous restaurant. Many days, he swam out to the boat and asked if we were coming in for dinner. He took Visa cards, so we lived well on our limited budget.

We met Lea'aetoa (Toa) when we visited the elementary school in the village of Pangaimotu. We carried two packages from New Zealand for one of the teachers in the school, where Toa was the headmistress. I immediately felt a rapport with her, and when she invited us to visit her home on Sunday, we readily accepted. This was the beginning of a warm friendship with her family, husband Panove, and six of their eight children. Sunday, a kind gentleman on his way to church delivered us to Toa and Panove's door. Their Catholic service was over by the time we arrived, and dinner was being prepared in the *umu* (spelled *omu* in Polynesia).

Daughter Jane was home from Nuku'alofa, where she was a student in teachers' training school. We soon learned that this family placed great importance on education, and even with two incomes, they lived humbly, as they paid for a son being educated at a seminary in Fiji, Jane in Nuku'alofa, and tuition for two children in high school, who would also go on to advanced education. In Tonga, it was unusual for children to be educated beyond sixth grade, which was mandatory. Panove, a fisherman, learned to play violin from his father and played with a band at the Paradise Hotel on Saturday nights to earn a little extra.

We felt awkward when we were seated at a small table on the only two chairs in their home. Before us, they placed lobster, piglet, octopus, corned beef with oriental fried noodles, baked breadfruit, and many root vegetables, as well as papaya baked with coconut cream. We were amazed at the amount of food. It was the custom for the guests to be offered the best food, and after they have eaten, the man ate and then the wife and children. We felt uncomfortable with this custom, and still do, even after having shared many meals in native homes. The family sat on the floor on mats, and throughout the meal, people dropped by, and they were given food. More plates of food were sent to other homes in the village. The people may be poor in money, but God has richly blessed this land, and nobody goes hungry.

We invited the family to visit *Fram*, and Panove suggested a picnic, Tongan style. We picked them up and sailed to a deserted beach, where an *umu* was prepared and Panove's spear gun produced a feast—octopus, fish, poisson cru, taro, breadfruit, and manioc root (tapioca), all prepared on the beach and cooked in the ground on hot rocks. During our stay, we enjoyed many good times with this family. We felt privileged to be included in their life and learn about Tongan customs and culture.

Wanting to give something useful to the school, we asked Toa what they needed, and she told us that English is a required subject, and they have language tapes supplied by New Zealand but no tape recorders to play them. We took up a collection from all the yachts and asked our son-in-law Doug to buy tape recorders that would operate on batteries since the school had no electricity. He also bought a large supply of batteries. His parents, Bob and Martha, brought this special gift when they arrived from Seattle for a visit; and they were with us when we gave them to Toa at her school. She burst into tears of surprise and gratitude and sent one of the children to fetch Panovi, who came and thanked us, saying they would have a feast for us.

An enormous feast was prepared by the PTA in our honor, and all the yachts were invited. We were simply overwhelmed. We heard about the exceeding abundance of a Tongan feast, but nothing prepared us for the huge amount of food placed before us on woven mats on the floor. Three piglets, fish, chicken, lamb, octopus, breadfruit, papaya, pineapple, and many root vegetables had been baked in several *umus*. We were seated on the floor around the food mat and ate Tongan style with our hands. Food dripped from our chins and ran down our elbows as we washed it all down with green drinking coconuts. We ate until we could eat no more, and still there were piles of food. The music started, and we danced and sang with the villagers and all the children while Ralph and I celebrated the joy of having spent several months with these good people. The next day, we left for Pago Pago.

Tongan Feast

I had injured my hand in a dinghy accident a few weeks before, and thinking there might be broken bones, the doctor immobilized it.

Martha took one look and asked, "How are you going to sail to Samoa with that?" I must have looked pretty pathetic, because then she said, "Why don't we help you sail the boat there?"

I don't think she knew what a relief that was, because I would have been poor help for Ralph as a one-handed crew. They were welcome company, and their help was hugely appreciated. Fortunately, the weather was good, and after three days, the high island of Tutuila rose out of the sea with the morning sun.

The first thing I did in Pago was have my hand x-rayed and was relieved to find no broken bones, so I tore off the wrappings and began the slow process of recovering the use of my hand. This minor accident made us realize how precarious our situation was when we need medical attention in a remote and backward country. We have been fortunate with good health and few medical problems. In general, ocean sailing was a healthy lifestyle.

October 23, we left *Fram* and the cat in Pago Pago in the able care of our friend Karl (*Arkenstone*) from the Duwamish Yacht Club while we flew home for the birth of our second grandchild. We wanted to be there when it was time for Sheri to go to the hospital, but Kelly was anxious to get started with life and couldn't wait for Grandma and Grandpa to make her appearance two weeks later. She arrived five hours before we did. Our two months at Dave and Sheri's home was a big grandparent treat. However, after spending a snowy Christmas with all the family, it was time to return to *Fram* and the tropics.

January 1991. Once again it was time to move. In the southern hemisphere, cyclone season is from December through April, and we were right in the area they liked to visit. We decided to go north toward the equator instead of south as we had the year before. Kanton Island in the Phoenix group of Kiribati lies within three degrees of the equator, which is outside the cyclone area. We provisioned the boat, got reacquainted with the cat (he loved Karl in spite of being called the dog), fueled up, and then waited and waited and waited. Weather determined our departure date. We were ready to go, but a convergence zone lay between us and our destination, and we did not relish the idea of vicious squalls and big seas.

This six-day passage felt strange with the bow aimed at the Big Dipper and the Southern Cross now over our shoulder. Orion still lay on the equator, but the sky looked a little more familiar the further north we went. However, we could only see Polaris in our memory since it was not visible below the equator. The further north we sailed, the more we thought about how far we have come since leaving Seattle in 1987. It was now 1991. The time has gone by quickly, and we have visited many destinations, which, just four years ago, were part of a vision. *Fram* was a comfortable home and carried us safely as we wandered across the face of the sea.

Ask Ralph his favorite place of all our cruising destinations, and he will answer unequivocally, "Kanton," a coral atoll that lies within three degrees south of the equator, where the weather is warm and dry. It is part of the Phoenix group, which along with the Gilbert Islands and Line Islands make up the Republic of Kiribati (pronounced *Kiribas*), which covers 1,370,000 square miles of ocean, both north and south of the equator. Tarawa is the capital. Kanton is located in the central Pacific Ocean about seven hundred miles north of American Samoa. Howland Island of Amelia Earhart fame is also part of the Phoenix group. You can't get there except by small boat or the quarterly supply ship out of Tarawa, which serves all the islands.

The U.S. government turned Kanton over to the newly created republic in 1979. Great Britain and the U.S. had shared control through the years. In the thirties, it was used as a refueling base for Pan American clippers on trans-Pacific flights. During World War II, it was a military base with thirty thousand troops and both a fighter runway and a bomber runway. In the sixties, NASA used it as a tracking facility for manned-space flights, and in the seventies, it was a secret U.S. military base for tracking ballistic-missile tests. WARNING: DO NOT APPROACH WITHIN 50 MILES, read our chart as we sailed toward the rising sun and into the lagoon at Kanton. In spite of this ominous message, we arrived at our most intriguing destination yet. We entered on an ebb tide and had to use full throttle to power against a strong outgoing current. Ahead, in the middle of the pass, sat Spam Island, a pile of spoilage dredged from the channel. A rusting WWII wreck stood on our starboard, a silent sentinel. To port loomed two large white fuel tanks. A rugged cement wharf materialized as we crept into the lagoon.

We anchored in about thirty feet of water on a white-sand bottom. After an uneventful six-day sail, it was nice to be in our new home. We were here for about four months—to wait out the tropical cyclone season—at this isolated atoll. Our new floating neighborhood would be four yachts with occasional visits from other yachts passing by.

A dinghy with three men made its way from shore and broad smiling faces greeted us with, "Welcome to Kiribati." They were soon seated at *Fram's* dining table with soft drinks and cookies. Berniti (pronounced *Bernis*), the police chief, was also the customs officer and the official representative of the government. Bakewa, the fireman, presented us with shell necklaces, and the medical officer, Biuta, represented immigration and gave us permission to lower the Q flag. Whenever we arrived in a new country, we flew the yellow quarantine flag from a spreader that indicated we were healthy and requested permission to enter their country. It was the responsibility of immigration to allow us entry and permission to take the flag down.

They looked around our main salon and admired the photo of our family. This friendly conversation was the beginning of a warm friendship with the families who accepted us as part of their lives as we came to visit their poor vandalized island.

We hiked a mile and a half from our anchorage to the village and passed many remnants of the U.S. presence. Wood power poles marched away to the north with transformers and floodlights, all askew, clinging to their tops. Rust-streaked buildings with gaping windows and sharp teeth of broken glass dotted the landscape. Inside, file cabinets tossed carelessly aside, their contents scattered, carefully recorded a past life. The only sound—the rustle of rats scurrying among the papers.

All around us was stark dry land with low-lying brush hiding random piles of rocky coral, and under the palms, we saw carcasses of dead trucks with hearts torn out by careless hands and lying amid motors, transmissions, gears, and nuts and bolts.

A few scattered low palm trees were visible but not the rank growth of other atolls. Stretches of white sandy beach were interrupted by scrub brush, hiding priceless electrical parts and motors—scattered about in reckless abandon and mingled with bleached shells. We were surrounded with the detritus of Uncle Sam's extravagance, generously given to the people of this island—now discarded and left to nature's relentless work at returning all man-made objects to the earth, which gave the materials in the first place.

Huge generating plants silently hovered over the darkened village. Near the shore, the water-desalinization plant lay still and at rest. Its lifeline of electrical power long since denied, it waited while the people worried about a brackish water supply, easily depleted on this island of little rain. On *Fram*, a watermaker working faithfully in the dark bilge provided the substance of life itself. Here on this desert island, we dared not take this precious gift from the villagers.

Behind locked doors, outdated medical supplies stood proudly on shelves next to sterile gauze pads stained with rat urine, beside vitamin tablets so badly needed by the nutrition-poor villagers. In the next locked building, carefully protected, was a fine table saw, which had never been used by the village carpenter, who thought it was a sewing machine.

In the distance, we saw two large spidery towers, which looked like construction cranes but were huge jagged antennas. Beyond, a large satellite-tracking antenna, used for the Mercury/Gemini program and later for ballistic-missile tracking, awaits its next assignment. An empty waiting room in a roofless building quietly waits for the airplanes that do not arrive at the perfectly preserved six-thousand-foot runway.

Amid the waste and chaos lived seven families, sent as caretakers by the government in Tarawa. It was a harsh existence, with little left to take care of. Because of few jobs in this poor country, they didn't have any choice. Once it was a tropical paradise but not anymore.

In the village, we stopped at Berniti's house. I brought cookies and balloons for the children and cooking oil and flour for Uanna.

"Come in, Ralph and Phyllis. Will you have lunch with us?" called Berniti.

One of the teenage boys shinnied up a palm tree and prepared drinking nuts for us. On a platform which began life as the raised floor in the computer facility, we joined the family for a visit. It was cool here under the shade of the corrugated tin roof. We sat on soft mats as the children came and played near us, unafraid of strangers with different-colored skin.

Mother and children

Scrawny chickens scratched in the sand near baby pigs asleep in a pen in the kitchen, their fat bodies preparing for a feast to come. I wondered if they knew they would be the feast. The refreshing effervescence of drinking nuts gurgled down our parched throats while we ate lobster and rice.

We visited Beronika's class of twelve students; small brown fingers grasped white chalk and wrote today's lesson in English. Betro's class of four young teens sat with furrowed brows as they decided which sentence was correct English when the teacher asked about a nuance of English usage.

School children on Kanton

The importance of learning English was accepted by most islanders and yet . . . did it help them as they yearned for the material things they could only dream to eventually own? Would it help them when there were no jobs on their island and no country wanted their unskilled hands? We gave of our meager supplies, believing in the importance of education, hoping one of these small lives might be changed for the better by our insignificant gift.

They wanted to learn of other cultures so different from their own, and yet on a dusty shelf lay forgotten classic literature, which once formed the library for young American minds seeking recreation through the magic of words in a lonely and desolate place.

When I asked, Betro politely said, "No, I haven't read any of these books. No, none of the students read these books either."

Our eyes gazed with hunger at the treasured works of such authors as Dickens, Melville, and Mark Twain . . . and we returned to our portable tradable shelves of quick adventures and throbbing love stories.

With no store on Kanton, supplies were ordered from Tarawa, which arrived on a small ship every three months. They didn't always receive what they ordered. Their basic diet was mullet, caught with cast nets inside the lagoon, and coconuts, along with rice and bread. The women boiled the sap from coconut trees until it was like coconut-flavored molasses. They used this in baking and also as food for infants after they were weaned. Quite nutritious, it took the place of milk, which wasn't part of their diet. The men made toddy, an alcoholic drink from the sap.

When we arrived, they were out of most basic supplies. I gave away most of our provisions from Pago Pago, a little for each family—oil, rice, onions, and flour. We could provision later in Fiji.

Berniti gave us permission to clean out one of the buildings by the wharf for a club house. Men came from the village in the fire truck (recently repaired by Steve and Randy) and helped drag out the big useless electric transformers. Now in this clean and tidy place, we gathered for yoga, exercising, social events, and sail repairs. The villagers enjoyed it too and came with kids, babies, food, and sleeping mats to watch movies. We set up a TV and VCR for them, hooked up to a small generator. They stayed all night until the generator ran out of fuel. On this ruin of an island, we found a complex community of lonely, good-natured people with whom to share four months of our lives.

One day, the U.S. Coast Guard Buoy Tender, *Sassafras*, on their way from Hawaii to Pago Pago, stopped to give the men a little R & R. We watched with pride as the stars and stripes steamed through the pass. The villagers joined the party: steaks from a grill, salads, fresh vegetables, baked potatoes, fresh fruit, and ice cream, cake, and cookies. Did the ship's captain know we were all starved for such food? The children hungrily ate apples and oranges, filling their pockets with more. Boxes of toys added to the joy on happy little faces.

Playing volleyball with the villagers was good exercise, but Biuta and Berniti worried that Ralph was too old, until he spiked the ball a few times. They also worried about him riding his bicycle all over the island. He thought this was quite funny since he didn't feel old, in spite of his gray beard.

Berniti asked us to take them out ocean fishing. Boston Whaler dinghies were left behind by the U.S., but they had no engines. So with our outboards on their sixteen-foot boats, we took the men outside the reef to fish. Bakewa, a strong, gentle giant of a man, fished with Ralph, and they caught trevally, barracuda, tuna, wahoo, and rainbow runners about five miles offshore.

These big fish were caught using a five-sixteenths-inch nylon rope attached to the dinghy with a rubber snubber. Next was a 165 pound-test steel leader and a large double-prong stainless steel hook about two-and-a-half-inch long. In front of the hook, a handmade lure of a wood plug with a shiny skirt made from a mylar wine bag. After catching a fish, Ralph maintained their speed while Bakewa brought it in hand over hand as fast as he could, and Ralph flipped it into the boat with a gaff before the sharks took it. We lived on fish. After taking some for each of our galleys, the rest went to the villagers, where they were filleted, dried, and then sent to Tarawa to be sold for cash.

Ralph and Bakewa

One day, Berniti and the two teenage boys, Nga Nga and Tai, drove us around the island to the British side of the lagoon. We were in high spirits for a full day's adventure as we piled under a canopy in the back of the small pickup. When we had the first flat tire, we were barely out of the village. All the men helped change it. We hadn't gone far before we had the second flat. Berniti didn't seem worried, but I worried all day about how we would get back to our boats after the third flat with no more spares. Tires weren't meant to drive on sharp coral.

The British side was the old seaplane landing area. The smashed remains of the seaplane, Big John, with an engine rusting in the surf, its broken wings overgrown with plants, and a deteriorating rubber tire on the sand were grim reminders of WWII.

The few remaining buildings—including the hotel with hermit crabs its only guests—were rotted and falling down. Windows stared through vacant eyes, with shards of glass twinkling in the sand. Most of the roofs were gone, having been removed by visiting ships, leaving the insides exposed to weather and the ravages of nature. Rusted cars and trucks were parked in underbrush growing over the unused road. Old bottles and rusted fifty-five-gallon drums lay in heaps. After a picnic among the ruins, complete with fresh-speared grilled fish, the day was as much fun for the villagers as for us.

Old truck on Kanton

We invited each family to visit *Fram*, an important occasion for most of the women and children, who had not been on a yacht before. They came dressed in their finest and brought gifts of shells, and sometimes lobster or a precious egg. I served cake and juice, and we showed a movie. It was always a pleasure to invite local people to our floating home, but it was especially sweet on Kanton.

As interesting as it was to spend time with the villagers, we enjoyed many activities and good times among ourselves. Every week, we invited all the yachties to Sunday brunch and movies on *Fram*. Bonnie and Steve invited us all to a formal dinner on their anniversary. We shared recipes and books and gathered often on each other's boats for good conversation over a glass of wine.

Ralph found a soul mate in Steve from *Windrose*. They rode their bicycles all over the island, scrounging in hidden bunkers, exploring collapsed buildings, finding more treasure for overloaded bilges. One day, he came home grinning with, "Here is your new wringer." I looked at his latest treasure trove: a couple of aluminum rollers with bearings, a length of a large-diameter rubber hose, leaf springs, a big wing nut, a hand crank, a pile of odd metal pieces, and, on top of it all, the seat from a crashed Catalina. I was laughing so hard at this preposterous suggestion I took a picture. A week later, I was the proud owner of a one-of-a-kind, adjustable, custom clothes wringer, complete with leaf springs. Another picture of the finished product reminded me never to doubt Ralph when he promised me something.

Time passed quickly and soon it was April. Week after week, we delayed our departure. We did more boat projects and maintenance in this ideal climate. I put together songbooks for the village, with songs they knew in English, using file folders I found scattered in the office debris as covers. Finally the thought of mail waiting for us in Fiji overcame our reluctance to leave, and we set a departure date.

Farewell parties filled humble homes with good food, singing, and dancing as each family—mothers, fathers, and children—delivered farewell speeches, gave gifts they made, and wept when we left.

Here in this isolated place, two degrees and forty-eight minutes south of the equator, we hid from the cyclones of the South Pacific. With three other yachts, we became a part of the lives of the seven families who lived there. They became our families for a moment in time. We left with many gifts of shells and weavings and treasured memories. In exchange, we left a part of our hearts.

Kam na toua te kabaia ma te tekeraoi—when your footsteps take you to good experiences, you have a treasure between your toes (old Kiribati proverb).

Our next destination was Wallis Island seven hundred miles away and about four hundred miles north of Suva, Fiji. As Kanton faded behind our stern, the light wind also faded away, and in brilliant sunshine, we motored on calm seas. Night watch was bright with star shine reflected in the dark surface of the water. The next morning, the sun rose on a calm sea without a whisper of wind. There were squall clouds and lightning in the distance, but none came our way. As the day progressed, it became more beautiful. We sailed under a pale blue sky with a few fluffy white clouds, some lying beyond the horizon with only their tops peeking above. The water was the deep, deep blue that only exists on a clear deep ocean. We could see forever into its depths. The surface was oily smooth as we ghosted along through its shining mirror. The long swells were disorganized, and the surface seemed to undulate in random searching. It was too vast and unruly to lie flat and peaceful. The horizon went to the edge of the earth, and we alone could see it.

On the morning of the fifth day, we saw Wallis lying under an umbrella of black clouds and rain. As we drew near, the wind picked up, and on that last morning, we were once again a sailing vessel. The sailing directions warned that the narrow pass through the reef into the lagoon at Wallis has strong currents and must be entered at slack tide, preferable low slack. Even though we arrived a little early, we decided to go ahead and enter. After the rushing current washed us backward out to sea, we believed the directions and waited a half hour to try again. We anxiously eyed the squalls as they marched relentlessly over the island, hiding everything from view. Once inside the shallow coral-infested lagoon, we had several miles to traverse from marker to marker through the coral to the anchorage. We said a nervous prayer for some clearing, and thankfully, the black clouds and rain found the mountaintop, and the sun shown like a spotlight on each marker leading us through the dangers.

We breathed a thankful sigh of relief when we were safely anchored and then the sky opened. Wind built up inside the lagoon while huge ocean waves exploded over the nearby reef. Our anchorage was safe but frightful with the onslaught of big waves while thunder and lightning cracked overhead. We gratefully eyed the radio tower high on the mountain above us, hoping it would be a much more attractive target for the slashing streaks than the small boat riding below.

I fixed a simple meal, and we huddled together in the main salon, wondering why we were here. We spent an anxious night trying to sleep in the tumult that only ended with the low tide that kept the ocean waves outside the reef, where they belonged.

Wallis was an intriguing destination, and we long anticipated visiting this out-of-the-way, high, mountainous island surrounded by a wide, shallow lagoon with small islands dotted here and there. Pictures showed a lush green gem in a beautiful turquoise setting, surrounded by the reef and deep lapis-blue of the sea. Not many yachts stop here, and we looked forward to a unique experience.

It was a French territory, so once again, there would be a language challenge. We decided not to check in the day we arrived since the weather was so horrible we thought the French officials would understand.

The next day we were up early and dressed in our respectable "going ashore to check in" clothes. I put on makeup and fixed my hair. Ralph trimmed his beard and moustache. We went outside and prepared to put the dinghy in the water. It was still blowing hard, and the waves created large surf on the beach where we had to land. Then the black clouds poured out their contents in a tropical downpour. After four dry months on Kanton Island, maybe we had forgotten about rain, but there was no way we were going to get ashore, much less hitchhike five miles to town and not get wet. I did not want to mess up my hair.

"Please don't make me go ashore yet. Let's just wait until it clears and the tide is lower so the reef will block the big waves," I pleaded with the captain.

"Okay, we'll wait," was his relieved reply.

We changed into our regular "lounging around the boat" clothes. It was hot and humid, and we sweat profusely inside the boat, closed up against the driving rain. I wore a *pareau* with panties and Ralph, briefs. We read books.

The clouds lifted and we prepared to go ashore. Oh! Oh! It was pouring again, and waves were still breaking enthusiastically onshore. We had lunch. What should we do? Maybe the French didn't notice we arrived yesterday, even though we were the only foreign yacht in the lagoon. Maybe they won't mind if we wait until Monday to check in. Today was Friday, and you never check in on the weekend if you can avoid it (overtime charges). Finally, at around three in the afternoon, our consciences convinced us the weather had improved. We did not want to have to explain (in French) why we arrived on Thursday and didn't check in until Monday.

Landing through the surf was not a good idea, so we decided to take the dinghy five miles through the lagoon to Mat 'utu, where we had to check in. This sounded like a better plan, and the weather even improved. So off we went, carefully. The direct line from *Fram* to town was filled with coral reefs. We maneuvered our way through the maze to the wharf, where we secured the dinghy and climbed up the rocks. We were a little dirty, the hair a lot messed up, and our clothes real wet from the wind and waves. In less than bandbox condition, we presented ourselves to the gendarmerie. Once again, we found the French extremely polite and friendly. They did not even laugh out loud at my terrible French. They just had trouble understanding me. I seemed to have forgotten all the vocabulary I learned in French Polynesia. With formalities taken care of, we asked where to find the bank to exchange U.S. dollars for French francs.

"Oh, the bank won't be open until Tuesday," the handsome young man said with a smile.

I tried hard not to cry. For four months and a five-day passage, I dreamed about oranges, potatoes, onions, and fresh vegetables. It was a cruel disappointment to have to wait four more days. Since we had no local currency, we returned to the boat. We were deluged with warm tropical rain, and the dark sky made it almost impossible to see the reefs. We saw *Fram* far across the lagoon, waiting, a dry refuge. We also saw the lightning streaking down all around her with each crack of thunder. What if our lives ended here in a rubber dinghy in a lagoon with only French-speaking people to bring the sad news of our demise to the kids back home?

Our ten days at Wallis Island were one nasty squall after another. It seems that the dreaded convergence zone lay right on top of us, which we learned was normal at this time of year. We left the boat four times in ten days. What we saw of this lush and tropical island and her people made us wish for a longer stay.

One day, a friendly woman gave us a basket of oranges and papaya and two wonderful sweet pamplemoose (grapefruit). Another day, we were given a ride to town in a tiny car already stuffed with three large women before adding two more passengers. I don't remember if Ralph sat on one of the ample laps or if it was me, but five miles seemed like a long ways in our sardine-can vehicle. We thanked them profusely and were equally fortunate when we hitchhiked back. We discovered the supermarket took credit cards, so we could go shopping even though the bank never did open while we were there. With outrageously high prices, maybe they did not use money anymore, just plastic.

We would have liked to explore the lagoon and snorkel on the reefs. We would have liked to move the boat and anchor behind some of the small islands. We would have liked to take our bicycles ashore and explore the land. But every time we left the boat, we were drenched with the never-ending rain, and we understood why everything was so green! The natives told us they have a lot a rain on Wallis.

A French family with twin girls anchored nearby after we had been there a week. We visited back and forth, and it was a great improvement in our shoreside communications to go to town with Isabelle. Finally we all checked out to leave the next day, Saturday. After the paperwork was finished, the gendarme said he really wished we would not leave since the weather was so bad. A big ship had not been able to enter the pass for the last twenty-four hours due to the big seas, and a local boat was feared lost at sea (they showed up later okay). After a conference, we all decided to stay until Monday, and on Saturday, we went to the gendarmerie once again to notify them of our change of plans. A call to the metrological office advised us that there was an improving trend in the weather, so on Sunday morning when we awoke to sunshine, we had a conference with *Farquar*, who was also heading for Fiji, and decided to leave. We had an hour to stow the boat for sea and motor to the pass to arrive at the proper state of the tide. The ship had been able to enter, and sunshine made the world look like a much nicer place. So off we went.

We followed *Farquar* out the calm pass, passing close to the reefs on either side. After waving good-bye to the Wallisian fishermen in the pass, we immediately lost sight of each other in the huge seas. No problem, we were on our way to mail and pictures of family; a few lumpy seas could not diminish our happiness to be on this last leg to Suva. The wind was blowing twenty-five to thirty knots, and we were still in squalls. The sunshine had been only a momentary break, and as we looked back, Wallis disappeared in the black clouds and rain, looking much as we had seen it the first day. We sailed with double-reefed main and a partially rolled-up jib and, for twenty-four hours, had quite a bumpy ride. This was the first time I remembered feeling a little queasy. Boy, when I feel bad, it is rough! The boat sailed well and the sat nav was working without any hiccups. What more could one ask on the briny deep? When the weather moderated, we knew we were out of the nasty convergence zone, and the sailing should be better the rest of the way. Now our only worries were the notorious reefs and currents in Fijian waters.

We entered Nanuka Pass at 0400 as planned and were able to spot the small island that was the key to visual navigation between the numerous reefs guarding this northern entrance to Fijian waters. Now we could breathe a sigh of relief and let the sat nav and radar guide us through the night. We were 175 miles from Suva, which meant we would have to spend two nights passing through the islands. Fortunately, there was only one other place along our passage with treacherous reefs that we wanted to pass during daylight hours. We reduced sail to slow the boat down and enjoyed a beautiful night sailing past the high island of Taveuni, clearly visible in the brilliant moonlight. We experienced no adverse current and were able to hold our planned course between the dangers.

The following night found us slowly sailing along the barrier reef that forms Suva harbor. In the clear night, the lights of the city were bright when I went on watch at midnight; however, it looked like we were much too close to the reef. I turned on the radar, which showed us twelve miles from land and puts us six miles from the reef. Yes, that reef stuck out six *big* miles from the land. The navigation light that I needed to verify our position was right where it was charted to be, and I breathed easy. We recently ordered a Global Positioning Satellite (GPS) unit that we will pickup in Fiji so we will have continuous fixes for the rest of our voyage. This will reduce some of the anxiety we experienced in the past, when we had to wait for a good fix. I thought of how frightening it would be to rely on celestial navigation and visual-only piloting in these dangerous waters. Many yachts were lost each year in Fiji; in fact, an acquaintance of ours lost his off of Lautoka at the same time we were approaching Suva. A week later, a German yacht sailed right up on the reef beside the light I was now watching so attentively. The specter of lost ships was an eerie companion as I sat in the cockpit with Katisha in my lap keeping me company, along with the ghosts, during the lonely night watch.

Chapter 25

Melanesian Islands to the Land of Oz

On our last night out, the sat nav was not able to get a good fix. We were nervous when we made the turn toward Suva based only on radar and dead reckoning positions. In the early morning as we made our way closer and closer, we finally saw the tall buildings in Suva and the shipwreck on the reef. Then we saw the white line of breaking seas on the reef and finally the range markers leading us to safety. We relaxed when we knew we were right on course. We anchored in the quarantine area at 0945. We were finally in Fiji.

Sixteen thousand sailing miles from Seattle, the crossroads of the South Pacific, east meets west, Melanesia meets Polynesia, high mountainous islands, low coral atolls, deep passages, treacherous unmarked coral, brilliant blue lagoons, shipwrecks, and a Mecca for hundreds of yachts. Now we patiently waited for the check-in process. It seemed needlessly time-consuming and frustrating, but we just reminded ourselves we had to pay the admission price to paradise once in a while. When we finally anchored off the Royal Suva Yacht Club with our seven packages of mail, pictures, and videos of the family, the bad weather of the past few weeks could not dampen our joy at this important touch from home.

Checking in at Suva

After four months on a desolate atoll near the equator, this small city was filled with wonderful sights. First, the polyglot of humanity caused one to pause and watch the cauldron of colorful costumes swirling all about. Fijians, Indians, Caucasians, Orientals, and, of course, the ever-present tourists and slightly scruffy-looking yachties in shorts, faded T-shirts, and thongs. Shopping to replace our depleted stores was easy. Eating out was a test of our endurance as we explored the many options, all at reasonable prices. My love of curries was easily satisfied in restaurants and hole-in-the-wall eating places.

We found Fiji as wonderful as its reputation. In spite of continuous political unrest, the people were especially friendly. Greetings of *bula* met us everywhere we went. On the streets, we saw the Fijian police dressed in distinctive uniforms—white skirts with a zigzag hemline and dark-blue shirts with a touch of red at the waist. The people seem to be a part of the twentieth century, and yet there was a strong sense of their customs and traditions. The Indian presence dominated most government offices, as well as the businesses and shops. It was interesting. When I went into a darkened store, the lights were turned on as long as I was inside. They practiced energy conservation less because of the environment but more to save money.

The huge public market was ablaze with abundant vegetables and fruits and featured everything I needed along with exotic spices that perfumed the air with the scent of curry. I took advantage of the inexpensive, good-quality beef and canned a good supply for our food lockers. I carried a large pressure canner that I used all the way from Canada throughout our cruising years. This saved money and assured us of an adequate supply of protein, regardless of where we were. I canned beef cubes, chunks of roast, meatballs, hamburger, and chicken; as well as salmon, and crab in the Pacific Northwest. We preferred fresh fish, but my home-canned meat was particularly handy on long passages.

Provisioning in Fiji

Hardware stores seemed to have everything the captain needed, and I enjoyed the luxury of bookstores, fabric stores, and real department stores. New Zealand had been the last port of call for many of these things. Any service needed by a cruising yacht could be found here, and engine mechanics were able to fix any problem. Some yachts even had reupholstering done. We hauled out for bottom maintenance and painting, a necessary evil of owning a boat.

We enjoyed the camaraderie of the Royal Suva Yacht Club, where we gathered with international yachts and locals as well. We relished renewing friendships with yachting friends, who spent the cyclone season in various locations, returning to the tropics for the winter season. Membership in the yacht club gave us several privileges besides free anchorage and a safe landing for our dinghies. They collected our mail and held it for our arrival. Every Tuesday, they served a fabulous curry buffet dinner, and we all enjoyed this special evening with local members.

Royal Suva Yacht Club

The Yacht Club was across the road from the prison. Each morning, we watched as the prisoners were marched out with their guards to work on the roads. To our amazement, the prisoners all had machetes needed for their work while the guards guarding them had no weapons. The prisoners weren't even chained together. When someone was sent to prison, they were tattooed with a butterfly on their shoulder so the public knew they were convicts. Apparently, this was enough to protect the population against machete-carrying prisoners.

Kava, also known as *yaquona* or *grog*, was a mild narcotic that caused a feeling of euphoria. It was prepared using the root of a plant in the pepper family. First the root was pounded into a paste and then strained, traditionally through the fibers of a coconut, and mixed with water in a special kava bowl. It was served in a coconut shell, from which it was drunk after receiving it with a clap. It was often used for ceremonial purposes, and Ralph was welcomed both to Nukualofa, Tonga, and Suva, Fiji, by participating in a kava ceremony. In Tonga, it was only men who could drink kava. In Fiji, I could have participated but declined because it looked too much like drinking muddy water. Ralph liked it.

We bought kava at the public market. When visiting a village, it was customary to present the chief with a gift of kava root before asking permission to enter. If it was picked up, permission was granted. Therefore, we needed kava when we visited some of the outer islands.

After several weeks in Suva, we moved *Fram* around the island to Mololo Lei Lei and Musket Cove Resort in the Mamanuca Island Group. Beautiful music on the stereo accompanied us on the pleasant overnight motor cruise under a full moon while we thread our way between the outlying reefs and found the pass through the reef. Our new GPS navigating system we ordered was waiting for us when we arrived at the resort. This piece of equipment will replace our sat nav, which didn't always receive information when we needed it. GPS provides our exact position twenty-four hours a day, every day—very important for safety, particularly in this area of reefs and scattered small islands.

Here we enjoyed a more touristy view of Fiji. We were now members of the Musket Cove Yacht Club. Very exclusive. You had to sail here on a yacht from somewhere else to be members. This was our base until we left for Port Vila, Vanuatu, with the race on September 21.

While here, we took scuba-diving lessons from Lino a Fijian, who spent many years in the U.S. learning to dive and where he became a certified PADI diving instructor. It was three days of intensive work. Since we were his only students, it was indeed personalized teaching. What a wonderful classroom on a white-sand bottom in warm water surrounded by living coral and beautiful tropical fish. We made three open-water dives and earned our PADI diving certificates, proving that age was not a limiting factor if you were determined to accomplish something. We received our certification on Ralph's sixtieth birthday. We now looked forward to the wonderful world of underwater exploration.

Doug and Lisa arrived for a three-week visit, dive certificates in hand, so we enjoyed spending time underwater together. Lino took us on a shark dive in one of the passes, and we were not as fearful with an experienced diver compared to when we first encountered those terrors of the deep. We sailed to one of the outer islands and presented the obligatory kava root to the chief, which he accepted, and we enjoyed visiting a traditional village. Doug thought the dead-looking, dried-up root was a strange gift for a village chief in exchange for visiting another exotic tropical island.

Our friends Alan and Charlotte Cochran arrived about a week before Doug and Lisa left. Alan was also a certified diver, and it was a pleasure to share one of life's great adventures with him and our kids. The living coral and the fish life were endlessly interesting, and we were soon comfortable with our new diving skills.

Alan and Charlotte were our classmates in high school, and it was a special treat for them to be with us at the same time as our kids. During the last week of Doug and Lisa's visit, we were into the social activities of the Musket Cove Regatta Week. We had invited Alan to sail with us on the Port Vila race while Charlotte takes the more civilized way of travel via 737. They would stay with us for ten days in Vanuatu, so it will be fun to discover a new experience in a different country together. We told Alan we didn't expect him to be a sailor when we leave Fiji, but he should know something about it when we arrive in Vanuatu five hundred miles and four days later. Besides, we needed a *good* fisherman onboard.

As part of the preregatta festivities, we sailed to another island, where we were all captured by pirates and were made to eat, drink, and dance the day away. Another day, there was a parade of decorated yachts. We enjoyed feasts, native dancing, and singing, all leading up to the big event—the actual race to Port Vila, Vanuatu. Doug and Lisa waved good-bye from shore as they prepared to return to Seattle, and Charlotte kissed Alan good-bye as he prepared to sail his first ocean race with us.

As we mentioned before, *Fram* was no racing machine, but when she is surrounded by wildly tacking, aggressive racers, she could pick up her skirts and fly with the best of them. We were in a fleet of about thirty boats, ranging in size from thirty feet to eighty feet. There were trimarans, catamarans, monohulls, and even one powerboat! There were Aussies, Kiwis, Finns, Japanese, Canadians, Americans, and Pommes (that's what they call the English in this part of the world). Old, young, it didn't matter. We were having a great time. The rules required us to check in each day by radio, and we did. The rules required us to motor some of the time, and we did. The rules required us to be overloaded with stores, and we were! At dawn of the third day, the island of Efate, Vanuatu, rose from the sea, and after five hundred miles, *Fram* crossed the finish line following a rocking and rolling downwind run. We arrived with five fish, a landlubber who knew how to sail (*Fram* style), and a respectable finish in the middle of the fleet.

Port Vila was a delight. Our early morning arrival was met with a gift basket of fruit, cheese, beer, and fresh baguettes from the race committee. After a long wait, the officials finally arrived and checked us into the country so we could go ashore and find Charlotte, who was relieved that we returned her husband not much the worse for wear. There were parties, banquets, awards, more gifts, and a very warm welcome by the Port Vila Yacht Club. Alan entered the casino-night blackjack contest and, in spite of our encouragement, came in second to a crafty and obviously more experienced Aussie gambler. Too soon, we bid good-bye to our good friends and were happy to have again shared a little part of our adventurous life with them.

Children selling ducks at market in Port Vila

Formerly the New Hebrides, Vanuatu was made up of many volcanic islands thrust up from the sea. There were still active volcanoes and earthquake activities. We visited three islands: Efate with Port Vila—with many reminders of the U.S. Navy presence during WWII— and also the islands of Malekula and Espirito Santo.

The native people were referred to as ni-Vanuatu and were Melanesian, an ethnic group that also includes the islands of New Guinea, the Solomons, New Caledonia, and Fiji. The language of Vanuatu is Bislama, a form of pidgin English, a mixture of English, French, and Melanesian words set to a Melanesian syntax. They tend to express a general concept, rather than specific words. There were hundreds of different languages among the different villages, and a common language was essential for Vanuatu's transformation into a nation. There was also a need to communicate with English- and French-speaking supervisors on their jobs. I found it a fun language with a simple charm.

Some examples are the following:

What's your name?   Wanam nem blong yu? (What name belong you?)
My name is . . .   Nem blong mi . . . (Name belong me . . .)
Thank you very much Tankiu tumas (thank you too much)
A saw   Pulem I kam, pushem I go, wood I fall down.
                                   (Pull them I come, push them I go, wood I fall down.)
Bra   Basket blong titi (my favorite—quite explicit!)

Our stay in Port Vila was an astonishing contrast in cultures. The people had intense dark skin with big bloodshot staring eyes and wild fuzzy hair. The men looked downright fierce. In traditional custom dress, they were naked, except for a penis wrapper called a *namba*. This was a length of a fine basket weave with fringed ends they wrapped around their penis, leaving the balls hanging out, and then after achieving an exaggerated length, the fringes were tucked into a belt around their waist with said appendage pointed up. Imagine my shock one day in the grocery store when I came around an aisle and was momentarily stunned. There in front of me was this strange apparition with his penis wrapper pointed straight at me. I have to say my heart skipped a beat. Women dressed more modestly in only a skirt.

As a contrast, I was invited to a rehearsal of a stage production of *The Rocky Horror Picture Show* being prepared by an Australian ex-pat theater group. The lead character was played by a fine ni-Vanuatu actor, and the production was surprisingly good but seemed to be an odd choice, considering where we were. This same group of ex-pats finally convinced me I needed to sample all the culture offered, so one night, Ralph and I went with them to a kava bar.

We entered a dark cave of a room and stumbled our way up to a bar, where we were served kava in small coconut shells. Then we went with our new Aussie friends and sat in a booth, where we slowly drank the concoction that tasted like spicy dirt. Nobody spoke; it was not only dark but also silent as well. Soon my lips became numb and my tongue and throat also. We sat quietly and let the kava take effect and then went back to the bar for more. I don't remember how many times Ralph and I went back, but at the end of the evening, I definitely felt quite placid. Beware of Aussies . . . they could lead you astray.

In Port Vila, we were tied, stern first, to the quay with an anchor off the bow to hold us in position. We would be sorry later about that anchor. We used a boarding ladder as a bridge from the boat to the shore and the most wonderful steak house we have ever enjoyed. The beef was a breed of cattle imported by the French, which was flavorful and tender enough to cut with a fork. Every night, we chose a steak from the showcase at the Waterfront Restaurant and watched as it was cooked to perfection. For cruising yachties who live from the sea, there was nothing more gratifying than a juicy steak. Topped off with a slice of rich, fresh coconut pie, it helped me maintain my sumptuous figure.

One evening, we invited friends over to watch the video of The Three Tenors. This was especially meaningful to me since I sang with Placido Domingo years ago during the time I was with the New Orleans Opera. Hearing his golden voice was as thrilling on a sailboat tied to the quay in

Vanuatu as it had been on stage in the opera house, when I was a young singer. What an amazing turn of events.

We were ready to leave for Malekula, but our anchor wanted to stay. It seems all the anchors down there did some kind of crazy dance in the current, and ours had jammed underneath a huge rock. It was obvious all our maneuvering could not free it, and if it wasn't for the diving help of a young Aussie, it would be there still. This was a bad situation requiring several dives. At sixty years of age, it was beyond Ralph's capability.

We left the next morning for Malekula, one of the largest islands, but without any main village. As we entered and motored to the anchorage, canoes came out of every nook and cranny in every direction and began following us. We felt like an insect caught in a web. When we started the anchor down, they hung on the sides of the boat, asking for T-shirts, beer, windsurfers, and engines. By the time we were safely anchored, we felt extremely uncomfortable and threatened with all the aggressive begging. They were a frightening, wild-looking bunch.

One canoe had a woman dressed in rags, holding a toddler also covered in rags, while the man sat in the back, dressed in a stylish T-shirt. When I was in Pago Pago, I bought many lengths of cotton fabric to give away. When this man offered a few bananas and asked for a T-shirt, I brought out some fabric and gave it to the woman. Then we told them we were tired and needed to sleep, went below, and shut ourselves in. This was a creepy experience, and with no other boats nearby, we felt quite vulnerable. We were relieved when we left the next day.

Sailing in Vanuatu

Luganville, on Espirito Santo, was occupied by the U.S. forces during the war. All of the South Pacific was in danger of invasion from the Japanese, and the only thing protecting the islands was Allied troops and the U.S. Navy. We were still in the areas including Tarawa, in the Gilberts (now Kiribati), Guadalcanal in the Solomons, New Guinea, New Caledonia, and Australia, which were under the Japanese threat.

James Michener had been stationed on Espirito Santo during the war, and his book *Tales of the South Pacific* was based on his experiences there. When we arrived, I wanted to burst into song—"Bali Hai," from the musical based on his book. I played the role of Bloody Mary, and the story became real to me in this place. In my imagination, I heard the Seabees stationed here singing, "Bloody Mary is the girl I love."

But we came here to dive. During the fighting, the troop ship *President Coolidge* ran aground in the harbor. There were two entrances, and one of them was mined by U.S. forces, and the other was clear so ships could enter safely. The captain of the *Coolidge* made a mistake and took his ship in the wrong entrance. He hit a mine and, in backing up, struck another. The ship began to sink, and to save lives, the captain ran his stricken vessel up on the reef. His actions saved over five thousand troops, with the loss of only five lives, before it slid off the reef into deep water. This was a fascinating dive, and we came to visit this site, which was featured years ago in National Geographic, showing a double row of toilets lying on their side. I was determined to see those toilets for myself.

The dive master was not too happy about taking such old people on a dive of this depth. We insisted. We walked across the reef approaching the bow. Our first dive was to about 125 feet and required a decompression stop on the way up. The first thing we saw on the sunken ship were empty lifeboat davits reaching toward the surface with tufts of black coral looking like a bad haircut. Along the starboard rail, three-inch guns aimed helplessly into the depths. It was fascinating to swim through a ship lying on its side, with everything in place but askew. We saw guns, jeeps, tires, typewriters—all jumbled together in the hold. In the enlisted men's starboard head were the ranks of toilets I had seen in the photo. We both did several dives, but I did one last dive to 141 feet because I wanted to see the ceramic Elizabethan figure over the fireplace in the main smoking lounge. It was the highlight of this magnificent vessel that started life as a luxury ocean liner, only to be lost in a war.

With Brits Phil and Mary from *Philmar*, we made another interesting dive on Million Dollar Point. After the war was over, the French wanted the Americans to give them all the leftover buildings, vehicles, and equipment. The U.S. government tried to negotiate a sales price, which the French refused, so everything was bulldozed over the reef into the water. We dove to ninety feet on a wall of sunken Quonset huts, trucks, jeeps, typewriters, and more. It went beyond our dive in all directions, and the vast extent was overwhelming. It was sickening to see the waste of war.

While in Vanuatu, we changed our minds about where to go next year. Originally we planned to check out of here for the Solomon Islands, but friends convinced us we should not miss Australia. We could always sail to the Solomons from there. So as simple as that, we made a decision that changed the course of our lives, but we didn't know it at the time. We motored out the pass from Espirito Santo and were greeted by dolphins playing beside us, and in the distance, the hazy outline of Michener's Bali Hai (Aoba Island) thrust mysteriously into the sky.

We sailed past Ambrym Island, covered with clouds on the volcano, and after dark, we saw flashes of red in the clouds as it lit up the sky. Nature's fireworks were a fitting farewell from these fascinating islands that were rumored to still practice cannibalism and witchcraft. Fortunately, we experienced neither.

We appreciated having a GPS along with radar, which helped us dodge through some of the islands and reefs we passed on the way to New Caledonia. We listened to music in the cockpit as we read and enjoyed the glorious world around us. The ocean was deep indigo blue, crystal clear as we watched squid and flying fish just below the surface. The terns flew close to the surface, also watching, and when they banked to make a turn, their bodies rose a few inches as their wing tips skimmed the water. *Fram* slipped quietly along in this deep, intense blue, with the sky nearly white at the horizon before it deepened to a soft cornflower blue overhead. There were only two puffy clouds in all the heavens.

The Milky Way was a blaze of stars overhead as I sat on watch in the cockpit, naked in the warm night air. By 0700 of the fourth day, after an uneventful passage, we woke to glassy calm after motoring most of the way with no wind. The stark mountainous island of New Caledonia was visible in the distance. We arrived at Havana Pass and hardly believed our new GPS when it showed we were caught in a strong crosscurrent and being swept toward the reef. All other visual indications showed that we would pass safely without changing course. It was deceiving when our eyes saw one reality and we had to force ourselves to accept a different truth. After this experience, we understood how boats could be set on the reefs here without knowing they were in trouble.

New Caledonia

New Caledonia was a long mountainous rock formation with creases and outcroppings emerging from the South Pacific Ocean and set in the biggest lagoon in the world. The rocky land produces 20 percent of the world's nickel, and mining was the biggest industry. The lagoon contains clusters of small islands, rock formations, and coral outcroppings. In the south, the Isle of Pines is unique and offers good anchorages among stunning pine-covered islands with white-sand beaches.

Noumea is the capital of this French territory and reminded me of Papeete. We walked the streets past neat little cottages with red roofs and flower boxes of red geraniums on the porch. Paved walkways, swept clean of debris, took us past beautiful gardens of tropical flowers with exuberant bougainvillea piled high against walls in mounds of magenta. A Victorian bandstand painted white was the centerpiece of a pleasant little park in the center of town. Noumea was a beautiful bustling small city, and near the marina, the farmer's market was filled with a riot of flowers, in an explosion of fragrance and color. Beautiful fresh fruits and vegetables, cheeses, pâtés and baguettes, pastries, and a bottle of good wine were all we needed for a delightful light supper.

Near the small park was a monument dedicated to the U.S. armed forces, who kept them safe from Japanese invasion in WWII. We were proud to be Americans when we saw the gratitude expressed all across the South Pacific for our service members. Unfortunately, we couldn't stay long since we came here for Australian visas and needed to be on our way. Once again, we prepared *Fram* for a vigorous passage.

We were cautious while we moved around inside the reef since not all dangers were marked. On our way to the western pass, we threaded our way past some of them and were relieved when we arrived at the lighthouse that marked the pass. We lined up with the lead marker that led us safely through to the sea. We were sad when we saw a sailboat wrecked on the reef beside us, especially since it was one we knew.

Now that we had our visas, we had to decide where to make landfall. Australia is a big country (about the same size as the United States), so we had some choices. Its coast is notorious for bad weather that storms out of Antarctica and brushes along the east coast of the continent with strong winds from the south.

We decided to go into Brisbane, even though the authorities there had the reputation for being the most stringent in all Australia since they were responsible to guard against any imports that could damage their agriculture. Their concerns were the same ones we encountered in New Zealand. Again, they did not allow any foreign animals to be landed in their country, and we knew Katisha would again be quarantined to the boat. Not a problem since he is used to being confined to the boat.

Brisbane looked like a good choice, because of its location on the Brisbane River that empties into huge Moreton Bay. We thought this would give us some protection from the prevailing weather when we made landfall. Little did we know!

We had no Australian charts because we hadn't planned to come here. The only chart we had for Brisbane was hand drawn from another yachtie's chart of Moreton Bay. That large bay was filled with shifting shoals, and we had to follow the markers of a narrow, dredged shipping channel for several miles. The channel didn't look too intimidating, but it would have been nice to have a better chart for the location of all the shoals. We lived to rue those words.

But for now we were at sea again, and after a day of rough weather, it turned out to be a pleasant crossing of the Coral Sea. We didn't have an Australian courtesy flag to fly when we entered the country, so I made one. Our red Fijian courtesy flag has the same union jack in the corner as Australia, so I sewed red fabric over the Fiji shield and added the appropriate white stars. We would buy a proper flag when we arrive, but this had to do for now.

After six days at sea, the last twenty-four hours before our arrival, we were in extremely rough conditions with strong southerly winds. It was so bad I tried to sleep on the floor in the main salon. Ralph couldn't sleep either and was feeling bad in the big seas. Added to our troubles, the cockpit cover was flapping wildly in the thirty-five-knot winds, and we struggled to take it down before it tore itself to pieces.

The closer we came to the coast, the wind built in intensity, and big seas washed over the boat. At dawn, we were ten miles from the entrance to Moreton Bay and worried we could not find the entrance buoy in these conditions. Our hand-drawn chart did not show its position. We weren't sure what to do, so we called the coast guard for advice. When they did not answer, we contacted Mooloolaba Coast Guard, the nearest harbor to the north.

"Mooloolaba Coast Guard, Mooloolaba Coast Guard, this is the sailing vessel *Fram* on passage from New Caledonia."

"*Fram, Fram*, this is Mooloolaba Coast Guard."

"Mooloolaba Coast Guard, we are a fifty-foot sailboat with two people aboard, approaching Moreton Bay. We're afraid we can't find the entrance buoy of the shipping channel in these weather conditions. Can you advise?"

"*Fram, Fram*, Mooloolaba Coast Guard, be advised that it would be dangerous for you to enter Moreton Bay at this time."

We explained that we had not slept for twenty-four hours and were exhausted. Even though Mooloolaba was not a port of entry, could we come in and anchor and rest, until the conditions moderated? They told us it would be all right and to call customs after we arrived.

It was an easy run downwind to Mooloolaba, and when we entered the channel into calm waters, we knew our ordeal was over. Just then, Australian customs called on channel 16 and told us that under no circumstances were we to enter. We had to go to a port of entry. Heartsick, we turned around and beat our way back out to sea. It was then 1100.

Phyllis called her friend Don on the ham radio, and he assured us that the weather would improve. He gave us the coordinates for the entrance buoy so we could find it with our GPS. We turned around and set a course toward the buoy. It was lost in the rain and mist, and we didn't see it until we were right next to it. It was now 1530.

Once inside, instead of refuge, we found ourselves in a terrible situation. The waves built up in the shallow bay and were so steep and boxy we were unable to power forward. *Fram* plunged up and down with ship traffic passing on both sides. The wind tore at our rigging, and we felt helpless as the engine struggled to overcome the turbulence. After awhile, we gradually began to creep forward, but the visibility was so poor in the moisture-saturated air we couldn't see the channel markers lost in the haze.

Our hand-drawn chart was confusing, and we had trouble identifying the correct markers. We were blindly traversing a shallow bay filled with shoals in constant fear of running aground or being run over by a ship. By nightfall, the wind and seas moderated, and it was easier to follow the lighted channel markers. We hope we are never in such a situation again.

We were exhausted after having little sleep the night before and then sailing all day, trying to find a respite from the awful sea conditions. Hour after hour, and mile after mile, we took turns driving the boat in the endless channel until, at last, we were able to turn off and anchor near Moreton Island in about fifty-eight feet of water. Ralph was so tired he was falling asleep on his feet. It was midnight. We didn't have a friendly welcome to Australia.

After a good night's rest, we were ready to leave miserable Moreton Bay behind and were underway in sunshine for the entrance to the Brisbane River. We pulled up to the customs and quarantine dock at 1100. Clearance took until 1530, as they were professional and thorough but friendly. We did not have any contraband except for Katisha. They weren't happy to see him, but we signed a stack of papers that basically said he was quarantined to *Fram* and he wouldn't get off the boat. If he did, we would be fined several thousand dollars. No up-front bond, no regular cat inspections, just our word (signed by us on paper).

When we were finished, we head up river to the botanical gardens, where the pile moorings would be *Fram*'s home while we were in Brisbane. The fact that we were really in Australia finally sank in. The delightful trip upriver took about two hours, and the terrible time we had coming here was forgotten. Lovely homes lined the waterway with all kinds of boats going back and forth and little passenger ferries darting across. Ahead of us was a modern city we would grow to love and enjoy. We were glad we made the decision to come to the Land of Oz.

Ralph at Botanical Gardens

The facilities at the botanical gardens were beautiful. On the lower floor of one of the big luxury hotels, we had washing machines, showers, and restrooms—all spotlessly clean and included in the $15-a-week mooring fee. The dinghy dock was right next to the city ferry dock, and leaving dinghies was prohibited, except there were usually about twenty tied up, and it was tough wedging into the crowded dock. We didn't dare tie on the outside, where the ferry came about every ten to fifteen minutes.

Our cruising neighborhood was waiting for us. We were surrounded by friends: Kat and Joe on *Champagne*, Connie and Vern on *Tainui*, Jeannie and Bill on *Northmoor*, Jim and Gwen (and Charlie cat) on *Princess Del Mar*, and Pat on *Southern Cross*. We were so happy to see all of them after we had gone our separate ways we invited everyone for a potluck Thanksgiving dinner on *Fram*.

We explored Brisbane, and I enjoyed shopping in the heart of the city, a short walk from the Gardens. It was a festive atmosphere with buskers playing music on street corners, and aboriginal buskers added the distinct sound of the didgeridoo on others. They wore body paint in distinctive dream designs. I spent a lot of time walking among this lively and colorful scene that made me feel happy and joyous.

We took ferries, buses, and trains everywhere, so we did not buy a car here. To go grocery shopping, we hopped in the dinghy and ran upriver to a shopping area with a big mall, grocery stores, meat markets, and bakeries, as well as hardware stores for Ralph.

We were in civilization! Our first week was one culture shock after another—magnificent shopping malls, beautiful buildings, clean streets, attractive people in nice clothes, restaurants, and American-style fast-food places. One day, my friend Kat and I went shopping in a department store. We stood with our mouths open and stared at exquisite crystal and china and other beautiful things we had lived with in our former lives. I felt a little twinge of regret, but considering our amazing journey among nature's beauty, it soon passed.

We became tourists and visited animal parks, where we saw the unique creatures of Australia. We walked among kangaroos, peacocks, and even held a cute koala. Eww. They stink and have sharp claws! Every evening at cocktail hour, the fruit bats, squeaking over our heads, left in squadrons from the trees, where they roost all day. Kookaburras giggled at us from the treetops, and the gardens were alive with beautiful, colorful birds singing and chattering.

Before Christmas, representatives of the city asked us to be part of a special event called the River Sings. They furnished us with colored lights to string in the rigging, and we invited a boatful of friends aboard. We paraded up and down the river as the radio stations broadcast Christmas carols with people onshore singing along. It was a beautiful and joyous affair, except it did rain on our parade. And did it *rain*! A squall came through with thunder and lightning! We sure didn't like pointing our tall mast toward the storm clouds.

Before the evening was over, everyone was wet, and it took all the guys to help us tie to our pilings as wind gusts kept blowing us off. With drinks and snacks, we ended the evening having a great party with good friends. Christmas down under is summertime with attendant hot, muggy weather and summer storms.

We were not going home this year for Christmas since we would be going in May for Lynn's wedding instead. Christmas Eve, we sat around our main salon with friends, singing Christmas carols and eating and laughing and having a wonderful time, even though we were all halfway around the world from our families. The next day, we exchanged gifts—nothing expensive, just nice mementos of our time together. Later, Bill cooked a traditional Christmas dinner for us all on *Northmoor*.

After Christmas, we flew to Sydney to visit Michael and Jessie from *Ishara*. They were renting a house and invited us to stay and use the house and their car while the family was in Tasmania after Michael sailed *Ishara* in the Sydney/Hobart race. This was a lovely invitation, and we thoroughly enjoyed Sydney.

Meantime, Bill and Jeanne and Kat and Joe had sailed *Northmoor* to Sydney, and we were invited onboard for New Year's Eve and the famous fireworks. We were anchored off the zoo in a perfect place to watch the display over the opera house and the Sydney Harbor Bridge. It was a spectacular show and a great way to end an eventful year. We welcomed 1992 with a pleasant sail in Sydney Harbor. President George H. W. Bush was a guest on a big motor yacht and waved to us as they passed by. We were sure he was waving at our huge American flag.

Sailing past Sydney opera house

We took the backstage tour of the stunning Sydney Opera House and attended an opera and several concerts. We visited art museums and the nautical museum. We walked in their botanical gardens, which were beautiful and full of colorful birds. We enjoyed many tourist attractions, and having a house and a car made it possible to take in many interesting things.

One evening, the weather news on television showed the satellite image with a cyclone heading straight for Brisbane. Not a word was said about it, but Ralph flew back immediately to prepare *Fram* for a storm while I stayed a little longer with our friends in Sydney. We asked about this and were told that they didn't report such things because they did not want to discourage tourists. Actually, the cyclone turned away, but we were always cautious when *Fram* was in danger.

Back in Brisbane, our life took on a wonderful routine as we enjoyed living in the beautiful city. Every morning, we walked in the botanical gardens and were soon in great shape after spending so much time the last few months on the boat. I deleted all fats and sugar from my diet, and the pounds began to melt away.

Earlier, we noticed an article in the Sydney paper about a conference in Paris on Solar Power Satellites. Ralph was surprised because he thought there was no activity on this concept. He went back to work and finished the book he started years ago on the subject. He sent out forty query letters to literary agents in the States and sent proposals or manuscripts to seven. He had several replies with mixed responses. He planned to follow up when we were in the States in the spring.

One trip we looked forward to was a visit to my ham radio friend Don, who followed us all across the South Pacific. Several of us hams drove to his home and "ham Shack," south of Brisbane. He went to bat for us with customs after we were denied entry to Mooloolaba and gained permission for us to anchor for the night off Moreton Island. I heard later he was in trouble with the Australian government over his interference on our behalf. I hoped not. Unless you have been out on the ocean in a small boat, you just wouldn't understand what it was like. Most of the hams on the Mobile Maritime Net were experienced sailors.

Ham friend Don in his "ham shack"

I was planning our trip home and wound up taking advantage of a promotional offer for a round-the-world flight with United Airlines that included several layovers along the way and included crossing the Atlantic on the QE2. Since it was not much more expensive than a round-trip Brisbane to Seattle ticket, we booked it and made plans for leaving the boat. Since we expected to continue sailing on around the world, we planned to take the boat north to Townsville, closer to the passage around the top of the country.

The day before we were going to leave Brisbane, I was out shopping and came back to the boat with my mind on other things and, without looking, started down the stairs into the wheelhouse and fell into the engine room. I forgot Ralph was working on the engine and had removed the floorboards. A trip to the emergency room at the hospital showed I had broken ribs and bruises. I think the bruise on my butt was as painful as the ribs, and I didn't feel like going to sea the next day, especially when I remembered how awful it was getting here a few months ago. Spending a few days getting the boat ready for a passage kept Ralph busy while I rested. After a week, I thought I could tolerate the motion, and we left for the Whitsunday Islands on our way to Townsville. But it was too early, and by the time we left Moreton Bay, I knew I needed a few more days rest, so we entered Mooloolaba after all.

It was a delightful small town, and since there was no anchorage, we tied to the dock. Katisha sat in the wheelhouse window and cried when he could see a dock out there but was locked up inside. We could only take a couple days of his loud complaints, so off we went again. The ribs were better, but the bruise on my butt was truly impressive. A doctor on another boat heard me describing the size of the lump to my nurse friend Gwen, and he invited us over to his boat so he could take a look at it. After draining the fluid, the relief was immediate. When he learned I was a cancer patient in remission, he insisted I go to the hospital in Townsville and have some tests. Since I would be seeing my oncologist in a couple of months, I didn't think it was that important. But I remember him as a compassionate doctor when I needed one.

The Whitsundays were islands very much like our San Juan Islands, except the water was warm. They lay between the mainland and the Great Barrier Reef, so even though there was an ocean surge in the anchorages, the conditions were generally good. We wanted to spend more time there, but with the delay, we were running out of time.

Once in Townsville, we had to make plans for Katisha. We were going to leave him with Scott and Gretchen on *Shadowfax* until we catch up with them later in Indonesia around Thanksgiving time. They were traveling behind us and had an engine break down as they hurried to meet us for the cat transfer.

With our travel reservations just days away, this became a serious problem that soon engaged the help of several of our yachty friends as they rushed to the rescue of *Shadowfax* and, therefore, the rescue of Katisha and *Fram*. We were getting nervous, but the necessary engine part traveled by land and sea (yacht), arriving in Airlie Beach in time for them to get underway and arrive in time for the big day.

Transferring a cat from one American yacht to another American yacht turned out to be a big deal. We were not allowed to put Katisha on any other nationality yacht—I guess because he is American? Anyway, we had all his stuff together, ready to go. Cat food, litter box and litter, and, most important, all the paperwork we signed to bring him into the country. We had to transfer the responsibility for him over to Scott and Gretchen.

When Agriculture arrived, we had quite a parade of cat transfer dinghies. First, one official boarded *Shadowfax* to await his arrival. Then Ralph and I and a second official were in another dinghy with the cat, followed by friends in yet another dinghy with all his stuff. Only Ralph and I and Katisha were allowed to board.

After the papers were signed, we stayed to make sure he was okay with a new boat. He was all over the boat, exploring his new home, investigating the galley; the main salon; the bilge, where his extra food and litter were now residing; and the stateroom, where he would sleep. Finally he jumped into Gretchen's lap, and with a purr, he was her cat.

Now that hurt. The only reason he was out here in the first place was because I was sure if I found a new home for him in Seattle before we left, he would miss me so much he would grieve to death. Boy, was I wrong. Actually, he already knew Scott and Gretchen because whenever they visited *Fram*, he was all over them. He was already in love with Gretchen and that was that. They spoiled him rotten, called him Little Buddy, and fed him lobster all the way up the Red Sea.

The time had come for us to put *Fram* on the hard in a long-term storage yard and pack our bags for a wedding and circumnavigation of the world by way of jet planes and a cruise ship. Ralph was going to interview agents for his completed book, and we expected to return after about two months to continue our own circumnavigation—the slow way on *Fram*. We didn't understand the publishing world, and our circumstances would be changed by forces outside our control.

Once Ralph found an agent, it was just the beginning. There was a lot more work to be done before the agent could submit to the publishers. She believed in the book and was confident that, in the end, she would find a buyer and he would have a contract offer.

We were acutely disappointed that it would be so long before we could return to *Fram* and continue our sailing adventure. Sadly, we bought a house by the ocean and asked permission from Australian Customs to leave *Fram* in their country for a year. They reluctantly agreed.

Part IV

Conclusion of the Dream

Fram at home on Lopez Island

Chapter 26

Our Return to *Fram*

This is Ralph back to tell you about our journey bringing *Fram* home to the United States. I will take you with us on this difficult five-thousand-mile passage to windward and our return to the Pacific Northwest.

In the spring of 1993, we were still in the United States when we received a message from Australian Customs telling us that we had to get *Fram* out of the country by May 12. My book was ready to present to the publishing industry, and my agent insisted I could not leave since she expected to have several offers for me. I decided to ask Australia for another year's extension. I wrote them a letter and sent it off. The reply arrived by telegraph.

"Under no circumstances will we give an extension, and the boat is to be out of the country by May 12, 1993."

Friends who just happened to be in the customs office the day my letter arrived described how the supervisor exploded and spent ten minutes ranting about Americans, who thought they could leave a boat in their country for over a year. In Australia, rules are rules, so we didn't have any choice. With heavy hearts, we made the decision to bring *Fram* home.

We now faced the formidable task of sailing five thousand nautical miles to windward back to the United States because we could not take the time to go on around the world as planned. Katisha, now on *Shadowfax,* was in the Red Sea gorging on lobsters. Our original plans to pick him up in Indonesia was not to be, so he is now their cat, renamed Little Buddy, and on his way around the world.

When we arrived in Townsville, our hearts sank at *Fram's* forlorn condition, but after a fresh paint job, she was respectable again and ready for the first leg of our sail home. We had only a few frantic days to prepare for an ocean passage after a year away from the boat. Our first stop would be Noumea, New Caledonia, where we would leave her for a few months while we returned home to the book. It's good we could not foresee the misery that lay ahead of us.

One final Australian experience awaited us at the fuel dock. A fair dinkum Aussie character with a ruddy complexion straight out of *"Crocodile Dundee"* dressed in shorts with gum boots and a slouch hat, lay stretched out along the dock as he filled our diesel tank while regaling us with stories and wild tales of the bush.

"G'day, mate, and ooroo", he said as we left, wishing us a good day and good-bye.

"Ta and good on ya," we replied. "Thanks, and a good job."

This bloke was a last reminder of how much we enjoyed the Australian people.

Once we were fueled and watered, it was time to say farewell to Townsville and the fascinating country of Australia. The weather was as nice as it gets, and by 1200, we checked out of Australia, just in time to avoid the wrath of customs, and motored out to sea. It felt good to be underway again.

Fueling in Townsville

That day, we had an incident that scared me to death. Phyllis was on the ham radio, listening for weather, so I was hand steering from the wheelhouse because the autopilot interfered with reception. I started up the companion way to take a look around, and there dead ahead was a large fishing boat stopped with its stern toward us, less than fifty yards away. We were doing seven knots straight for it. I made a lunge for the wheel and spun it to port. We missed it with little room to spare as one of the fishermen, busy pulling in a net, looked up at me with a shocked look on his face. I was shaking like a leaf. I have no idea how I missed seeing it sooner, except it was stopped right in our path and the bowsprit must have hidden it from my view. Our first day back on the water might have been our last.

That first night, Phyllis was on watch as we motored south in a dark night without even stars to light our way. She sensed a presence near us but didn't see anything.

"Ralph, come see if you can see anything. I think there's a ship close by running without lights," she called down to me.

We both had an eerie feeling there was something on our port side.

"There, it looks like an aircraft carrier running dark," I confirmed, looking through the binoculars. "I hope he sees us."

We stared into the darkness and barely made out a faintly darker shadow ghosting by. Then the blackness revealed the outline of a U.S. Navy aircraft carrier running with absolutely no visible lights. It was going at least twenty knots as it swept by on its way to Townsville. There was a big event taking place the next day, honoring the Yanks for saving Australia from being invaded by the Japanese during World War II. We hoped they saw us.

We were motoring southeast inside the Great Barrier Reef in near-perfect weather, when we received a weather forecast on the ham radio from John on Norfolk Island. He warned us there was a low, north of the Coral Sea, that was strengthening and could develop into a cyclone.

The last place we wanted to be was crossing the Coral Sea in a cyclone! We were in a quandary about what to do and decided to continue on this course for twenty-four hours, which would put us near the southern tip of the Great Barrier Reef. We could run into Gladstone and wait if it looked like it would come our way. Going into Gladstone meant reentering Australia and suffering the challenge of the customs officials.

However, our experience with Australian officials in different locations led us to believe they didn't talk to each other, so they might not know we had been kicked out of the country. By dawn the next morning, the barometer was falling, and it was decision time, so we turned to head for Gladstone as our weather deteriorated. We entered the well-marked fifteen-mile channel at dusk. By the time we approached the end, it was dark; looking back at all the lights flashing together was like looking down an airport runway with green lights on one side and red on the other, with white range lights in the middle. We carefully made our way to the marina and tied up at an end dock.

When we checked into customs the next day, they didn't say anything about us being kicked out of the country, and neither did we. We enjoyed our week in Gladstone but were anxious to be on our way. The weather reports were discouraging. Even though the cyclone went to New Guinea instead of the Coral Sea, a high over the byte of Australia was causing strong winds.

We had already changed our flight reservations out of Noumea, and we couldn't delay any longer. We had no choice but to go anyway and just take our lumps in heavy winds and big seas. By the time we reached open water, it was extremely uncomfortable as we motor-sailed into the wind and waves. One of the things we learned about sailing in Australian waters was the effect the continent had on wind patterns. The combination of the sun and terrain characteristics influences atmospheric pressure changes that create wind patterns affecting the seas around the continent.

The weather forecast remained discouraging, and our conditions continued to deteriorate with rough seas of ten to fifteen feet and wind gusting to thirty-five knots. We were miserable with waves washing over us continuously. We finally shut ourselves up in the wheelhouse, as it was impossible to stay dry in the cockpit. We were thankful for a reliable autopilot that never failed to steer the boat no matter the conditions. We certainly were not looking forward to five thousand more horrible miles like this. Water was coming in everywhere, and on top of that, I was worried about a problem with the engine starter that acted up the last time I started the engine, so I'm going to keep it running until we dock in Noumea.

After a week, the high mountains of New Caledonia, barely visible through a misty veil, promised an end to all of this. We were exhausted as we approached our GPS waypoint for the pass through the reef. We could see the lighthouse inside the entrance, but out of the churning ocean appeared breaking surf on the reef ahead. No pass. We had based our waypoint on our charts, founded on surveys made by Captain Cook a few centuries ago, and he didn't have GPS. At least we saw the breakers in time to stay off the reef, but which way was the pass? I guessed it was to the left and soon spotted the opening with the markers that led us safely inside.

It was a huge relief to be out of the nasty seas and on an uneventful run into Noumea. We resolved to find another way to bring *Fram* back home other than doing it ourselves. We couldn't face another passage like the one we just completed. It had been a difficult return to the sea, and we had many more miles to go. We yearned to be sailing west, running before the wind, instead of beating the boat and ourselves up like this. It was a relieved crew that tied up to the guest dock and shut down the engine. We had sailed 1,243 nautical miles from Townsville to Noumea.

We looked forward to a week playing tourist, but instead, it turned out to be a week of frantic work. Sunday morning I solved the starter problem that turned out to be loose terminals on the batteries, but then, I checked the oil and found the engine full of emulsified oil and water. I spent the week trying to find where the water came from. I checked water pumps, the heat exchanger, the manifold gasket, and the head gasket. It was a mystery that wouldn't be solved before we had to fly home.

Phyllis prepared the boat for a delivery crew that we hired to sail *Fram* back to the United States. A yachting friend, David, agreed to watch the boat for us while we were gone and helped me move it over to the long-term storage. We left Saturday morning, June 6, a week after we arrived, and caught the bus to the airport for the long flight back to our home at the beach.

Public market in Noumea

Chapter 27

Passage Through Hell

We returned to Ocean Shores and the house we bought by the sea, only to find many rejections from publishers for my book. This was a big disappointment in light of the terrible passage we just completed, because my agent insisted I had to return as soon as possible to sign any offer. We walked the beach and gazed southwest across the sea, yearning to be on *Fram* instead of stuck on land, waiting at the whim of the publishing industry.

Disturbing news arrived with a call from David in Noumea that there was serious dry rot in the base of the mizzen mast. We received more bad news when our prospective delivery crew faxed us that they would be unable to make the delivery. We didn't have much choice, so we decided to dredge up our courage and sail her back ourselves. We left Seattle September 15 for Noumea, with a checked bag full of large pieces of spruce to repair the mizzen mast.

The flight from Auckland was on a lightly loaded 767, with only thirty-five passengers aboard. We told one of the flight attendants about our sailing experiences and that we were going back to our boat in Noumea.

"Oh," she said, "I bet you would like to see what New Caledonia looks like from the air. Come with me."

We followed her forward, where she ushered us into the cockpit. We clearly saw the reef we had approached a few months ago. This view of the safe pass was easy to see from here. All the coral in the lagoon was obvious, and we thought how much safer it would be if we had this prospective, instead of from the deck of a small ship. The view from the cockpit was spectacular, and it was a rare experience to be in the cockpit of a commercial airliner in flight, and certainly impossible today.

When we arrived at the marina, we found the boat in good condition, except for the rot in the mizzen mast. Since there wasn't any boatyard that could pull the mast, I rebuilt it in place by using temporary supports. When I checked the rigging, I found rot in one of the spreaders on the main mast. This had been a continuing problem throughout the years, so I was an expert at repairing spreaders.

September 27, we checked out and left New Caledonia filled with anxiety for the long windward passage to Hawaii via Pago Pago. We spent the first night in a fine anchorage just inside the reef twenty-five miles from Noumea. We had a nice dinner and enjoyed a pleasant evening at anchor again after so long. It was a lovely start to what would turn out to be a horrible voyage.

We were up at dawn, and I spent a little time setting up GPS waypoints and learning the peculiarities of our new Garmin GPS. We now had a GPS at the navigation station below and the Garmin under the dodger in the cockpit. It was a little after 0700 on the first full day of our long passage to windward, when we motor-sailed out the pass heading east and shut down the engine. We were leaving through Havana Pass, where we first entered New Caledonia, going west in 1991. As we looked back at the rugged island from a distance, it reminded us of Desolation Sound in Canada.

The first squall hit us at lunch time, and then the wind dropped for a while but picked back up as the afternoon wore on. I was beginning to feel pretty bad as the seas rose, and it turned into a miserable day that became worse through the night—lots of squalls on top of an already strong wind from the southeast. The boat motion was cement-mixer terrible as we plowed into the waves. Before dark, we put the second reef in the main and rolled up some more of the jib. I was sick, and we even had to put a patch on cast-iron-stomach Phyllis!

The wind was twenty to twenty-five knots and gusting to thirty. By about 2130, we could no longer hold a course to our waypoint between two reefs, so we turned northeast to pass north of them. The weather helm was so strong the always reliable autopilot couldn't steer the course, so I was forced to hand steer for about three hours. Normally, hand steering is exhausting, but I felt better while I was outside steering, except for being miserably cold and wet. After we cleared the reef, we took down the mizzen and changed course to ease the weather helm so the autopilot could steer. I was sick again, so Phyllis took over while I tried to sleep in the dinette. Our course was farther north than we liked, but maybe the wind would shift or slacken so we could make some corrections. It was a miserable night. *What are we doing out here?* At least the moon was almost full.

FROM THE SHIP'S LOG

September 29, 1993 (Wednesday)

Phyllis let me rest until 0500. She was falling asleep on her feet. The conditions were unchanged. We are still making much more northing than we should. Not much we can do about it without running the engine and beating straight into the wind and waves. I was feeling better.

Our noon position was lat 21°22'70" S, long 169°16'21" E with a noon-to-noon run of 123 nautical miles.

Conditions stayed fairly constant the rest of the day and into the evening with occasional small squalls. It was a bumpy ride, but we were starting to become accustomed to all the motion. The seas were four to ten feet. Having a full moon helped at night. It has been tough becoming used to a sea passage—particularly beating to windward.

I checked the oil in the engine in the afternoon and found it was much too full—at least two to three quarts. I felt it must be more water, but when we pumped a sample out of the crankcase, it was very thin oil. The only conclusion I could reach was diesel had leaked into it. The only three ways I could conceive of it getting there was (1) an injector was malfunctioning so the fuel wouldn't burn and part of it leaked past the piston rings, (2) a valve was stuck or adjusted wrong so the cylinder wouldn't fire and the diesel leaked by the piston rings, or (3) the engine fuel pump was leaking diesel directly into the crankcase. I think it is one of the first two options, because the last day we ran it, it smoked much more than previously, and when it was idling, I thought it sounded like it was missing. We decided to head for Suva to do the repair. The course we were on headed that way. With the wind direction, we could hold fairly close to a direct shot to Suva, Fiji.

September 30, 1993 (Thursday)

More of the same except it didn't seem quite as rough, and we were able to correct the course close to the Suva rhumb line. The sky was clearer than yesterday, so the sun was shining most of the time. Our noon position was lat 20°29'60" S, long 171° 04'800" E with a noon-to-noon run of 115 nautical miles. We are getting used to the motion and spent our watches below, checking the horizon every fifteen minutes. It really helps to be out of the wind and noise. We have been able to read also. It is nice having the moon out.

October 1, 1993 (Friday)

Phyllis woke me for my 0300 watch a little early, as there was a boat very close to us, and she couldn't determine which way it was going. The bow and stern lights used by ships indicated it was going one direction, but the green running light, the other. It had been moving around us and we were both nervous. I finally concluded it must be a fishing boat, and the white lights were only for boat illumination. Anyway, it finally crossed our stern going to the port side at less than a half-mile range. I was glad to see them disappear below the horizon.

The wind was still from the same direction (ESE), blowing fifteen to twenty-five knots with gusts to thirty. We have been sailing with a reefed mizzen, double-reefed main, staysail, and a little bit of jib. We have never used that combination before, but it works good beating to windward in these strong winds. We are rail down most of the time and water coming over the bow with nearly every wave. Didn't even go outside today.

Our noon position was lat 19°39'464" S, long 172°46'644" E with a noon-to-noon run of 109 nautical miles.

October 2, 1993 (Saturday)

It was the same conditions it has been since we left New Caledonia, except the wind has shifted just enough for us to make a more southerly course than previously, so it looks like we may be able to make the Kandavu Pass without a major tack. I sure hope so. I'm squeezing the wind as tight as possible and still have decent sailing.

Decided I better work on the engine and find out what is wrong—how the diesel got in the oil. I pulled the valve-cover gasket to look at the return line from the injectors and the valves. Everything seemed to be fine. I am nearly positive it must be the fuel pump. Rather than mess with trying to repair it in these rough seas, I bypassed it with a new fuel line around the pump. The fuel tanks are high enough that when they have a reasonable amount of fuel, it can be a gravity feed to the engine. When I was through after replacing the oil and one engine fuel filter, the engine ran very nicely, so I don't think it was the injectors or valves. The only other thing it could be is if there was a leak in the return line. I didn't run the engine with the valve cover off, so don't know for sure. I'll check the oil tomorrow and see if it is okay. Our noon position was lat 19°14'037" S, long 174°56'559" E with a noon-to-noon run of 124 miles.

October 3, 1993 (Sunday)

More of the same except the wind shifted a little toward the east, and we couldn't keep our tack. We tacked at 0945 Unfortunately in this strong wind, our progress to windward is miserable—we were nearly backtracking on our path. By noon, our position was lat 18°49'269" S, long 175°55'038" E with a noon-to-noon run of only 60 nautical miles.

We decided to run the engine and motor-sail to see if we could make any better headway. So we rolled in the jib so it wouldn't slat and tried it for a few hours. That did not go well. We couldn't make much speed, and the engine was laboring in the heavy seas. Its RPM would change slightly with the wave surges and then have a burst of what sounded like a gas engine knocking. I had never heard that before and was very concerned. Also after checking the oil, I determined that diesel was still getting in and filling the crank case. We shut it down after about ten hours of running. Very discouraging.

October 4, 1993 (Monday)

The struggle continued as the wind was unabated and out of the ESE. It shifts a little bit north and south during the twenty-four-hour period. We need to try and time our tacks to take advantage of it, but we did a poor job today in both directions. We actually ran reciprocal courses for a while. The noon position was lat 19°15'579" S, long 176°33'441" E with a noon-to-noon run of only 45 nautical miles.

Went back to work on the engine after fixing a battery problem. We hadn't been able to use the #1 battery bank, as the voltage would drop when it was switched on. Had replaced the switch in Noumea and thought that had fixed it. It turned out to be a lose nut on the positive terminal. We ran the engine with the valve cover off, and it appeared that there was leakage of diesel out of the #2, #3, and #4 injector return fitting. I was not sure and it seems very strange. I took the return line loose, but there was nothing obviously wrong. Also checked the return line for blockage, but no joy. Ended up changing oil and we will have to find out in Suva. Two mysteries now: how did the water get in the crank case in Noumea and how is the diesel getting in now?

We were back on the starboard tack for my evening watch—hope to hold it through Phyllis's watch in the middle of the night. This is getting frustrating. The only good thing is the boat rides reasonably smooth, even though it is being tossed around by the waves and water is coming over the decks nearly continuously. It could really be miserable in a smaller or lighter boat. Sometimes when we jump off a wave or a wave breaks against the bow, it is like hitting a rock; the impact and noise are pretty bad.

October 5, 1993 (Tuesday)

We were supposed to be in Suva by now but, instead, switched over to the port tack (away from our destination) when I came on watch at 0300 At least our track was improving through the night, and one of the small islands north of the pass was visible on radar at ten miles. If we had been real brave, we probably could have cleared it on that last tack, but there was another reef farther in, so it is not worth the gamble. We tacked south and maybe this will be the last one. At least we have a good chance that we can make it on the next one. We should start to see the wave size diminish as we come into Kandavu Pass. There is some protection.

We tacked at 0845 with 80 nautical miles to go to Suva Harbor. We were able to stay south of our rhumb line to the waypoint in the pass so should be able to make Suva on this tack. Our noon position was lat 19° 01'45" S, long 177° 42'34" E with a noon-to-noon run of 68 nautical miles.

Our generator has been making strange noises for the last several days, and this morning it went belly-up. I think it is a bearing on the alternator. We will have to nurse our batteries today to make it into Suva.

The wind has not let up since we left New Caledonia. Water has been coming in from everywhere. It is always nerve-racking to make a landfall, particularly at night. We made one last tack to take us far enough south so we could make the waypoints to Suva. The moon finally broke the horizon at around 2000 There were enough clouds that it had to peak through. That was about when we made the final turn on the lead line to Suva Harbor. We were on GPS, as we could only make out the lights of Suva in the distance and not the lead lights. As we approached, we dropped the staysail and the mizzen. Our speed dropped from a crashing seven knots to a more relaxing five knots. We were both up and watching by now. At least the wave action was down some. It has been very nice while we were in the shadow of Kandavu but had picked up again as we made the final run into Suva.

I had started the engine to have emergency power as we approached the reef. The engine was running terrible. On every little wave surge, it would knock something terrible. We had rolled in the jib and were sailing on the double-reefed main alone with the engine at a fast idle.

October 6, 1993 (Wednesday)

Midnight came and went as we plowed on through the night toward the lights and reef of Suva. This was going to be a nerve-racking landfall. By this time, I had picked out the red range lights leading into the pass. The markers for the pass itself were much harder to find. Phyllis finally was able to identify most of them, but it was the range lights and the radar that gave us the most confidence. We found our way in by using GPS. Even though the moon was out part of the time and there was a fairly big sea running, we could not see the breakers on the reef until we were actually in the pass surfing down the face of a wave. This is a terrifying maneuver with thirty-five tons of boat. Fortunately, it is fairly broad, and we were able to stay lined up on the red lead lights so we just kept going. It was a real relief to pass the flashing red marker on the inside end of the pass so we could turn toward the harbor and try and find the Yacht Club anchorage. We came up on the far outer edge and decided that was close enough and dropped the hook in about thirty feet of water, and we went down and had a drink to celebrate a safe arrival. The boat was stable for the first time in eight days.

Our position was lat 18°07'41" S, long 178°25'43" E with a noon to arrival at 0130 of 68 nautical miles. We were 766 nautical miles from Noumea.

The morning was very pleasant to have the boat still. We called the harbor control and told them we couldn't move the boat, so they told us to come into the wharf by dinghy and check in. It took most of the day, and in the afternoon, the customs man came out with me in the dinghy to finish the papers and look at the boat. I think he just wanted the outing, as he really didn't look at anything.

After formalities were over, the rest of the day was amazingly productive. I called Collin Dunlap at Tradewinds Marine, who recommended John Taylor, a diesel mechanic at Maxlane Engineering. John identified the problem as injectors and sent me to Batteries South Pacific to see Calvin Moon, who was just opening a diesel service shop. By 1500, the injectors were tested, finding three that were bad. Fortunately, Calvin happened to have four rebuilt injectors for a Ford 254-cubic-inch displacement engine like mine. I was soon on my way back to the boat, and by the end of the day, the engine ran great. Fiji was an incredible place, where you could find just about anything you need and a versatile workforce for any problem.

NOW BACK TO OUR STORY

We needed the rest, but after a week in friendly Suva, it was time to go. We were checking out of a foreign country for the last time. Honolulu was the next stop 2,800 miles away, the longest passage of all.

Saturday, October 16, we motored out the pass at about 0520—no more Friday departures for us. Ten miles outside the pass, we came upon a fisherman in an open boat out of fuel, so we gave him a jerry jug with gas and a can of oil—our final thank-you to Fiji. We were sailing in warm, sunny weather again with a steady fifteen-knot wind. The waves were rough, however, and neither of us felt good. We were both nervous since we had a couple more passes to go through to escape Fijian waters. By evening, we were headed out the last pass with the waves building up in the freshening wind. We could just barely maintain our desired course and used the engine to help out part of the time. We still had not gotten our sea legs back, and sailing to windward was not my idea of fun. It was much more pleasant when we used to sail downwind. We were both feeling better by nightfall but were very tired.

The next day was October 16 again since we had crossed the international date line. Two things went wrong on my watch. The radar died, and the main bilge pump would not turn off even though it wasn't pumping. I just did not have the energy to fix them. Later in the day after I charged the batteries, the bilge pump was working right, but the radar could not be resurrected.

The boat was taking a beating as it plowed through the waves, with the rail under water most of the time and water coming over the bow in great torrents. It was as tough on us as it was the boat. It was extremely difficult to move around inside the boat. We could not let go of a handhold without falling. When it impacted a wave, the whole boat shuddered; we were thrown about and the noise was frightening. The howling of the wind never stopped.

Water, wind, spray, and noise were the accompaniment to a bouncing ride. We were well into reading John D. MacDonald's books about Travis McGee's adventures, which was a great help because they were interesting enough to distract us from our relentless situation.

I was reading the next morning at around 0800, when I heard a loud report that sounded like a gunshot. I rushed out to the cockpit to investigate but did not see anything wrong. All the stays and shrouds were in place. I decided something must have hit the boat.

A couple of hours later, we were smashed by a particularly large wave that jarred the boat violently, accompanied by another loud report and the clattering and banging of something loose. The staysail stay had broken loose, and the sail was being shredded in the thirty-knot wind as it streamed aft on the port side. We brought the boat around into the wind and rolled up the jib so we could heave to. It took a half hour to get untangled and secured. The eye securing the stay to the bowsprit was broken, and the staysail stay was badly kinked.

I thought it would not be a big job to jury-rig a new eye. But that was forgotten as I made my way aft on the starboard side and saw that the lower aft mainmast shroud was a bunch of splayed wires with only the core holding it up. All the rigging looked pretty loosy-goosy as we rolled in the waves, hove to with double-reefed main and reefed mizzen. We took the main down as fast as we could and rigged the staysail halyard as a temporary stay, lashing the loose stay to the bowsprit. At least I got a bath in the process, as the bow plunged into the waves while I was working there. This was a most discouraging day as we realized the standing rigging could no longer be trusted. We had been pushing it hard for over 2,000 miles, nearly all on the starboard tack, and we still had almost 2,500 to go.

We decided to stop in Samoa to make repairs and evaluate the situation. We were just approaching the north end of Savaii, the westernmost island of Western Samoa. Unfortunately, Apia, the capital on the island of Upolu and the only good harbor, was still ninety miles away dead to windward. The wind was blowing twenty-five knots, and the seas were ten to fifteen feet. Our speed under power was only about two knots, and we soon found there was also a current running against us.

I didn't dare carry any sail except the mizzen in anything short of an extreme emergency. Since we had plenty of fuel onboard, we just buckled down to slug it out with the wind and waves. The ride was extremely rough as we drove on with power alone. It was a gruesome time.

The waves and motion were totally chaotic as the rollers and seas built up by the strong east southeast and southeast winds were merging with waves and current coming around the top side of Savaii. It reminded me of some of the riptides in Canada, except on a grand scale. I thought we would never get through it, but it seems that all things come to an end, and this did too, as we finally came into the wave shadow of Upolu. The motion smoothed out, the wind moderated, and the sun came out in a brilliant clear sky. We thought at last things were going our way. We expected to be in Apia at the end of the day.

That lasted for about an hour, and then I heard an odd noise coming from the engine room. Strangely enough, it is usually Phyllis who hears unusual noises first, but this time, she didn't. I knew we had trouble. By the time I opened up the engine room, it was screeching, and I discovered a bearing was gone on the cruise generator. I shut down the engine, and we raised the mizzen and hove to while I attempted a repair. We could do without the generator, but it also disabled the freshwater pump for the engine. I sat there and stared at the engine as we drifted backward in the wind and current until we were once again in the huge waves we had so recently escaped. Our rigging was broken, the engine couldn't be run, and we were in the clutches of horrible seas. What were we going to do? It was without question the lowest point of my life. I felt utterly defeated.

The worst day of my life

Gradually, my mind revived, and I remembered the spare bearing I bought in Suva. It was an easy task made extremely difficult by the sea conditions, but eventually we were underway again. It took us five hours to make up the distance we had drifted back. It was terribly discouraging to watch the bow reach toward the sky as we climbed up the mountainous seas and then crashed down on the other side with the bow buried in the next wave, bringing the boat to a stop as the prop tried to get thirty-five tons moving again. It was better not to watch since we were making such little headway.

The severe jerking, pounding motion woke me up during Phyllis's watch. It was the very worst for me. I could hear the wind howling, and even after a full week of continuous motion, I didn't feel good. I was about to give up and go lay on the floor in the salon, when it seemed to moderate a little, and I stayed in the bed where I was. By morning, it moderated somewhat when we were only eighteen miles from Apia. By the time we came through the reef into the harbor, the weather was beautiful. We were weary to the bone and thankful to be there.

An exhausted Ralph checks in at Apia

The next day, it was time to make what repairs we could. I replaced the broken eye for the staysail stay with one I found on Kanton Island. I was able to replace the unraveling shroud on the mast using a spare end fitting I carried for just such emergencies, with one of the original forestays that was replaced when we installed roller furling in New Zealand. Now we were back in business as a sailboat. Our spare storm staysail was smaller than the staysail that was shredded but would work just fine until we could replace it.

But now it was time to find something to help us forget our troubles, so we went out to dinner. The next morning, we were up early and went to town to watch the police band in their uniforms of powder-blue shirts and skirts—topped off with white bobby helmets and wearing huge sandals—marching down the street to raise their flag in front of the government building. It was a stirring event and a display of the pride of the people for their country. Samoan people are *big*, and nobody messes with the police. They didn't need to carry weapons.

It was about noon when we motored out through the reef in lovely light airs for Pago Pago. With a nearly full moon, we enjoyed the first really glorious day and night at sea in over two years. It was daylight by the time we entered the harbor for the third time and pulled up to the customs dock for check in. The distance traveled from Noumea to Pago Pago was 1,433 nautical miles.

We were here to make repairs to *Fram*, so the sooner we started, the sooner we would be on our way to Hawaii. It began with a phone call to Seattle, and by the end of the day, we were in business. New stainless-steel rigging was ordered from the same supplier that fabricated our original set, so the dimensions were in their files, and it would be shipped by air within the week. Ouch, that will hurt the bank account!

I found extensive rot in the bowsprit, and the repair turned out to be difficult, as I had to work from the dinghy bouncing around in the harbor waves, but by the time the rigging arrived, the repair was finished. Installing the rigging was no fun working at the top of a mast that was in constant motion.

Replacing rigging in Pago Pago

We had been in Pago Pago fifteen days when we checked out for Honolulu. Our radar had been repaired, our water tanks were filled, the boat was provisioned, and a fuel truck topped off all of our fuel tanks to maximum capacity, and it only cost eighty-five cents a gallon, the cheapest fuel in a long, long time.

November 11, we were up before dawn and ready to go as the sky lightened and we cast off the dock lines and headed out of this most spectacular harbor. As we left, the cruise ship *Rotterdam* arrived, and later that day, at around 1930 it came over the horizon behind us on its way to Christmas Island. They were an impressive sight at night with all their lights blazing.

For the next five days, the conditions were nearly perfect—a welcome change after what we had been through. The light winds and small seas reminded us of the pleasant days years before as we sailed west through the South Pacific. We motored much of the time, so we decided we'd better stop at Christmas Island, Kiribati, to add fuel. We were now within eight degrees of the equator, and it was hot. The water temperature was eighty degrees, and we sweat profusely. Fans brought some relief below, and the cockpit cover was essential to shade us from the intensity of the tropical sun.

Late one afternoon, we sat in the cockpit enjoying a gin and tonic, remembering many similar passages over the last six years. It seemed strange to be going home, but we were ready. We felt our age, and these last couple of months have been hard on us. Sailing the boat home was different than the outbound journey, when we looked forward to new places and people. Now it was just a relentless trip with endless miles to cover.

My early night watch was a joy. The moon was out, the sea was flat, and I sat in the cockpit enjoying the night with a sparkling ocean stretching into the distance. My, how fast things change while one is sound asleep in bed. With lightning all around us, Phyllis woke me early for my predawn watch so I could disconnect the radios. We were in the middle of a huge squall, and the boat was bouncing around as we dove into the waves under power. We raised sail and fell off to an easterly course, motor-sailing against short steep waves that slowed us to a crawl. This went on all day, giving us an uncomfortable ride and slow progress in the persistent squalls. It was another hard day on both of us. At least we were heading east, but the contrast to yesterday was stark.

On November 23, Phyllis woke me late for my watch. The sky was already bright with an incredible dawn—hardly any clouds at all but a panorama of changing color as the sun made its way above the horizon. We were only a minute and a half below the equator when I got up. We both watched the GPS display as the numbers marched toward zero, zero, zero, zero, zero, zero, zero. It was 0508:24 Pago Pago time when they started climbing again, this time with an *N* after them. It had been four years since *Fram* was last in the northern hemisphere. Many adventures and ocean miles later, I doubt we will ever cross the equator again in a small boat.

Phyllis prepared a special lunch with a bottle of sparkling wine, so we celebrated crossing the equator in fine style, giving a little sip to King Neptune so he would smile kindly on *Fram*.

The next morning, Phyllis woke me at 0400 with our chart position showing us twelve miles from Christmas Island, but there was nothing on the radar. By the time I plotted our new position, we were nine miles from the island but still nothing on radar. I went topside to check again as the sun rose. Lo and behold, there it was, stretching out on the horizon as a line of palm trees sticking out of the ocean. Now that I knew it was where it ought to be, I fiddled with tuning the radar and finally brought it up on the screen.

We approached the open roadstead anchorage off of the fuel storage tanks onshore and dropped the hook near a couple of small Japanese ships and one sailboat. We received instructions from the authorities on channel 16 on where to check in. We assembled the dinghy and outboard and had a long choppy ride through the shallow lagoon to the wharf.

The island reminded us of Kanton, also in Kiribati, with discarded junk everywhere, radio towers, satellite dishes, scrubby trees, and coral sand beaches. The officials were quite friendly and helpful. We arranged to check in and out since we would only be staying one day. We also arranged to have two fifty-five-gallon drums of diesel delivered to *Fram*. Everything was taken care of efficiently, and the customs agent stopped by our boat later with our clearance papers. The distance traveled from Pago Pago to Christmas Island was 1,075 nautical miles.

The next day, we celebrated Thanksgiving at Christmas. After a nice dinner, we were soon underway for Hawaii on a course east of north with 1,150 miles to go. For this entire passage from New Caledonia, we have fought for easting since the trade winds blow from the southeast below the equator and northeast above. Hawaii was west of our position, but we needed to work our way as far east as possible before we met the northeast trades. We should then have a favorable point of sail when we turn west to the islands.

We have been dragging our fish lines since Pago Pago with no luck. We haven't seen a single flying fish or dolphin since we left Australia. When we were on our way west across the ocean, we caught all the fish we could possibly eat. On this passage, we passed many Japanese and Korean fishing vessels that drag gill nets up to fifty miles long that caught anything that was alive. It's very discouraging. It was as if the sea had been emptied of life.

One night on Phyllis's watch, she spotted a ship that she thought was probably a fishing vessel and called on the VHF radio. "Ship at (position), this is the sailing vessel *Fram* starboard of your position. Please answer on channel 16."

Usually we have no response from ships at sea, but a heavily accented voice came back asking, "Why are you out here in the middle of the ocean?"

She wasn't sure if they understood her answer, "I am sailing with my husband on a sailboat bound for Honolulu."

They seemed puzzled. "Why would your husband bring you out here?"

And they soon disappeared over the horizon.

Sunday, we were taking heavy seas over the bow once again with the now-familiar bad weather conditions. Neither one of us felt well. We had to sleep in the main salon since it was too uncomfortable in the aft cabin. Hawaii seemed terribly far away right now. It is a big ocean and this was getting old. King Neptune must not have been satisfied with a little sip of sparkling wine. I guess we should have given him the whole bottle.

By Wednesday, we are both extremely tired, and our bodies were taking a beating, but *Fram* just crashed on and on. She is a tough boat, but now we were having a problem with the sails. The trailing edges of both the jib and mizzen were fluttering, and we worried they would flap themselves to death. There's not much we could do about it as the leach line (which tightens the trailing edge of the sail) was broken in the jib, and we can't get at the one in the mizzen with it reefed. We just hoped they hang together.

It was worse when there was a moon, because we could see the huge waves as they crept up on us out of the night. At least we were making good time, averaging six knots or better. The little position crosses kept marching up the chart. We were well over halfway from Christmas.

We kept expecting the weather to moderate, but it didn't. Instead the wind and waves just kept getting bigger and stronger. We were leaping and bouncing and crashing through the waves, constantly burying the bowsprit and continuously heeled over with the lee rail under water. The rigging was howling, but the worst was the fluttering of the jib and mizzen. I couldn't believe it was all hanging together, but we were being driven at incredible speed.

Finally, I decided we had to get the jib and mizzen off before they destroyed themselves. To ease the pressure on the sails, we fell off and ran downwind while we rolled it up. It was absolutely amazing what a difference that made. One minute we were beating into thirty to thirty-five knots of wind shrieking and tearing at us, with sheets of spray cascading off the boat. The next minute, we were surfing down the face of the waves with the wind at our backs in relative quiet with no spray. We turned back into the wind, and I started the engine to maintain our previous speed. We were determined to make Honolulu by Sunday. Enough is enough. As daylight came, we were still climbing mountains in the middle of the Pacific Ocean.

We had scotch for breakfast. That made us feel better, but the best was *not* yet to come. The weather report out of Hawaii was for strong trade winds dominated by a large stationary high north of Hawaii. Each day, the report gave higher velocity winds that were exactly what we were experiencing.

As we approached the southern tip of the island of Hawaii, we stayed about twenty-five miles offshore to avoid the worst concentration of wind and waves. We couldn't sleep because of the motion. It was still pretty wild, and then suddenly the wave heights dropped dramatically, and the wind simply quit. The wind shadow of the big island finally gave us a brief respite for our weary bodies and minds.

But it was not long until the wind and seas started to build again as we approached the infamous Alenuihaha channel between Hawaii and Maui. This channel magnifies the wind and waves and is truly dangerous for small boats in the conditions we were experiencing. We soon found that true, even though we were about sixty-five miles off of the main channel. We were beam on to the seas, and I was glad we had taken down the jib and mizzen; they would never have survived this wind.

Even though we were healed over about thirty degrees with just the double-reefed main and the storm staysail, *Fram* was handling the seas well. Its weight and hull configuration were great in heavy seas. Waves occasionally broke against the side of the hull, but one really scared us when it broke against the wheelhouse. It felt like we were hit by a truck. The impact slammed us over another twenty degrees, and it sounded like a cannon shot. I was glad I had built the wheelhouse windows strong.

Crossing the channel took about eight hours before we found calm again in the wind shadow of Maui and Molokai Islands. We had one more hair-raising experience waiting at the end of this horrible windward journey across the Pacific. As we approached the channel between Molokai and Oahu, the latest forecast out of Honolulu was for thirty-four-knot winds and seas of twenty-two feet with gale warnings for all channels. The wind on the highest peak of Oahu was estimated at one hundred knots.

Dawn found us approaching the channel where we would receive the full brunt of the storm. What we saw was terrifying. The wind picked up surface water and blew it sideways in streamers of mist. The surface of the sea was covered with white tendrils of foam, and waves broke in great patches of frothing, foaming water. As our bow plunged through the waves, the spray blew off in horizontal sheets, with water crashing onboard. The rigging was wailing.

We listened as the coast guard responded to emergency calls of boats overdue or in trouble. We also listened to radio communications with the U.S. Navy aircraft carrier, Abraham Lincoln, so we knew it was out here somewhere. We couldn't see anything but the angry sea. We held each other while we braced ourselves in the wheelhouse, hanging on with white knuckles as waves slammed into the windows, sending water and spray completely over the top into the sea behind. We prayed that nothing would break, because it would be a dangerous for us to go outside to fix anything. Poor old *Fram* was taking her worst beating yet and so were we.

When Diamond Head on the island of Oahu appeared on the radar screen, we knew it would soon end, but we had a little further to go before its steep slope rose out of the mist. We knew it was over when we rounded up in the calm of the lee and took down sails as we called customs on VHF channel 16.

We did not hear from any officials, but an old friend, Bob Bitchin from Redondo Beach, California, who we first met in 1987, was at the Ala Wai Yacht Club, where he saved a place for us on the dock behind his boat. We couldn't believe the call. After meeting in Redondo Beach, we next saw Bob in San Diego, where he saved a place at the dock for us, and also Cabo San Lucas, when he directed us to an anchoring spot near his boat. This was a "small world" experience, and it was appropriate somehow that he was there to welcome two exhausted sailors.

We made 5,031 nautical miles from Townsville, Australia, to Honolulu—all of it to weather. We had been at sea for a total of fifty-three days since we left Townsville.

I called customs when we arrived, but their marine office didn't work weekends, so they told me to call them back on Monday morning and to call Immigration and Agriculture. Immigration came out a short time later, looked at our passports to verify we were U.S. citizens, and welcomed us back to the United States. That was it. Agriculture said they would send someone out on Monday.

On Monday, I walked to the Customs office in downtown Honolulu and checked in. It was a very casual, easy process.

"Hi," he said to me, "how long was the boat out of the United States?"

"Six years," I replied.

"Welcome back," he answered.

That was it. Agriculture came to the boat while I was gone and completed the process.

We made preparations to return to Ocean Shores. We were fortunate to find a slip at Ala Wai Boat Harbor, where we could leave *Fram*, but it was not easy, as Hawaii did not allow people to leave boats in the islands. What we had to do was sell her to the guy who was leasing the slip from the Yacht Club. So that is what we did, at least on paper. We changed the homeport from Seattle to Honolulu and flew home on December 11.

Rough sailing to Hawaii

Chapter 28

Coming Home

Fram had been in Honolulu for six months, and now it was time to bring her home. When Phyllis and I discussed this final passage, we decided she would stay home and follow us through the Mobile Maritime Net, and I would make it a "guy" trip. I invited son David and sons-in-law, Doug and Mark; but Doug and Mark couldn't get away, so Mark's thirteen year old son, Matt, took his place. When I asked Matt if he wanted to make the trip, I also asked, "Hey, Matt, have you ever been seasick?"

"Naw, I never get seasick," was his answer.

It was a big job getting a boat ready for an ocean passage after sitting for six months. Phyllis and Matt flew to Honolulu to get started two weeks before we were to sail, and I arrived June 16 to help finish the job. Phyllis had the sails repaired and cleaned up the interior, and we both worked on the exterior that looked terrible after taking such a beating. We sanded and painted the cabin, replaced halyards, installed a radar detector, rebuilt a spreader to eliminate dry rot, and reinforced the mizzen masthead fitting, where screws had pulled out and the stainless steel top plate was bent during our wild passage from Pago Pago last December. I changed engine oil and filters and had the bottom cleaned. The home port on the stern again read Seattle instead of Honolulu.

David arrived on the evening of the twenty-second; and Friday, the twenty-fourth, we were underway at last for Ocean Shores and home. Aboard as crew were David and Matt on their first ocean passage in a small boat. We put a transdermal seasick patch on Matt, just in case. I hoped leaving on a Friday doesn't jinx our trip. Oh well, leaving on Saturday certainly didn't make our last passages uneventful. This will be quite a change for David, who spent his time in the navy on a nuclear-powered cruiser. This was the first time Phyllis was not onboard for a passage. We were in high spirits, but she looked forlorn standing on the dock as she sadly waved good-bye.

The weather was perfect as we raised the sails in twenty knots of wind. Several navy ships were maneuvering off Pearl Harbor as we headed west around the island to avoid the Molokai Channel that gave us such a wild ride coming into Honolulu last year. We made good time as we rounded the island of Oahu. At about dusk, we cleared the northwest corner of the island and met strong winds and big seas. We were beating into north-northeast winds and Matt was seasick. We were barely able to hold our course heading north, and at this time, we were heading for Alaska. Alaska?

I checked into the Mobile Maritime Net and talked to Phyllis, who was still in Hawaii on a friend's boat. She closed with, "I wish I was going with you. Be careful. I love you."

I miss her already.

On Saturday, Dave and I traded off short watches. With all the motion on the boat, Dave and Matt were having trouble sleeping, but I was able to sleep fairly well. Dawn found us with big seas, overcast skies, and squalls. Our speed through the night was good, and Dave was really impressed with the size of the waves. They look a lot different from the deck of a small boat compared to his navy ship. Poor Matt, the motion inside the boat was rough, and he didn't leave his bunk.

As the day progressed, the wind shifted farther north, and our course gradually turned west. Now we were heading toward Japan. I checked into the MM Net and tried to call Phyllis, but even though the reception was poor, the message came back that she had arrived home safely. After a short nap, I came on watch at 2100. The wind moderated, and Matt was feeling better after he ate some gummy bears and drank a can of 7UP. We had taken the patch off of him in the afternoon on the chance it was contributing to his being sick.

It didn't seem like Sunday. Dave woke me at 0230 with lightning to the west and north. It appeared to be quite far away, but I unhooked the ham radio and put the Garmin GPS in the microwave oven, where it should be well protected from an electromagnetic impulse if we were struck. Fortunately, the lightning eventually disappeared. One of the things that really worried us was lightning. On the ocean, the only thing sticking up inviting a strike was our sixty-two-foot mast.

The ride was still rough as we kept the boat pointed as high as possible, but we still made good speed. We couldn't get a good weather fax picture because of poor reception, but the barometer continued to rise, so we must be entering a high, which should bring better sea conditions.

Matt was seasick again, and we are beginning to worry about him becoming dehydrated. Dave had him sit the cockpit after lunch so he could get some fresh air and look at the horizon. He refused to wear his glasses, probably because the big waves were too frightening, especially with no land in sight. The boat was taking a lot of water over the decks and bow, so it was a pretty scary thing to see if you're not used to it. It was worse when we passed through a squall and the wind drove us crashing through the waves with the lee deck awash. The next day when the motion eased a little, we did get Matt to eat a slice of bread for lunch and drink a little water, which he kept down. I had a hamburger for supper, and Matt thought that sounded good to him, so I gave him a half, and when that was gone, he wanted the other half, so I thought he would be okay.

David's first watch started while it was dark, now that the moon is past full. He had been afraid of the dark since he was a little boy, so dark nights with no lights truly were frightening for him.

"It's like riding a freight train to hell," was Dave's comment about *Fram's* passage through the dark night and rough seas.

I think Dave was surprised at how well *Fram* sailed in these conditions with a double-reefed main, the storm staysail, and the jib partly rolled out. Our speed varied from four and a half to eight knots.

The next day, I woke to a lovely dawn with fluffy trade-wind clouds, and with a perfect wind, we let the jib all the way out. But the squalls returned in the night, and we had to roll the jib in again. This was discouraging, but with more wind, the boat was flying at speeds as high as eleven knots. Less sail area makes the boat easier to control. There were squalls throughout the rest of the night, but the weather was beautiful by morning, and we were back to trade-wind sailing.

The air temperature was definitely down this morning. Even with jeans and a sweatshirt, it was a little chilly. Matt was still in his bunk but could keep food down. The weather fax today was encouraging, and the satellite picture showed clear skies all the way to the West Coast. When we reach the latitude of Ocean Shores, we will turn east. The distance to go was 1,853 nautical miles. This was our fifth day at sea.

Matt spotted the first ship we have seen since leaving Honolulu. It looked like a tanker heading south, eight miles off of our starboard beam. We were now in the middle of the high, and it was enjoyable running under sail and power in the small seas. I took a nap in the morning after fixing Spam, fried potatoes, and eggs. I woke up at 1300 to the sound of Dave and Matt getting out the gaff. When I got out there, they had a yellowfin tuna onboard. We had it for lunch, and it sure tasted good. The sailing conditions have been good for sailing but not for fishing. We had the fishing line out most days but hadn't caught anything, so they were quite excited. It was our ninth day at sea.

Matt and David with tuna

Sunday, July 3, was Matt's fourteenth birthday. It was calm enough to bake him a cake, and it was done before he woke up. It was a little lopsided because of the heel, but it should taste all right. David was making pizza for lunch, and we caught another tuna. We were finally in the center of the high, and the seas were flat calm as we motored along on our tenth day at sea. My ETA is the afternoon of the thirteenth or fourteenth.

Monday, July 4, dawned with a brilliant red sunrise that reminded me of sunrise over the Baja peninsula when we were sailing along the Mexican coast. Over my morning coffee, I remembered July 4, 1976, eighteen years ago. It was the two-hundredth anniversary of our nation, and *Fram* was still sitting in our backyard. I was working to finish construction, and it was going so slow I wasn't sure I would ever finish. It was a beautiful day when I climbed the ladder and sat down on the stern hatch looking forward over the bow. Firecrackers were going off as the neighborhood celebrated, but my spirits were low, and I sat there in despair. That day, I resolved to finish the boat and launch the next year. Two years later, we did.

We had 1,225 miles to go. It was a long crossing, and we were only halfway home. The daily position marks were so close together they seemed to be barely crawling across the chart. Today I dug out the Grays Harbor chart and marked our waypoint at the mouth of the harbor just south of the green whistle buoy. I expect to run in with an afternoon incoming tide. I also found the chart of the Washington Coast that showed our outbound track seven years ago. We were off of Ocean Shores at noon on August 13, 1987. How well I remembered that day. We were at the start of our great adventure on our first full day at sea, heading for Mexico, and we were filled with anticipation of adventures on the oceans of the world. We were excited and a little scared. That day the seas were large with a strong following wind, and *Fram* was surfing down the face of the waves. We knew even then we were embarking on the adventure of a lifetime.

We were back in tuna territory when we caught two albacore that I filleted and put in the freezer. We caught our first tuna seven years ago on our outbound trip at this same latitude off of Ocean Shores. Over the years, we caught many in other parts of the ocean, but the tuna circle was completed here at this spot. I fixed a nice lunch to celebrate the Fourth of July, preparing a special recipe Phyllis had onboard and cooked some of the fresh tuna that was delicious. We would catch two more tomorrow.

On this long passage, I have had time to think about many high points in our cruising experience. One of the most important people in our lives after leaving Mexico was my brother-in-law, Dick Borton. Dick became a licensed amateur radio operator in his teens, and he is the youngest eighty-plus-year-old you would ever meet. After Phyllis and I received our ham radio licenses, Dick contacted us every week from the time we left Mexico in 1989 to today. He was a constant presence in our lives, and he has no idea how much it meant to us to know he was always there and to hear his voice so far from home. He brought us news about family and was able to patch telephone calls through to our kids, even though we were oceans away. He was there today, our thirteenth day at sea, and made a phone patch for David to Sheri and another to Mark and Lynn for Matt.

The sea was flat calm with no wind even though the night was heavily overcast with rain and fog. We used the radar eyes to look for ships that we couldn't see. With the engine running, we had plenty of electrical power. Today we saw dolphins and we even saw a seal yesterday. In the afternoon, I spent some time removing rust stains from the deck so the boat wouldn't look so ratty when we arrived. This was our fourteenth day at sea.

In all our thousands of miles, I have never seen the ocean so flat calm and glassy smooth. It was hard to believe we were in the North Pacific Ocean. We were 462 nautical miles from Grays Harbor and Ocean Shores.

The next day, we saw the strangest-looking creatures on the smooth seas. When we shut down to check the engine oil, David snared one and brought it aboard. It was some kind of jelly fish with a black body about one and a quarter inch in diameter, floating on the water with little tentacles underneath; and on top, sticking into the air was a transparent sail semicircular in shape.

They looked like bubbles floating on the water in great masses clustered together like foam on an ocean beach in a storm. They went on and on to the horizon as far as we could see all afternoon, billions and billions of them.

Another Sunday and still no wind as I gazed out across the calm sea and reminisced about the years we spent living such a wonderful experience that had taken us to beautiful exotic places and people. We particularly enjoyed the time by ourselves on ocean passages. Sometimes the ocean was fierce, and we were challenged to the extremes of our capabilities, but other times, it was peaceful and quiet, like now. We knew each other so well we often didn't have to speak when handling *Fram*. We enjoyed simple meals and the companionship of reading and listening to music.

I look back at the long frustrating years of struggle to learn and build until we were ready to go and follow our dream. Now this bittersweet passage without Phyllis by my side was coming to an end.

"Aren't you afraid when you sail out of sight of land?" was one of the questions many people asked.

"No, when the land dropped below the horizon, we felt safe. It was land that struck fear in our hearts," was my answer.

The weather fax said we should have wind, but there was only a slight breeze from the northeast as we motored along. The weather was overcast with light winds when we were 313.7 nautical miles from our waypoint off Grays Harbor. The high had been following us for days now. When the Mobile Maritime Net controller gave me the weather report, he made the comment, "Look up, and you will see a big *H* in the sky. It has been following you."

Finally on this our seventeenth day at sea, the wind picked up, and we were surging along under sail. After roll call, David took over, and I went to bed but couldn't sleep in anticipation of arriving home. The boat was rolling, and after a week of calm motoring, it was quite uncomfortable. David reported speeds of over ten knots during the night with the average over seven and a half. We were still going fast when I came on watch at 0300. It was overcast and dark. The coast guard could be heard on channel 16 from Astoria to Port Townsend with their security announcements. I was able to talk to Phyllis, and they will be waiting for us tomorrow. Our voyage was nearly over, and it was exactly one month short of seven years today since we left. Cruising was everything we hoped for, but I am looking forward to bringing *Fram* home. Now it is time for other adventures.

We upped our ETA to noon on the twelfth at the outer buoy. It will bring us across the bar at maximum flood and give us a rising tide into the marina. Matt stayed in bed until noon, and with the boat rolling in the beam seas, he was seasick again. He improved as the day progressed and had pizza for lunch and a carrot for dinner. I'm sure the prospect of getting off this gyrating hellhole contributed to his recovery. I don't expect he will be interested in ocean sailing anytime soon!

We lowered the mizzen to slow down a little but were still averaging a little over six knots. I hoped it will be clear in the morning, because we should be able to see land at dawn. The wind moved a little aft the beam so the sailing is great. Below you could hardly tell we were moving, even though we were still going over six knots. This was our eighteenth day at sea and the last night watch!

Tuesday, July 12, we were running under power when I came on watch at 0300. The stars were still out, and I watched the sunrise as we crossed our outgoing track this morning. However, land was lost in a low-lying overcast, but I expect it will burn off early and stay clear. We were right on schedule to arrive at our waypoint at noon, local time. As we approached the entrance to Grays Harbor with all our courtesy flags flying, we put up the sails in the light breeze so the family could watch us sail in from the sea. We saw Phyllis and Sheri and the kids and Lynn and Mark on the shore waving us home from this, our final voyage.

The weary sailors were home, and the adventure of sailing the world in *Fram* was over. The distance traveled from Honolulu to Ocean Shores was *2,545* nautical miles. Total distance traveled since leaving Seattle on August 10, 1987, until our return to Ocean Shores on July 12, 1994 was *26,619* nautical miles.

Fram at the end of the voyage in Ocean Shores

Epilogue

For the next twelve years, we continued our odyssey with *Fram* in the Pacific Northwest, revisiting our favorite places in the San Juan Islands and Canada. What began with a family and their first sailboat has come full circle: a new generation with a love of the sea.

As we sit in front of the fireplace in our home overlooking Mud Bay on Lopez Island in the San Juan Islands, we write this story of our adventures in our beloved *Fram*.

Our daughter Lisa and her husband, Doug, and their children, Dana and Derek, also live on Lopez, not far from us. They uphold the boating tradition, although with a powerboat that can get places in a hurry.

Our daughter Lynn and her husband, Mark, live in Tacoma and are working toward the day they can retire to a life of travel on ships, not sailboats. Matt is the father of a little girl. He has never gone ocean sailing again.

Our son, David, and his wife, Sheri, who both made passages on *Fram*, have two grown children, Nick and Kelly. They also plan to retire on Lopez Island.

We are home.
Our dream started forty-two years ago.
Together, we shared an amazing journey.
We lived it as few others have done.
A marvelous moment in time.
To our readers, we offer a simple message:
Follow your dreams and visions.

Fram was sold to Tim O'Brien in 2006.

Fram's wings of power for 26,000 nautical miles

Brief Bio for Ralph and Phyllis Nansen

Ralph and Phyllis Nansen grew up in a small wheat farming town in Washington State. They first met when Phyllis came to live with her grandmother when she was in the first grade. They played together as children and began dating in middle school. Their romance grew through the years and they married while attending Washington State University. Ralph was studying to be an engineer and Phyllis was studying music.

After spending two years as a lieutenant in the Air Force, Ralph went to work for the Boeing Space Division in Seattle. When the Saturn/Apollo moon program was started by President Kennedy, Ralph joined the Boeing team that designed and built the first stage of the Saturn V moon rocket in New Orleans. While in New Orleans. Phyllis's singing career blossomed as she sang with New Orleans Opera, became a choir director, and formed a teenage singing group.

It was also in New Orleans that their interest in sailing was born and they bought their first sailboat and learned to sail with their three children. After the first manned landing on the moon, they transferred back to Seattle where Ralph worked on the Space Shuttle Definition and later as the Solar Power Satellite program manager. Phyllis continued to expand her music interest by singing in musical theater as well as directing choirs, teaching voice, and forming a new teenage singing group.

Ralph and Phyllis soon bought a larger sailboat and sailed the inland waters of the Pacific Northwest, where the dream of ocean sailing was born. They came to realize that they needed an even bigger and better boat to fulfill their dream, so they bought the bare hull of a 49-foot ferro-cement boat. Over the next eight years of trials, tribulation, and hard work they finished building the stone boat called *Fram*. For the next nine years they explored the Pacific Northwest and Canadian waters and prepared to sail the oceans.

On August 10, 1987, Ralph and Phyllis left on *Fram* for their ocean sailing adventure, ranging over seven years and 26,000 nautical miles from Seattle, to Mexico, and on to the South Pacific, completing the odyssey that began with their first sailboat in the bayous of Louisiana.

Today, Ralph and Phyllis reside in the San Juan Islands of Washington State, the beautiful island group they first discovered from the deck of a sailboat.

Other books by Ralph Nansen

SUN POWER: The Global Solution for the Coming Energy Crisis
(Ocean Press 1995)

ENERGY CRISIS: Solution from Space (Apogee Books 2009)

CPSIA information can be obtained at www.ICGtesting.com
Printed in the USA
244316LV00002B/49/P